CERTIFICATE
HISTORY & CIVICS

In accordance with the latest syllabus prescribed by the Council for the Indian Certificate of Secondary Education Examination, New Delhi.

CERTIFICATE
HISTORY & CIVICS

CLASS IX

By

K. S. S. Seshan
Professor of History (Retd.)
University of Hyderabad
Hyderabad

Dipankar Prakash Rai
M.A., B.Ed (N.B.U)
Dr. Graham's Homes
Kalimpong

OSWAL PUBLISHERS
1/12, Sahitya Kunj, M. G. Road, Agra-282 002

No Part of this book can be reproduced in any form or by any means without the prior written permission of the publisher.

Edition : 2019

ISBN : 978-93-87660-68-7

OSWAL PUBLISHERS

Head office	:	1/12, Sahitya Kunj, M.G. Road, Agra-282 002
Phone	:	(0562) 2527771- 4, +91 75340 77222
E-mail	:	contact@oswalpublishers.com, sales@oswalpublishers.com
Website	:	www.oswalpublishers.com
Facebook link	:	https://www.facebook.com/oswalpublishersindia
Available at	:	amazon.in, Flipkart, snapdeal

Preface

It is a matter of extreme satisfaction and pride to present the latest edition of Certificate History & Civics Textbook for the students of Class IXth of ICSE Board.

History is the study of past events, particularly in relation to human affairs. It is important to study history if one wants to learn how and why the world and its people came to be as they are today. Keeping this in view, this book narratively presents the sequence of past events, so that the students can objectively analyse such events and study the reasons and the effects that have determined them.

This book has been completely designed to incorporate the extensive changes effected in the new ICSE syllabus and to enliven the study of History and Civics. The book has been divided into two sections- **Section A** (Civics portion) and **Section B** (History portion). The text is written in a lucid and engaging manner, which adds to the student's perspective and understanding and helps them envisage the whole concept easily.

We sincerely hope that this book will enhance the student's understanding of the world, as well as inculcate the right attitude and ideas about the inter-relationship between the history of all nations and their developments. The book has thus been patterned on the basis of guidelines issued by the Council and goes a long way in preparing the students for their oncoming examinations.

Utmost care has been taken to present the book in an error free manner. However, there is always scope for improvement. Constructive suggestions for the further improvement of the book are welcome. We shall try to incorporate as many of such suggestions as possible in the future editions.

Publishers

SYLLABUS CLASS IX

Aims

- To provide an understanding of the working of the Indian government necessary for the student to grow into a responsible, enlightened citizen in a Secular democracy.
- To enrich the understanding of those aspects of Indian historical development which are crucial to the understanding of contemporary India.
- To awaken a desirable understanding in pupils of the various streams which have contributed to the development and growth of the Indian nation and its civilisation and culture.
- To develop a world historical perspective of the contributions made by various cultures to the total heritage of mankind.

- There will be one paper of two hours duration carrying 80 marks and an Internal Assessment of 20 marks.
- The paper will be divided into **two** parts, Part I and Part II.
- **Part I** (30 makrs) will contain short answer questions set from the entire syllabus.
- Candidates will be required to answer **all** questions.
- **Part II** (50 marks) will consist of Section A and Section B. Candidates will be required to answer **two** out of **three** questions from Section A and **three** out of **five** questions from Section B. The sections will correspond to the sections indicated in the syllabus.

SECTION A : CIVICS

An elementary study is required of this section without verbatim study of the Constitutional Articles in detail.

1. **Our Constituion**

   Definition of Constitution : date of adoption, date of enforcement and its significance. Features : Single Citizenship, Universal Adult Franchise, Fundamental Rights and Fundamental Duties, Directive Principles of State Policy (meaning), Welfare State.

2. **Elections**

   Meaning; Composition of Election Commission (in brief); Direct and Indirect election; General election; Mid-term election and By-election.

3. **Local Self Government**

   (i) *Rural; Three-tier system of Panchayati Raj, Gram Panchayat, Panchayat Samiti, Zila Parishad-their meaning and functions.*

   (ii) *Urban; Municipal Committee and Municipal Corporations : Meaning and functions.*

SECTION B : HISTORY

1. **The Harappan Civilisation**

   Sources : Great Bath, Citadel, seals, bearded man, dancing girl, dockyard, script.
   Origin, extent, urban planning, trade, art & craft, and its decline.

2. **The Vedic Period**

   Sources : Vedas and Epics (brief mention); Iron Artifacts and Pottery.
   Brief comparative study of Early and Later Vedic society and economy.

3. **Jainism and Buddhism**

   Sources : Angas, Tripitikas and Jatakas (brief mention).
   Cause for their rise in the 6th century. B. C.; Doctrines.

4. **The Mauryan Empire**

   Sources : Arthashastra, Indika, Ashokan Edicts, Sanchi Stupa.
   Political history and administration (Chandragupta Maurya and Ashoka); Ashoka's Dhamma.

5. **The Sangam Age**

   Sources : Tirukkural and Megaliths.

   A brief study of society and economy.

6. **The Age of the Guptas**

   Sources : Account of Fa-hien; Allahabad Pillar Inscription.

   Political history and administration (Samudragupta and Chandragupta Vikramaditya); Contribution to the fields of Education (Nalanda University), Science (Aryabhatta) and Culture (works of Kalidasa, Deogarh temple).

7. **Medieval India**

   (a) **The Cholas**

   Sources : Inscriptions; Brihadishwara Temple.
   Political history and administration (Rajaraja I, Rajendra I).

   (b) **The Delhi Sultanate**

   Sources : Inscriptions; Qutab Minar.

   Political history and administration (Qutbuddin Aibak, Alauddin Khilji and Muhammad Bin Tughlaq).

   (c) **The Mughal Empire**

   Sources : Ain-i-Akbari, Taj Mahal, Jama Masjid and Red Fort.

   Political history and administration (Babur, Akbar and Aurangezeb).

   (d) **Composite Culture**

   Sources : Bijak, Guru Granth Sahib, Ajmer-Sharief, St. Francis Assisi Church (Kochi).

   Significance of Bhakti Movements and Sufism (Mirabai, Sant Jnaneswar and Hazrat Nizamuddin).

   Influence of Christianity (St. Francis Xavier).

8. **The Modern Age in Europe**

   (a) *Renaissance :* definition, causes (capture of Constantinople, decline of Feudalism, new trade routes, spirite of enquiry and invention of the printing press) and impact on art, literature and science (Leonardo Da Vinci, William Shakespeare and Copernicus).

   (b) *Reformation :* causes (dissatisfaction with the practices of the Catholic Church and new learning); Martin Luther's contribution, Counter Reformation.

   (c) *Industrial Revolution :* definition. Comparative study of Socialism and Capitalism.

INTERNAL ASSESSMENT

Any **one** project/assignment related to the syllabus.

Suggested Assignments

- The Indian constitution protects the rights of children, women, minorities and weaker sections. Elaborate on the basis of a case study.

- 'Fundamental Duties complement Fundamental Rights.' Illustrate with the help of a Power Point Presentation.

- Highlight the civics issues of your locality and what suggestions would you offer to address them.

- Visit a museum or local site of historical importance and discuss its significance.

- Discuss the art and architectural features of any of these monuments : Buddhist Caves, Ajanta; Iron Pillar, Mehrauli; Gol Gumbaz, Bijapur; Mattancherry Synagogue, Cochin; Kamakhya Temple, Guwahati; St. Thoms Basilica, Chennai; Tower of Silence, Mumbai.

- Make a pictorial presentaion of inventions and innovations as a result of the Industrial Revolution.

- Make a comparative study of the Harappan and the Mesopotamian Civilisations.

CONTENTS

SECTION A : CIVICS

1.	Indian Constitution	13–20
2.	Salient Features of the Constitution	21–31
3.	Elections in India	32–39
4.	Local Self-Government-Rural	40–50
5.	Local Self-Government-Urban	51–58

SECTION B : HISTORY

1.	The Harappan Civilization	61–73
2.	Emergence of Vedic India	74–84
3.	Jainism and Buddhism	85–99
4.	The Mauryan Empire	100–111
5.	The Sangam Age	112–117
6.	The Age of Guptas	118–126
7.	The Cholas	127–134
8.	The Delhi Sultanate	135–145
9.	The Mughal Empire	146–154
10.	Emergence of Composite Culture	155–164
11.	The Renaissance	165–177
12.	The Reformation	178–185
13.	Industrial Revolution	186–192

SECTION-A
CIVICS

CHAPTER 1

INDIAN CONSTITUTION

- ◆ Definition of Constitution, Date of Adoption, Date of Enforcement and its Significance.
- ◆ Meaning of the terms given in the Preamble.

Indian Constitution

Constitution
The Framing of Our Constitution
- Date of Adoption and Enactment of the Constitution
- Commencement of the Constitution
- Historical Significance of 26 January in India

The Preamble
- Objectives of the Indian Constitution
  - Sovereign
  - Socialist
  - Secular
  - Democratic
  - Republic
- Ideals of the Constitution
  - Justice
  - Liberty of Thought, Expression, Belief, Faith and Worship
  - Equality of Status and Opportunity
  - Faternity assuring Unity, Integrity and Dignity of the Nation
- Significance of the Preamble

The constitution of India is the supreme law of India. It was adopted by the Constituent Assembly on 26 November, 1949, and came into effect on '26 January', 1950. On this day, India became a 'Sovereign Democratic Republic'. In its aftermath, the Union of India assumed the modern status of Republic that superseded the Government of India Act, 1935. In order to establish Constitutional Autochthony, the framers of the constitution annulled the previous Acts of the British Parliament through Article 395 of the constitution. After coming into effect, India observes 26th January as 'Republic Day' each year. Presently, the Indian Constitution comprises the Preamble, 12 Schedules, 448 Articles in Parts I to XXII and an Appendix to Part IX.

THE CONSTITUTION

The constitution is a comprehensive document comprising laws and rules according to which a State is governed. It is also known as the **Fundamental Law of the Land**. The aim of the Constitution of a Nation is to ensure the welfare of its citizens by means of smooth governance. It defines and determines :

- The democratic and parliamentary form of the government adopted by our country.
- The powers and position of the various organs of the government the executive, the legislature, and the judiciary and how they are inter-related.
- The limitations on these powers.
- Rights and duties of the people

Our Constitution moderates relations within the government and governs and protects the interests of the citizens by restraining the government from taking arbitrary decisions. The aim of the Constitution is to deliver smooth governance for the welfare of its citizens. It contains lists of approved languages, rules for election and other details about the conduct of the government and caters to the needs of the citizens of India irrespective of caste, religion, race, language and culture.

THE FRAMING OF OUR CONSTITUTION

The idea of an independent constitution for India was first mooted by Pt. Jawaharlal Nehru, expressing his views in 1938. He advocated the formation of an elected Constituent Assembly to frame the constitution of a free India without interference from outside sources. On 24 March 1946, the British Government sent a delegation (Cabinet Mission) of three Cabinet Ministers (Sir Stafford Cripps, Lord Pethick Lawrence and Mr. Alexander). The Cabinet Mission decided that the members of the Constituent Assembly were to be indirectly elected by the Provincial Assemblies, while the Princely States would have their own representatives by way of nomination.

The Constituent Assembly of undivided India comprised 389 members, out of which 296 were from British India and 93 from the Princely Indian States. With the partition of the country, the number was reduced to 299, with 90 members forming a separate body to frame the Constitution of Pakistan.

The Constituent Assembly was the 'Mirror of the Nation', reflecting the diversity of caste, religion, race, language and culture of India. It included members from all sections of Indian society such as Hindus, Muslims, Sikhs, Parsis, Indian Christians, Anglo-Indians, Scheduled Castes, Scheduled Tribe and women. Some of the eminent members of the assembly were Dr. Rajendra Prasad, Sardar Vallabhbhai Patel, Jawaharlal Nehru, Maulana Azad, B.G. Kher, Sardar Baldev Singh, K.M. Munshi, Sarojini Naidu, Frank Anthony and others.

The first sitting of the Assembly was held on 9 December 1946, at the Central Hall of the Parliament which was attended by 207 members including 9 women. Demanding a separate state, the Muslim League boycotted the meeting. The assembly was presided over by the oldest member of the House, Dr. Sachchidananda Sinha, who was elected as the first temporary President of the Assembly. Dr. Rajendra Prasad was elected as the first permanent President of the Assembly while Sir B. N. Rau was appointed as Constitutional advisor to the Assembly. The Constituent Assembly took almost two years, eleven months and seventeen days to complete the Constitution for Independent India. The total membership of the Assembly thus was to be 389.

First day of the Constituent Assembly. From right: B.G. Kher and Sardar Vallabhai Patel; K.M. Munshi is seated behind Patel

The work of drafting the Constitution was started by the Constituent Assembly and on 13

INDIAN CONSTITUTION

December 1946, Pandit Jawaharlal Nehru moved the Objectives Resolution, which formed the Preamble of the Constitution. The 'Resolution' proposed :

- Free India will mean being 'republic'.
- The republic would grant Fundamental Rights to citizens.
- The ideals of political, social and economic democracy would be guaranteed to all people.
- The state would safeguard the rights of backward classes and minorities.

On 22 January 1947, the Constituent Assembly passed the Objectives Resolution. However, as a result of the partition of India under the Mountbatten Plan of 3 June 1947, a separate Constituent Assembly was set up for Pakistan and representatives of some Provinces ceased to be members of the Assembly. As a result, the membership of the Assembly was reduced to 299.

Lord Mountbatten with Nehru and Jinnah

Date of Adoption and Enactment of the Constitution

On 29 August 1947, the Constituent Assembly set up a Drafting Committee under the Chairmanship of Dr. B.R. Ambedkar to prepare a Draft Constitution for India. The Draft Constitution was published on 26 February 1948, after many deliberations and amendments. It was published in all the leading news-papers of the country in order to seek wide-ranging consultations and opinions. The Assembly considered the views of judges, lawyers, private individuals and public bodies and decided to revise the Constitution. The Draft Constitution was discussed in detail by the Drafting Committee.

On, 26 November, 1949, the Constitution was enacted and adopted by the Constituent Assembly. At the time of its signing, the Constitution comprised 8 Schedules and 395 Articles. Commenting on the completion of his work, Ambedkar said,

Dr. B. R. Ambedkar

"I feel that the Constitution is workable; it is flexible and it is strong enough to hold the country together both in peace time and in war time. Indeed, if I may say so, if things go wrong under the new Constitution the reason will not be that we had a bad Constitution. What we will have to say is that Man was vile".

Commencement of the Constitution

After many deliberations and some modifications, the Constitution came into force on 26 January, 1950. In India, this day is celebrated as the **Republic Day**. At the time of signing, 284 out of 299 members of the Assembly were present who signed two hand-written copies of the document (one each in Hindi and English). On this day, Dr. Rajendra Prasad started his first term of office as the President of the Indian Union. The eminent political thinker of the new constitution C. Rajagopalachari replaced Lord Mountbatten as the Governor-General. Under the

Pt. Jawaharlal Nehru and Dr. Rajendra Prasad signing the Constituion.

transitional provisions of Constitution, the Constituent Assembly became the Provisional Parliament of India until the new General Elections were held in 1951-52.

Historical Significance of 26 January in India

A resolution was passed by the Congress Session at Lahore declaring Complete Indepen-dence or 'Purna Swaraj' as India's goal. It was decided that 26 January should be observed as the 'Purna Swaraj Day' all over India. In fact, for the first time, the Complete Independence Day was celebrated on 26 January 1930 and continued to be celebrated till 1947. After India achieved Independence on 15 August 1947, it came to be known as the Independence Day and 26 January as the Republic Day of India. Therefore, these factors made the Assembly selected 26 January as the date of Commencement of the new Constitution of India.

> The Indian Republic's Golden Jubilee–The Republic Day's Golden Jubilee was celebrated by India on 26 January 2000.

THE PREAMBLE

The Preamble is an introductory statement, stating the aims and objectives of the constitution. It describes the 'soul and spirit' of the Constitution of India.

> We, THE PEOPLE OF INDIA, having solemnly resolved to constitute India into a SOVERIGN SOCIALIST, INDIA; SECULAR, DEMOCRATIC REPUBLIC and to secure to all its citizens :
>
> JUSTICE, social, economic and political;
>
> LIBERTY of thought, expression, belief, faith and worship;
>
> EQUALITY of status and of opportunity; and to promote among them all;
>
> FRATERNITY assuring the dignity of the individual and the unity and integrity of the Nation;
>
> In our CONSTITUENT ASSEMBLY this twenty-sixth day of November, 1949, do HEREBY ADOPT, ENACT AND GIVE TO OURSELVES THIS CONSTITUTION'.

The Preamble of the Constitution.

By the 42nd Constitution Amendment Act of 1976, some minor changes were made in the Preamble such as the addition of the words Secular, Socialist, Integrity and Unity. These words proclaim the solemn resolution of the people of India to constitute India into a 'sovereign, socialist, secular democratic republic'. For a long period, the Preamble was not considered an integral part of the Constitution by experts on constitutional law. Later, in 1973, in the Kesavananda Bharati case, the Supreme Court ruled that the Preamble is an integral part of the Constitution, containing the basic framework or structure of the Constitution. It serves the following purposes to the Constitution of India :

❏ It indicates the source from which the Constitution derives its authority; and

❏ It also states the objects, which the Constitution seeks to establish and promote.

Objectives of the Indian Constitution

The Preamble is considered to be prelude to the Indian Constitution, as the terms 'SOVEREIGN SOCIALIST SECULAR DEMO-CRATIC REPUBLIC' emphasize not only the nature of the Constitution but the nature of the Indian state. According to Chief Justice Hidaytullah, 'It lays down the pattern of our political society'.

Sovereign

By declaring India as a sovereign entity, Preamble entails complete political freedom. It implies that India is internally powerful and externally free. She is not a subject of any other country or state and is free from foreign interference. There is none within her to challenge her authority and it is free to choose her allies in war and peace alike. This suggests that sovereignty is one of the most important values of a state as it allows the state to frame her own social, economic and foreign policies and develop her resources the way she likes.

Though our Constitution does not specify where the sovereign authority lies but by mentioning the source of our Constitution as **'We the people of India'**, it announces to the world that the ultimate sovereignty rests with the people of India as a whole. It emphasizes that India is a sovereign republic, yet it continues to be a member of the Commonwealth of Nations without any domination of the British Crown. Infact, as stated by Pt. Jawahar Lal Nehru her membership of the Commonwealth of Nations does not compromise her position as a sovereign republic. The Commonwealth is an association of free and independent nations. The British Monarch is only a symbolic head of that association. Initially, it was known as the British Commonwealth of nations. It was established in 1926, when the British Empire began to disintegrate and the forces of den-colonization began to surface. At present, there are 53 member-states of the Commonwealth of Nations. Some nations such as the United States of America were initially in the Empire but are not incorporated in the Commonwealth.

Socialist

The word 'Socialist' was included in the Preamble in 1976 in for emphasizing the need to strive for socialism. Socialism, as seen by the Indian leaders, means equitable distribution of National Income to all sections of the people for the wellbeing of one and all. This means freedom from all forms of exploitation–political, social and economic. The State is expected to prevent the concentration of wealth in a few hands and bring about economic and social equality. In order to ensure a basic minimum for all, the Government of India has adopted a mixed economy, introduced five year plans and has framed many laws to achieve the value of socialism in a democratic set up.

Secular

The word 'Secular', which means 'Not Connected To Any Religion Or Faith' was also included in the constitution in 1976. Since India is home to most major religions in the world, therefore to keep the followers of all the religions together secularism has been found to be a convenient formula. The ideal of secularism implies that our country has no official religion and is not guided by any religion or religious considerations. It allows people to profess, preach and propagate any religion of their choice, unless it goes against the security, peace and integrity

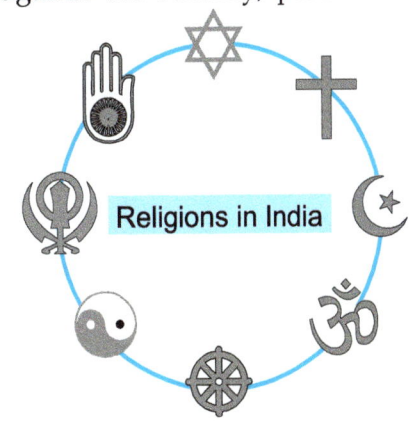

All forms of discrimination weaken our democracy

of the country. Everybody is considered to be equal before the law and enjoys equal rights, no matter to which caste, creed, colour or faith he or she belongs. The Constitution also restrains the State from making any discrimination on the grounds of religion.

Democratic

Democracy is defined as *'government of the people, by the people and for the people"*. It is that system of government in which people choose their rulers by voting for them in elections and the latter remains accountable to the people. A democratic government implies free and fair elections where people elect their government by a system of **Universal adult franchise** popularly known as 'One man one vote'. By Adult Franchise, citizens aged 18 years and above have been given the right to elect representatives for the State Legislatures, Union Parliament and local bodies like village panchayats and municipalities. Similarly, citizens have also been given the right to contest elections for these bodies, irrespective of their educational, social or financial background. The fundamental Rights provided by the Constitution give the citizens numerous democratic rights like equality before law and the independence of the judiciary and civil liberties like freedom of speech, expression and association.

Democracy contributes to stability in society and stands for the inalienable rights of citizens, rule of law, independence of judiciary, free and fair elections and freedom of press etc. Therefore, development of a democratic political culture has been an important objective.

Republic

The word 'Republic' refers to a State in which power is held by the people through their elected representatives. A Republican government is one in which no individual has a hereditary right to public offices. The President is the elected Head of the State of India, who holds office for a term of five years. The people also elect the legislators, i.e., the MLAs (Member of Legislative Assembly) and MPs (Member of Parliament). A republic makes no distinction between indirectly and directly elected head of the State.

Ideals of the Constitution

The ideals to be achieved are stated in the second part of the Preamble. The ideals are Justice, Liberty, Equality and Fraternity.

Justice

Society comprises various groups and sections of people. 'Justice' implies the administration of law in a reasonable and fair way without any privilege or prejudice. In order to achieve this object, the Constitution provides certain fundamental rights to all citizens. It also lays down the Directive Principles to guide the State in its entire works. The term 'justice' in the Preamble embraces three distinct forms—Social, Political and Economic.

- **Social Justice :** Social Justice avoids discrimination on the basis of religion, race, language, sex or caste. Each individual is given what is due to him, without privilege or prejudice. Though the State might make provision for the advancement of educationally and socially backward classes of citizens.
- **Political Justice :** Political Justice consists of various things like free and fair elections, right to vote and equal access to public offices. The citizens are free not going against the interests of the country. Every citizen of India can stand for election and hold office, except for those who are debarred on account of criminal offences.
- **Economic Justice :** Economic Justice means that the citizens are given their due without discrimination on the basis of their economic standards or wealth. The Directive Principles of State Policy are directed towards giving the citizens adequate means of livelihood, including the right to work. The government ensures that economic justice is carried out by legislations on minimum wages, no pay difference between men and women, equal work-equal pay, etc.

Liberty of Thought, Expression, Belief, Faith and Worship

The word 'Liberty' means freedom that has been ensured to every citizen through a set of Fundamental Rights by our constitution. The freedom of thought and expression provides the citizen the right to think, write or speak freely on any subject, especially in the matter of 'faith and worship', provided the restrictions imposed on this right are abided by him or her. The makers of our Constitution believed that the ideal of democracy was unattainable without the presence of certain minimal rights which are essential for a free and civilized existence. The British had placed various restrictions on Indians which have all been done away with under this ideal.

Equality of Status and Opportunity

The Indian Constitution guarantees its citizens social, political and economic equality for the development of the best in him. It also implies equal opportunity to all its citizens, in matters of public employment irrespective of caste, creed, colour or economic status. Every citizen of India is entitled to equality before law and equal protection of law.

Fraternity, assuring the Dignity of the Individual and the Unity and Integrity of the Nation

The word 'Fraternity' stands for the spirit of common brotherhood. It ensures the dignity of the individual as well as the unity and integrity of the nation. This is the foremost objective to achieve in a country like India, which is composed of diverse races, religions, languages and cultures. Due to the absence of these aspects, a plural society like India stands divided. As a result, the word 'fraternity' was added to the constitution in 1976, declaring that it is the duty of every citizen to promote harmony and the spirit of common brotherhood amongst all the people of India transcending religious, linguistic and regional or sectional diversities. According to Justice Basu, *'Fraternity will be achieved not only by abolishing untouchability amongst the different sects of the same community, but by abolishing all communal or sectional or even local or provincial anti-social feelings which stand in the way of unity of India.'*

SIGNIFICANCE OF THE PREAMBLE

The Preamble of the Constitution of India is a unique piece of document. It embodies the most important values and objectives of our constitution. It is the soul and the spirit of the constitution. It briefly states what our political leaders and constitutional fathers wanted India to be. Therefore, the Preamble is the actual mirror of India's Constitution and a yardstick by which one can judge the constitution. The Preamble seeks to establish what Mahatma Gandhi described as–'The India of my Dreams', *"...an India in which the poorest shall feel that it is their country in whose making they have an effective voice; ...an India in which all communities shall live in perfect harmony. There can be no room in such an India for the curse of untouchability or the curse of intoxicating drinks and drugs. A Woman will enjoy the same rights as man."*

In Retrospect

- **Constitution** : The system of rules and laws that specify the rights and duties of people and determine the government's organization.
- **The Framing of the Indian Constitution** : On 9 December 1946, the first sitting of the Assembly took place. Dr. Rajendra Prasad was selected as the President of the Assembly on December 11. The Drafting Committee's Chairman was Dr. Ambedkar. After 2 years, 11 months and 17 days, the Constitution was finally enacted and adopted by the Assembly, on 26 November 1949. On 26 January 1950, the Constitution finally came into force. The Purna Swaraj Day was first celebrated on 26 January 1930. After the Constitution came into force in 1950, this day has been celebrated as the Republic Day.
- **Meaning of Preamble** : An introduction to the Constitution is known as the Preamble. The Preamble states the source, contents and objects of the Constitution. Essential Features of the Constitution : People of India are considered to be the source of origin of the Constitution, Nature of the State or Polity: Sovereign, Socialist, Secular, Democratic, Republic, Ideals or Objects of Indian Constitution : Justice, Liberty, Equality and Fraternity.
- **Significance of the Preamble** : The Preamble is considered to be the most important part of our Constitution as it contains the Constitution's basic structure. Since the Indian Constitution is a written Constitution, the Preamble acts as a key to unlock the riddles of the Constitution.

EXERCISES

Part-I (Short Questions)

1. What do you mean by the term 'Constitution' ?
2. Which body framed the Indian Constitution ?
3. When did the Indian Constitution come into effect ?

4. Name any four prominent members of the Constituent Assembly.
5. Who was appointed as the permanent President of the Constituent Assembly ?
6. Why and by how many numbers the original membership of the Constituent Assembly got reduced after the partition of India ?
7. Who was the Chairman of the Drafting Committee ? When was it formed?
8. When was the Constitution of India adopted ?
9. What is meant by the term 'Preamble' to the Constitution ?
10. Which words were added to the Preamble by the Constitution (42nd Amendment) Act of 1976 ?
11. What is the source of the Constitution ?
12. Mention what the Preamble states about each of the following:
    (a) Justice   (b) Liberty   (c) Equality   (d) Fraternity
13. How does the Constitution ensure :
    (a) Social Justice   (b) Political Justice   (c) Economic Justice
14. What are the different Liberties ? How are they ensured by the Constitution ?
15. What is meant by Equality of Status and Opportunity ?
16. What is meant by Fraternity ?
17. What is the significance of the Preamble ?

Part-II (Structured Questions)

1. Define the Constitution and describe in brief the history of the formation of the Constitution.
2. With reference to the Preamble to the Constitution of India, answer the following :
   (a) What is meant by a sovereign state ?
   (b) India's membership in the Commonwealth does not affect her Sovereignty? Give reasons.
   (c) Why were the terms 'Socialist' and 'Secular' added in the Preamble by the 42nd amendment to the Constitution of India in 1976 ?
   (d) How does democracy contribute to stability in the society ?
3. Justice implies the administration of law in a reasonable and fair way without any privilege or prejudice'. In this context, explain :
   (a) What is meant by the term Justice?
   (b) (i) Social Justice   (ii) Economic Justice   (iii) Political Justice.
4. With reference to the basic ideals of Constitution of India, write short notes on the following :
   (a) Equality   (b) Liberty   (c) Fraternity
5. What do you mean by the term 'Preamble' to the Constitution? What is the significance of the Preamble in a written Constitution?

CHAPTER 2

SALIENT FEATURES OF THE CONSTITUTION

◆ Features : Single Citizenship, Universal Adult Franchise, Fundamental Rights and Fundamental Duties, Directive Principles of State Policy (Meaning), Welfare State.

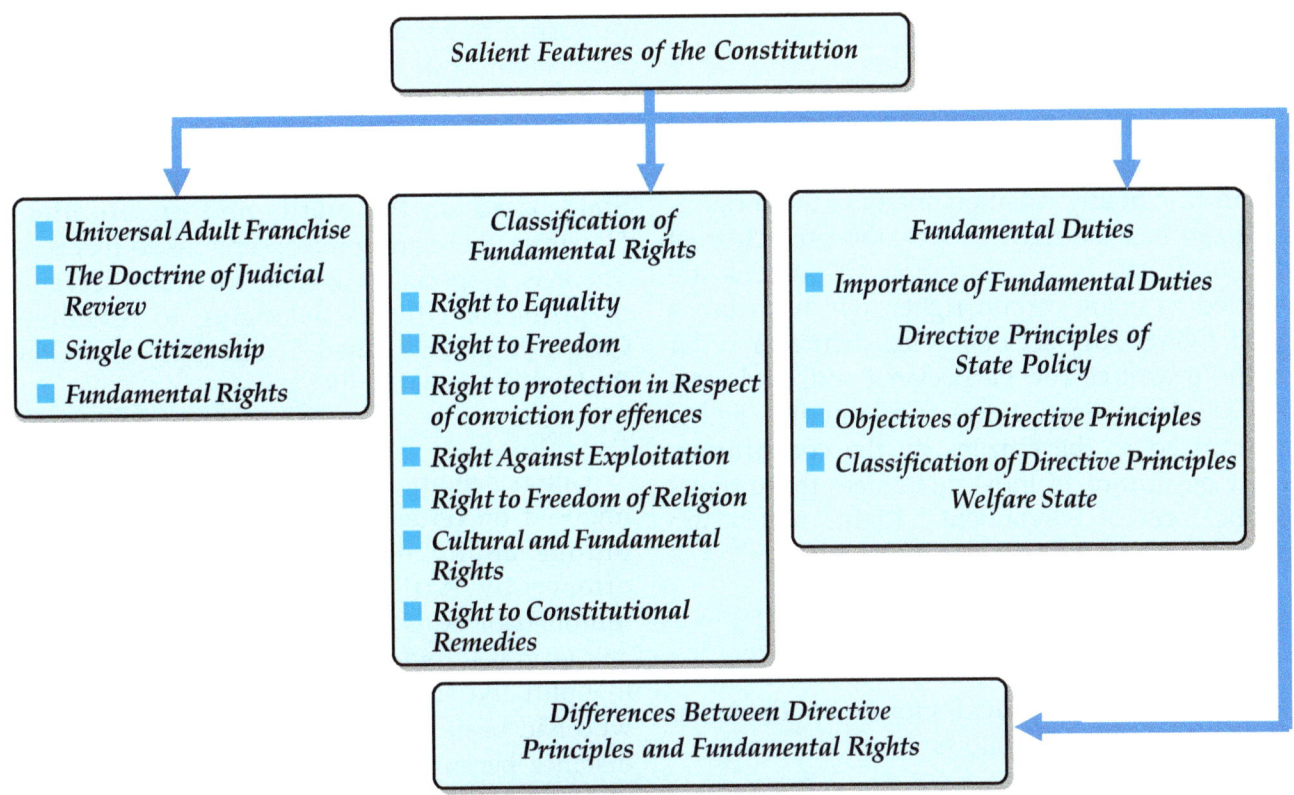

The term 'Constitution' can be applied to 'an all-encompassing' law that defines the functioning of a government. The Indian Constitution aimed at achieving many important goals during its formation like maintaining the unity of the Nation and removing the backwardness of the country. It established a democratic society that provides justice to all its citizens, irrespective of their cultural or social background.

Universal Adult Franchise

The adoption of Universal Adult Franchise by the Indian Constitution establishes political equality in India; which means every citizen of India who is 18 years of age or above is entitled to vote in the elections irrespective of caste, sex, race, religion or status. *'One person one vote'* is the policy adopted in Indian democracy, which maintains political equality in India.

Doctrine of Judicial Review:

According to the doctrine of Judicial Review, the power is included in Articles 226 and 227 of the Constitution of India, relating to the High Courts. As far as the Supreme Court is concerned, Articles 32 and 136 of the Constitution, the Judiciary in India regulates every component of governmental and public operations. It is laid down by the Judicial review.

Single Citizenship

Under a federal system, there is generally a dual citizenship, that of the State to which an individual belongs and of the Nation that represents a Union of States. In India, we have single citizenship that is, not of the respective states to which we belong. This provision helps in promoting unity and integrity among the people of the nation.

Fundamental Rights

Fundamental Rights are one of the important features of the Indian Constitution. These rights are protected by the judiciary and are inviolable, i.e., in case of any violation of any of these rights; a citizen has the right to seek the protection of the judiciary. In a democracy all citizens are entitled to enjoy certain rights, which ensure a good living. Any act of the legislature or order of the executive can be declared null and void if it violates any of the fundamental rights guaranteed to the citizens by the constitution. The Constitution of India guarantees those rights in the form of Fundamental Rights which, are present in part III (Articles 12 to 35).

CLASSIFICATION OF FUNDAMENTAL RIGHTS

The Constitution provides for six Fundamental Rights. These are as follows :

Right to Equality–Articles 14 to 18

The Right to Equality of citizens comprises social, political and economic components and the success of Indian democracy largely rests on it. However, certain restrictions are put on Right to Equality by the 42nd Amendment Act, 1976. A person cannot move the Court if his right to Equality is restricted to implement the Directive Principles of State Policy.

Equality before the Law

As per Article 14, the Constitution of India guarantees that all its citizens will be treated equally before the law. It means that if two persons commit the same crime, both of them will get the same punishment without any prejudice or partiality.

Prohibition of Discrimination

Article 15 ensures social equality by prohibiting discrimination against any citizen on the basis of race, religion, sex, place of birth, creed or caste. However, the State can make special provisions or concessions for women and children and socially backward classes of citizens.

Equality of Opportunity in matters of Public Employment

Article 16 states that there shall be equal opportunity for citizens *'in matters relating to employment or appointment to any office under the State'*. The State cannot discriminate against anyone in the matter of public employment. All citizens can apply and become employees of the State based on the merits and qualifications. However, there are some exceptions to this right. There is a special provision for the reservation of posts for citizens belonging to Scheduled Castes (SCs), Scheduled Tribes (STs) and Other Backward Classes (OBCs).

Abolition of Untouchability

Untouchability refers to the social disabilities imposed on certain classes of people. Practicing untouchability in any form is a punishable offence by Article 17 which declares that 'untouchability is abolished and its practice in any form is forbidden'. This provision is an effort to uplift the social status of millions of people who had been looked down upon and kept at a distance because of their caste or the nature of their profession.

Abolition of Titles

Article 18 abolishes all titles like Rai Sahib, Maharaja and Khan Bahadurs as they are considered to be a contradiction to the idea of equality. However, the President of India can confer civil and military awards to those who have rendered meritorious service to the nation in different fields. The civil awards such as

Bharat Ratna, Padma Vibhushan, Padam Bhushan and Padma Shri and the military awards like Veer Chakra, Paramveer Chakra, and Ashok Chakra are conferred.

Right to Freedom–Articles 19 to 22

Since democracy presupposes equality and also calls for individual liberty, our Constitution is inclusive of the Right to Freedom as stipulated under Articles 19-22. However, during an Emergency, the fundamental rights guaranteed under Article 19 remain suspended. The following are the six categories of the Rights to Freedom :

Freedom of Speech and Expression

Clause (1) (a) of Article 19 means the right to express one's convictions and opinions freely by word of mouth, writing, printing, pictures or any other medium. Article 19 thus, includes the expression of one's ideas through any communicable medium or visible representation, such as gesture, signs, etc.

Freedom to form Associations and Unions

Clause (1) (c) of Article 19, the citizens have the freedom to form unions or associations to protect their individual and collective interest without creating any turmoil but the state may impose reasonable restrictions on the right of freedom of association and union in the interests of public order, morality and the integrity and sovereignty of India.

Freedom to Reside and Settle

The Article 19 (1) (e) enables geographical mobility and freedom to people for settling in any part of India. They are also entitled to buy, sell or transfer their property.

Freedom to Assemble Peacefully and without Arms

According to Article (19) (1) (b) provides the right to citizens to assemble for public gatherings, protests, functions, discussions, etc. in a peaceful manner without possessing arms and weapons. Reasonable restrictions on assembly can be imposed if the same is harmful to the maintenance of public order.

Freedom to Move Freely Throughout India

According to Article 19 (1) (d) the citizens have the freedom to go wherever they like in the territory of India. They cannot be stopped without any legal sanction. However, reasonable restrictions may be imposed in the interest of the general public or to control an epidemic.

Freedom to Practice any Profession, Trade or Business

According to Article (1) (g), all citizens of India have the freedom to practice any profession or to carry on any occupation, business or trade that does not have any adverse effect on the moral standards of society. However, the State is permitted to lay down the professional or technical qualifications necessary for practicing any profession or carrying on any occupation, trade or business.

Right to Protection in Respect of Conviction for Offences

Article 20 provides protection to individuals who are punished or accused of an offence. The three such protections are :

- No individual shall be prosecuted and punished for the same offence more than once.
- No individual can be convicted for an act that was not an offence at the time of its commission. Moreover, no one should get a greater penalty than what is actually prescribed under the law.
- No individual can be forced to give witness against his or her own self.

Protection of Life and Personal Liberty

Article 21 states that 'no person shall be deprived of his life or personal property except according to procedure established by law.' The expression 'personal liberty' consists of all those freedoms that are not included in Article 19. Therefore, a punishment that is too cruel is considered to be unconstitutional.

Rights of a Person Arrested Under Ordinary Circumstances

Article 22 states the Rights that are conferred by the Constitution upon a person arrested under ordinary circumstances. They are as follows :

- Whenever a person is arrested, he or she should be informed, as soon as it is possible, of the grounds for arrest and should be allowed to consult and to be defended by a legal practitioner of his or her choice.

The individual must be produced before the nearest magistrate within twenty-four hours of the arrest. Without the orders of the magistrate, he/she cannot be detained in custody beyond the said period.

Right Against Exploitation–Articles 23 and 24

The citizens of India have been guaranteed the right against exploitation through Articles 23 and 24 of the Constitution. The Indian Constitution is inclusive of two main declarations against exploitation :

Prohibition of Traffic in Human beings and Forced Labour

Article 23 prohibits traffic in human beings and other forms of forced labour. Trafficking in human beings means 'dealing in men and women like goods, such as letting, selling or otherwise disposing of them'. Forced labour or 'beggar' means 'making a person work against his will and then not to pay him his wages'. The contravention of these provisions is declared punishable by law. Thus, a person who is asked to do any labour without payment or with payment less than his desire can complain against the violation of his fundamental right.

However, an exception is made for compulsory service for public purposes. Compulsory military conscription is included by this provision.

Prohibition of Employment of Children in Factories, etc.

Article 24 prohibits the employment of children below the age of 14 years in any mine or factory. A child should not be engaged in any hazardous employment.

Right to Freedom of Religion–Articles 25 to 28.

The Preamble to the Constitution ensures the liberty of belief, worship and faith to all citizens. The objective is realized by the following provisions of the Constitution of India :

Freedom of Conscience and the Free Profession and Propagation of Religion

Article 25 guarantees freedom of conscience and the right to practise, profess and propagate any religion to every individual. However, the State may impose restrictions on the freedom of conscience and the free profession and propagation of religion in the interests of health, morality and public order. Thus, no one can be allowed to hurt the religious feelings of any class of Indian citizens. Religious practices like sacrificing animals or human beings, for offering to gods and goddesses or to some supernatural forces are not permissible.

Freedom to Manage Religious Affairs

Article 26 of the Constitution guarantees the right to establish and maintain institutions for charitable and religious purposes and to manage its own affairs regarding matters of religion. The rights are also subject to morality, public order and health.

Freedom as to Payment of Taxes for Promotion of any Particular Religion

Article 27 states that no taxes shall be levied on the proceeds of which are meant for the maintenance of any particular religion. It is against the ideals of a Secular State to pay out any money out of the public funds for the promotion of any particular religious sect.

No Religious Instruction in Educational Institutions maintained out of State Funds

Article 28 of the Constitution aims to establish a Secular State by allowing equal freedom of worship and faith to all. In case of State recognized or State-aided educational institutions, there is no bar to giving religious instruction. No individual can be required to take part in any religious instruction without his consent and in case of a minor, the consent of his guardian has to be obtained.

Thus, the Constitution aims to establish a Secular State by allowing equal freedom of worship and faith to all.

Cultural and Educational Rights–Articles 29 and 30.

Since India is a country of different religions and cultures, the Constitution protects the educational and cultural rights of the minorities.

Protection of Interests of Minorities

Article 29 provides that any minority group having a distinct language, script or culture of its own shall have the right to conserve it. No citizen of India shall be deprived of admission into any educational institution maintained by the State or receiving aid out of State funds on grounds only of religion, race, caste, language.

Right to establish Educational Institutions

Article 30 states that all minorities have the right to establish and administer educational institutions of their choice, irrespective of religion or language. The State shall not, in granting aid to educational institutions, discriminate against any educational institution on the ground that it is under the management of a minority.

Right to Constitutional Remedies–Article 32.

Unless there are the means to make the Fundamental Rights effective, a mere declaration of it is useless. Article 32 provides the right to move the Supreme Court for the enforcement of the Rights conferred by Part III of the Constitution. It provides writs or legal remedies for the protection of our Fundamental Rights against the arbitrary actions of the State. The High courts are also empowered by the Constitution to issue orders or writs for the enforcement of any of these rights. The writs include :

Habeas Corpus

In Latin, Habeas Corpus literally means, *'you may have the body'*. It protects the sefety of any person held in prison or taken into custody. This writ can be issued where a person is illegally held even by a private individual. By issuing this writ, the Court can order the detaining authority to bring the detained person to the court to explain why such a prisoner is being held. This writ also acts as a deterrent to unlawful imprisonment of people under trial. The writ of habeas corpus is reckoned as "the popular and effective writ, as far as illegal confinement is concerned". It is a hope given to the meanest against the mightiest. It is to be noted, in some Spanish-speaking countries, "amparo de liberated (protection of freedom)" is tantamount to Habeas Corpus.

Mandamus

The Latin word *'mandamus'* means *'we command'*. The writ is issued when a petition is filed against any public official or unit who is not performing its duty. In such cases the higher court can command the concerned officer to perform its duty.

Quo Warranto

The writ of Quo Warranto is generally issued against a person who has illegally or forcefully occupied a public office. It also questions the bona fide of the person holding such an office. If a person illegally occupies a post, this writ is generally is issued against that person.

Prohibition

The writ of Prohibition is issued against a lower court to prevent it from exercising its powers when it is legally not empowered to do so. This writ is issued to limit the jurisdiction of the lower court in exercising its powers.

Certiorari

The word *'certiorari'* means *'to be fully informed'*. By this writ, the lower court has to hand over all the relevant records of a case to the higher court.

FUNDAMENTAL DUTIES

The Fundamental Duties were inserted in Article 51A of Part IV of the Constitution, by the 42nd Amendment Act, 1976. Duty means *'an obligation imposed by custom or law on a person.'* Every right has a corresponding duty and like rights, duties may be both moral and legal. The incorporation of fundamental duties in the constitution was thus an attempt to balance the individual's civic freedoms with civic obligations and thus to fill a serious gap in the constitution.

Earlier, there were ten Fundamental Duties under Article 51A by the 42nd Constitutional Amendment Act, 1976. However, the 86th Amendment Act, 2002 amended Article 51A of the Constitution and added a new Article that dealt with the Right to Education. Under these provisions, all citizens are expected to faithfully observe the following fundamental Duties :

FUNDAMENTAL DUTIES

Under Article 51A, it shall be the duty of every citizen of India :

- To abide by the Constitution and respect its ideals and institutions, the National Flag and the National Anthem.
- To cherish and follow the noble ideals which inspired our national struggle for freedom.
- To uphold and protect the sovereignty, unity and integrity of India.
- To defend the country and render national service when called upon to do so.
- To promote harmony and spirit of common brotherhood amongst all the people of India transcending religious, linguistic and regional or sectional diversities, to renounce practices derogatory to the dignity of women.
- To value and preserve the rich heritage of our composite culture.
- To protect and improve the natural environment including forests, lakes, rivers and wildlife, and have compassion for living creatures.
- To develop scientific temper, humanism and the spirit of inquiry and reform.
- To safeguard public property and to abjure violence.
- To strive towards excellence in all spheres of individual and collective activity, so that the nation constantly rises to higher levels of endeavor and achievement.
- To provide opportunities for education to his child or, as the case may be, ward between the age of 6 and 14 years.

The 11th fundamental duty was added in the year 2002 by the 86th Constitutional Amendment Act. It states that every citizen who is "A parent or guardian has to provide opportunities for the education to his child/ward between the age of six and fourteen years.

Importance of Fundamental Duties

The Fundamental Duties have been enlisted in the Indian Constitution to make the citizens aware of their economic and social obligations. These duties warn the citizens of our country to respect the National Flag and National Anthem as it stirs up patriotism and strengthens national harmony. It also intends to uphold the right of equality among all individuals, to disown violence, to offer compulsory education and to protect the environment and public property. The constitution does not make any provision to enforce these duties. However, any citizen violating these duties or showing disrespect to the National symbol is punishable under law.

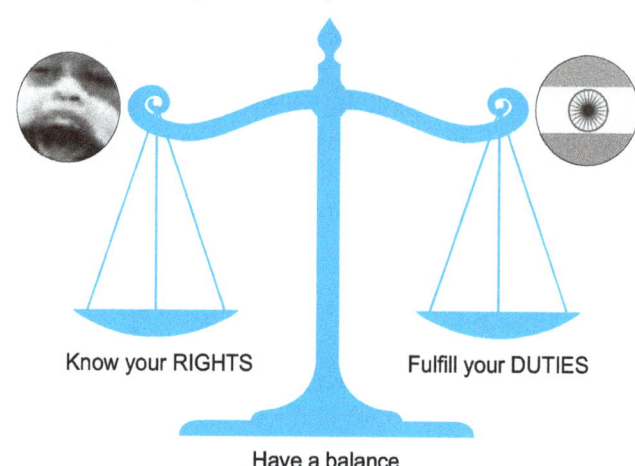

It is our duty to have a balance between our Fundamental Rights and Duties.

The Fundamental Duties remain ineffective if the citizens refuse to assume duties and are not enthusiastic to be active participants in the process of governance. These duties should be performed by each and every citizen of the country to protect their cultural heritage and also for taming the unruly elements in society.

DIRECTIVE PRINCIPLES OF STATE POLICY

The Directive Principles of State Policy are the instructions or guidelines to the central and state governments of India, to be kept in mind while framing laws and policies. These provisions, contained in Part IV (Article 36 to 51) of the Constitution of India embodies the Directive Principles of State policy, which are not enforceable by any court, but the principles laid down therein are considered fundamental in the governance of the country, making it the duty of the State to apply these principles in making laws to establish a just society in the country. The purpose of Directive principles is to provide social, economic and political justice to our people, like adequate means to livelihood, equal pay for equal work for men and women, free and compulsory primary education, right to work, public assistance in case of old age, unemployment, sickness and disablement, etc. These Principles added a new section to the constitution on 'Fundamental Duties' that enjoined citizens 'to promote harmony and the spirit of common brotherhood among all the people of India, transcending religious, linguistic and regional diversities.'

Indian Directive Principles of State Policy (DPSP) have been inspired by the Directive Principles, stated in the Constitution of Ireland. It also follows the principles of Gandhism.

Objectives of Directive Principles

The Directive Principles constitute a restatement of certain ideals and objectives mentioned in the Preamble. These are guidelines which should be kept in mind by the Union and State governments while making laws and implementing policies. Following are some of the directive principles of the state policy that are included in our Constitution which aim at establishing a welfare state where equal opportunities are granted to all in the social, economic and educational sphere.

- The State should aim at establishing a welfare state in India where there will be no concentration of wealth in the hands of a few. It needs to ensure equal pay for equal work for both men and women.
- The State should also work towards reducing economic inequality, and the inequalities in status and opportunity.
- The State should create social and economic conditions which ensure adequate means of livelihood under which the citizens can lead a good life.
- The State has to provide free education to all children till 14 years of age.
- The State should work for organizations of village panchayats and should secure a uniform civil code for all citizens from all sections of the society.
- The State should consider its primary duty to stop the use of intoxicating drinks.
- The State should extend all help in the cases of unemployment, child abuse, old age, exploitation of workers, sickness and disablement, etc.
- The State must ensure the living wage and proper working conditions for the workers.
- The State also has to work for the upliftment of the backward classes like Scheduled Castes, Scheduled Tribes, and others.
- The State should protect historical monuments and the environment from destruction and disfigurement.

The Directive Principles guide the State government to work for the welfare of all- children, women, men, villages and so on.

Classification of Directive Principles

Articles 36-51 of the Indian Constitution contain the main provisions of the Directive Principles of the State Policy. They can be classified under the following principle groups :

- Principles promoting economic equality.
- Political and administrative principles.
- Legal and Judicial Principles.
- Environmental Principles.
- Principles protecting national heritage.
- Principles promoting international peace and security.

CLASSIFICATION OF THE DIRECTIVE PRINCIPLES

ARTICLE	TITLE
36	Definition of state : The 'State' includes the Government and Parliament of India and the Government and the Legislature of each of the States and all local or other authorities within the territory of India or under the control of the Government of India.
37	Application of the principles.
38	State to secure a social order for the promotion of welfare of the people.
39	Certain principles of policy to be followed by the State. ❏ equal rights to men and women. ❏ ownership of resources. ❏ equal pay for equal work. ❏ protection of children.
39 A	Equal justice and free legal aid to citizens having economic or other disabilities.
40	Organization of village panchayats.
41	Right to work, to education and to public assistance in certain cases.
42	Provision for just and humane conditions of work and maternity relief.
43	Living wage, good working conditions etc. for workers.
43 A	participation of workers in management of industries.
44	Uniform civil code for the citizens.
45	Provision for free and compulsory education for children.
46	Promotion of educational and economic interests of scheduled castes, scheduled tribes and other weaker sections.
47	Duty of the State to raise the level of nutrition and the standard of living and to improve public health.
48	Organization of agriculture and animal husbandry.
48 A	protection and improvement of environment and safeguarding of forests and wildlife.
49	Protection of monuments and places and objects of national importance.
50	Separation of judiciary from executive.
51	Promotion of international peace and security. ❏ just and honorable relations. ❏ encourage settlement of international disputes by arbitration.

Thus, the Directive Principles of the State Policy are basically a code of conduct for the legislature and administrators of the country, which aim for the establishment of a Welfare State. With the help of these principles, the government can bring about more improvements in the condition of the people. It also serves as a yardstick to measure or assess the performance of a government.

Do You know

❏ *The Mahatma Gandhi National Rural Employment Guarantee (MNREGA) was introduced in 2005 as NREGA to enforce Directive principles embodied in the Article 39 and 41.*

❏ *Several schemes and programmes have been launched such as Mid-day meal scheme, ICDS, SABLA etc. by the government to enhance the nutritional level of the children and adolescent girls.*

WELFARE STATE

The famous sociologist T.H. Marshall identified the welfare state as a distinctive combination of democracy, welfare and capitalism. A welfare state is a concept of government in which the state plays a key role in the protection and promotion of the economic and social well being of its citizens. It is based on the principles of equality of opportunity, equitable distribution of wealth, and public responsibility for those unable to avail themselves of the minimal provisions for a good life. Otto von Bismarck, the first Chancellor of Germany, created the modern welfare state by building on a tradition of welfare programs in Prussia and Saxony.

One of the salient features of the Indian Constitution is the effort to establish a welfare state. Article 38 of the Constitution reads—*"The state shall strive to promote the welfare of the people by securing and protecting as effectively as it may a social order in which justice social, economic and political shall inform all institutions of national life."* While Article 39 (a) spells that all citizens, men and women equally have the right to an adequate means of livelihood, Article 43 enjoins that the state shall endeavor to secure to all workers work, a living wage and conditions of work ensuring a decent standard of living. Provision of employment opportunities, which is yet another objective of a welfare state is emphasized by Article 41, which directs the state for securing the right to work. Protection and special care of the weaker sections of the community are provided by Article 46. The Directive Principles of State Policy spell out the philosophy of the welfare state in clear terms.

The Directive Principles of State Policy are parameters for the framing of laws by the government.

DIFFERENCE BETWEEN DIRECTIVE PRINCIPLES AND FUNDAMENTAL RIGHTS

Directive Principles	Fundamental Rights
1. Contained in Part–IV (Articles 36 to 51) of the Constitution.	1. Contained in Part-III (Article 12 to 35) of the Constitution.
2. They are non-justiciable, which means no one can go to the courts to compel the State for their proper implementation. Hence, cannot be enforced by any Court of law.	2. They are justiciable, which means any individual can move the courts seeking legal assistance for restoring them. Hence, can be enforced by a court against the State.
3. These are aimed at securing welfare, social and economic freedoms by appropriate State action.	3. These are primarily aimed at assuring political freedom to the citizens by protecting them against excessive State action.
4. The Directive Principles are given a place of permanence by the Constitution makers.	4. The Fundamental Rights are given a pride of place by the Constitution makers.
5. These need legislation or policy intervention for their proper implementation	5. These are automatically enforced and no legislation is required for their implementation.
6. These are socio-economic instructions meant for the establishment of a welfare State.	6. These are meant for citizens to strive towards their individual good and to protect them from encroachment of their basic rights

TERMS TO REMEMBER

Adult Franchise : *The right to vote is given to individuals aged 18 years and above, irrespective of caste, creed, colour, qualifications, etc.*

Citizenship : *The right of an individual to be legally recognised as a member or citizen of the country.*

Single Citizenships : *In India, the concept of 'single citizenship is adopted from England. It means if one is a citizen of India, he/she can not simultaneously be a citizen of another country for example, USA.*

Federation : *A group of States with a Central Government.*

Residuary Powers : *The power to make laws on subjects that are not covered by any of the three lists.*

Unitary : *A single tier government in place of two or three tier system, as opposed to a federal structure.*

Conviction : *An instance of having committed a criminal offence.*

Constitutional Amendment : *Modifications, changes or additions to the Constitution.*

Exploitation : *Taking unfair advantage of someone.*

Minorities : *The relatively small groups of people.*

Reservation : *An arrangement where something is reserved like the reservation of posts for OBCs.*

Welfare State : *A welfare state is a concept of government in which the state plays a key role in the protection and promotion of the economic and social well being of its citizens.*

In Retrospect

- Universal Adult Franchise, Single Citizenship and Fundamental Rights.
- **Meaning of Fundamental Rights** : Some rights are considered to be fundamental as the Constitution or the 'Fundamental Law of the Land' incorporates them. The Fundamental Rights are enforceable by the Courts. Right to Equality–Articles 14 to 18, Right to Freedom–Articles 19 to 22, Right against Exploitation–Articles 23 and 24,

  Right to Freedom of Religion–Articles 25 to 28, Cultural and Educational Rights–Articles 29 and 30, Right to Constitutional Remedies–Article 32
- **Fundamental Duties** : The 42nd Amendment Act (1976) introduced the eleven Fundamental Duties. An individual's obligations to oneself and family, to society and the nation at large are specified by the Fundamental Duties.

The Fundamental Duties include duty to develop scientific temper, spirit of inquiry and reform; duty to provide educational opportunities for his ward or child and duties concerning the environment. The Duties towards the Society and State include the duty to respect the National Anthem and the National Flag and to abide by the Constitution. Duties towards the Nation include the duty to promote the spirit of common brotherhood and harmony amongst the people of India.

- **Directive Principles of State Policy** : These Principles aim at establishing a welfare state in India by laying down directives for social and economic justice to our people like adequate means to livelihood, equal pay for both men and women, free and compulsory primary education, right to work, public assistance in case of old age, unemployment, sickness and disablement, etc.
- **Classification of Directive Principles of State Policy** : Principles promoting Economic equality, Political and Administrative principles, Legal and Judicial Principles, Environmental Principles, Principles protecting National Heritage and Principles promoting International Peace and Security.
- **Welfare State** : It is a distinctive combination of democracy, welfare and capitalism. Based on the principles of equality of opportunity, equitable distribution of wealth, to every individual for a good life. Article 38 of the Constitution strives to promote the welfare State.
- **Difference between Directive Principles and Fundamental Rights** : Principles are not be enforced by any Court of law, Rights are enforced; Principles aimed at securing welfare, social and economic freedoms, Rights aim at assuring political freedom to the citizen; Principles are given a place of permanence, Rights are given a place of Pride by the Constitution; Principles need legislation for their proper implementation, Rights are automatically enforced; Principles are meant for a welfare state, Rights are meant for each and every citizen of the country.

SALIENT FEATURES OF THE CONSTITUTION

EXERCISES

Part-I (Short Questions)

1. Mention any three prominent features of the Indian Constitution.
2. What do you mean by Universal Adult Franchise ?
3. What is meant by Single Citizenship ?
4. What are the six categories of Fundamental Rights ?
5. What does the term 'Right to Equality' mean ?
6. Explain any two of the essential freedoms guaranteed to the citizens under Article 19.
7. Which Fundamental Right prohibits forced labour and 'beggar' ?
8. Define the Right to Constitutional Remedies.
9. Which courts are competent to issue writs ?
10. What are the Fundamental Duties ?
11. Mention two Fundamental Duties.
12. Which Fundamental Duty was added to the list by the 86th Amendment Act, 2002 ?
13. State two importances of the Fundamental Duties.
14. What is meant by the term 'Directive Principles'?
15. State the various types of Directive Principles.
16. Mention two principles related to economic equality.
17. What principles have been laid down in our constitution for :
    (a) Protection and Preservation of Environment
    (b) Protection and Preservation of our National Heritage.
18. Describe briefly the principle relating to the establishment of International Peace.
19. State the principles related to maintenance of administration and the rule of law.
20. What is a Welfare State?

Part-II (Structured Questions)

1. Define the term Fundamental Rights. Name the six main categories into which the Fundamental Rights are divided.
2. What do you mean by the term 'Right against Exploitation'? The Fundamental Rights can be suspended under what circumstances ?
3. Name any two Fundamental Rights which indicate that India is a Secular State. What are the three rights of an individual who is arrested under ordinary circumstances ?
4. In each of the following cases, which Fundamental Right will be violated ?
   (a) Some students of a school were disqualified from taking examinations without notice.
   (b) A person belonging to a certain religious community has been dismissed from Government service without reason.
   (c) A 10 year old child was found working in a 'bidi' factory.
5. What are the Fundamental Duties? Discuss the importance of Fundamental Duties ?
6. Define Directive Principles of State Policy. What are the Principles ?
7. What do you mean by a Welfare State ? How has the Indian Constitution tried to implement the principle of the Welfare State ?

CHAPTER 3

ELECTIONS IN INDIA

◆ Meaning; Composition of Election Commission (in brief); Direct and Indirect elections; General election; Mid-Term election and By-Election.

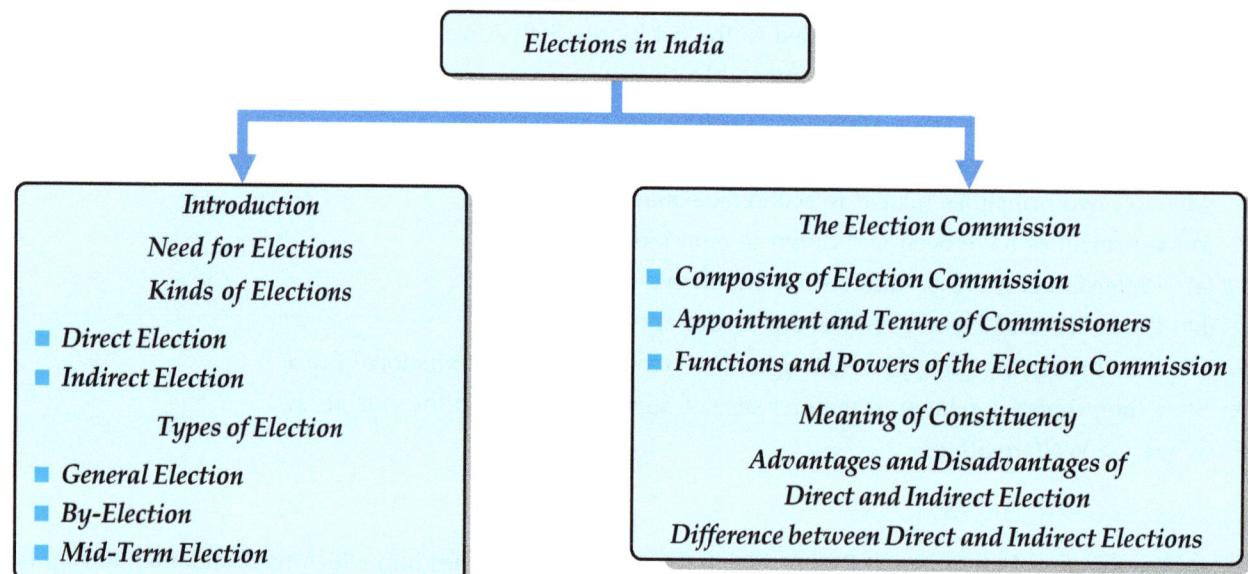

INTRODUCTION

Democracy is the form of government where people have the right to say and decide who is capable of holding power, and how they should be using that power. In a democratic nation, the citizens enjoy the right to elect or choose, either directly or indirectly, their representatives to govern the nation or the State. Thus, *Election is a process of electing or choosing the representatives who will run the government.*

India follows the policy of maintaining a democratic, representative and parliamentary form of government. As a matter of fact, Indian citizens freely elect their chosen representatives who form the legislatures and run the government. The Indian Constitution states that every citizen of India, who is not below the age of 18 years and has not for any other cause been disqualified under any law, shall be entitled to register himself or herself as a Voter. As per the Constitution, *'there shall be one General Electoral Roll for every constituency'* and no individual shall be barred from the electoral roll, on the basis of caste, religion, sex, or race. The electoral roll (also referred to as electoral register or poll book) represents a compelling list of persons who are entitled to vote in a specific electoral district.

NEED FOR ELECTIONS

India is a constitutional democracy with a parliamentary system of government, which is committed to hold regular, free and fair elections. These elections give an opportunity to the voters to indirectly participate in the administration of the country, to possess the membership of the two houses of the parliament, the State and Union legislative assemblies, and the Post of the President and Vice-President.

Elections in India are events involving political mobilization and organizational complexity on a huge scale. The representatives elected by the people retain power only for a fixed tenure. After this tenure, they need to be re-elected to resume power. Therefore, these representatives remain under the grip of the people. Moreover, election time is when the electorate or the common mass becomes educated and aware of the ideologies of different political parties. This is the time when the leaders arouse interest of the people in public affairs like economic, political and social problems affecting the entire nation. Beside this, by contesting elections either as members of a political party or as an independent candidate, people get a chance to participate in government formation and enact laws and execute policies for the good of the people and their country.

Kinds of Elections

India is the world's largest democracy where people under the system of **Universal Adult Franchise** vote to elect a representative government. The system of Universal Adult Franchise helps all the citizens to get involved in the governance of their state. This enables them to elect their representatives for the purpose of administering and protecting the interests of the people. As a matter of fact, India adopted the system of Universal Adult Franchise. Article 326 of the Indian Constitution maintains that the Elections to the House of the People and to the Legislative Assemblies should be organized based on this system. Every person, irrespective of religion or ethnicity, who attains the age of 18 is entitled to vote. It is in accordance with this principle that the people's representatives get elected at all levels from Local Self-Government to parliament. Our system of parliamentary democracy therefore is entirely dependent on elections which preserve the sanctity of the great ideals of Liberty, Equality and Fraternity.

There are two kinds of Elections in India, namely; Direct Election and Indirect Election.

"Liberty, Equality, Fraternity" is a hallowed legacy of the Age of Enlightenment. The adage first appeared during the French Revolution. The Preamble to the Indian Constitution adopted the great ideals of Liberty, Equality and Fraternity.

Direct Election : The voters directly choose their representatives to the legislatures. In other words, people directly elect the Members of Parliament in case of the 'House of the people' or lower house (Lok Sabha) and Members of Legislative Assembly in case of Vidhan Sabha or the legislative council or Vidhan Parishad in the lower house. Citizens of India who have attained the age of 18 years and their names have been included in the voter's list cast their votes in direct elections.

Indirect Election : The voters select their representatives indirectly, i.e., by electing intermediaries who choose the members of the legislature on people's behalf. The election of the members of the Rajya Sabha at the Union level, the Vidhan Parishad at the State level and the Vice – President and President of India also follow this method of indirect election. In this system, the common people do not directly participate in the voting process. On the other hand, the responsibility is divided among the shoulder of their representatives, whom they choose through direct elections.

Types of Elections

There are three types of elections commonly held in India, namely : General Elections, By-Elections and Mid-term Elections.

General Election : These are the regular elections, conducted after the completion of a period of five years of the Lok Sabha and State Assemblies. The First General Election in India based on Adult Franchise was held in 1952 wherein the adult citizens of the country elected their representatives to the first Lok Sabha and State Assemblies. The Second one was held in 1957 but after that year, the Lok Sabha elections and that to the State Legislative Assemblies were held at different times for the sake of convenience and ease.

By-Election : By-elections (known as special elections in the USA and by-polls in India) are used to fill the elected offices that have turned vacant or empty due to the death or sudden resignation of any member of the Central legislative Assembly or the State Legislative Assembly before the full-term expires. The newly elected member holds office only till the term of the existing government is not complete. By-elections may also be conducted to fill up the vacant seat of a candidate who has been disqualified under parliamentary law for some reason or the other.

Mid-Term Election : When the full term of five years of State Assemblies or Lok Sabha has not been completed and the house has to be dissolved, this type of election is held to bring a new house to power. However, the expression of 'Mid-term Election,' has legally no importance as only Lok Sabha elections are called General Elections, regardless of the fact whether the last House completed its term or was dissolved midway.

THE ELECTION COMMISSION

Meaning and Definition of Election Commission:

An Election Commission is a body entrusted with the responsibility of implementing election mechanisms. The use of exact terminology varies from country to country, including such terms like "electoral court", "electoral commission" or "electoral branch". The body can be governmental or judicial. It is indispensable for the Election Commission to perform election related activities in a systematic way.

FOUNDATION OF THE ELECTION

Elections in India are conducted by the Election Commission of India (EC), which has been established under Article 324 of the Constitution. It was established on 25th January 1950. Originally the commission had only a Solitary Chief Election Commissioner (CEC). However, the concept of a multi-member Election Commission has been in operation since 1993, which means the President can appoint the Chief Election Commissioner as well as two additional Election Commissioners.

Nirvachan Sadan, New Delhi

The Commission has its headquarters, called **Nirvachan Sadan** in New Delhi. The territorial work is distributed among separate units responsible for different Zones into which the 35 Constituent States and Union Territories of the country are grouped for convenience. At the state level, the election work is supervised by the Chief Electoral Officer of the State, who is appointed by the Commission from amongst senior civil servants. At the district and constituency levels, the District Election Officers, Electoral Registration Officers and Returning Officers, (In each constituency, an official deliberates on the process of an election and declares the result. This official is regarded as Returning officer) who are assisted by a large number of junior functionaries, perform election work. They all perform their functions relating to elections in addition to their other responsibilities.

Composition of Election Commission of India:

Article 324 of the Indian Constitution makes provisions for the Election Commission and its compositions. According to the Article 324 of the Indian Constitution, the Election Commission in India shall comprise :

❏ a Chief Election Commissioner, and
❏ two Election Commissioners

The name of the first Chief Election Commissioner of India was Sukumar Sen (1950-58) and the name of the present Chief Election Commissioner of India is Sunil Arora (December 2018). The other Election Commissioner is Ashok Lavasa.

Appointment and Tenure of Commissioners

The President appoints the Chief Election Commissioner and Election Commissioners. They have a tenure of six years, or up to the age of 65 years, which ever is earlier. They enjoy the same status and receive salary and perks as available to Judges of the Sup-reme Court of India. They do not hold any office of profit after retirement. Through impeachment by the Parliament, the Chief Election Commissioner can be removed from the office of the Election Commission. At the other end of the spectrum, other Election Commissioners can be removed by the president at the behest of the Chief Election Commissioner.

Mr. Ashok Lavasa (Election Commisioner, Mr. Sunil Arora (Chief Election Commissioner)

A voter identity card

of those who have turned 18 or have moved into a consti-tuency and to remove the names of those who have died or moved out of a constituency. The electoral roll is a list of all people in the constituency who are registered to vote in Indian Elections. Only those people who have their name registered in electoral roll are allowed to vote.

❏ To improve the accuracy of the electoral rolls and prevent electoral frauds. The Election Commission ordered the making of photo identity cards for all voters in the country in August, 1993. More than 450 million Identity cards have been issued till date. A voter's identity card, also known as Electors Photo Identity Card (EPIC) is a photo identity card, which is issued by the Election Commission of India. The photo identity card is given to all the citizens of India who are entitled to vote.

❏ To give recognition to political parties as All India Parties or Regional Parties on the basis of the votes received by them in the last elections.

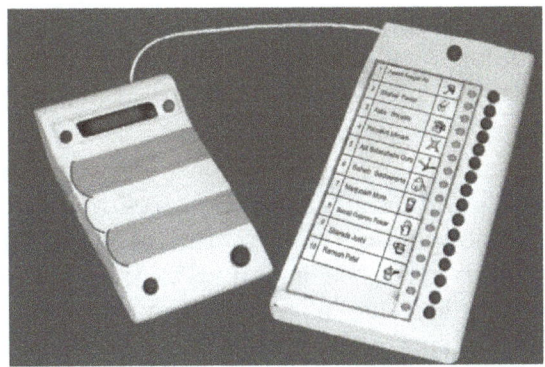

Electronic Voting Machine

❏ To allot election symbols to various political parties and independent candidates. The Election Commission is also responsible for hearing and settling all disputes with regard to such symbols.

Functions and Powers of the Election Commission

The main functions of the Election Commission are as follows :

❏ The superintendence, direction and control of elections.
❏ To conduct elections and to look after all the problems connected with such elections.
❏ To prepare electoral rolls and get them revised before every election so as to add the names

- To supervise the election machinery throughout the country so as to ensure that elections are held in a free and fair manner. A striking aspect of the democratic polity is holding of elections at regular intervals. Elections manifest the emblem of the democratic nation. Elections display the integrity and sovereignty of all the citizens of the nation and legitimize the power of the government. Thus, free and fair elections are essential for the democracy. The Election Commission is responsible to maintain free and fair elections. It is an autonomous unit and is free from the grip of external pressure. It is indispensable for the election commission to hold free and fair elections to the legislative bodies in the country and ensure the maintenance of democracy.

- It is the duty of returning officer to scrutinize the nomination papers of each candidate thoroughly. According to the law of the Indian Constitution, the returning officers receive the nomination papers of the scheduled date for scrutiny in the election time table published under section 30 of the representation of the people Act, 1951. The Returning Officer is exclusively responsible for the scrutiny of the nomination papers. This responsibility cannot be passed down to the Assistant Returning Officer by the returning officer. The nomination of any candidate with incomplete and invalid papers is rejected by the Commission. The candidates have to be genuine, qualified and fulfilling all criteria like election symbol, deposit money, election agent, etc.

- To scrutinize the election expenses incurred by a candidate during the election process. The nomination of a candidate is declared invalid if he/she is found to transgress or make illegal use of this expenditure limit set by the commission. In 2003, the limit for election expenses was fixed by the commission. A candidate seeking election to a Lok Sabha and Vidhan Sabha seat may spend 25 lakhs and 10 lakhs of rupees respectively during elections. The monitoring of Election Expenditure follows a coordinated mechanism. There are several aspects of monitoring Election expenditure. The management of Expenditure overseers and Assistant Expenditure overseers, Video Surveillance Teams, Media Certification and Monitoring Committee and Video viewing Team are needed for the serutiny.

- To conduct the elections of President, Vice-President, members of both the Houses of Parliament, members of Legislative Assemblies and Legislative Councils of various States.

- To advise the President of India about the possibility of holding elections in a State under President's rule after the expiry of a period of six months.

- To cancel polls in case of large scale rigging, irregularities or violence during the election process.

MEANING OF CONSTITUENCY

During the time of elections, a State or the entire country is divided into smaller geographical units, as far as possible with an approximately equal population called constituencies, from where representatives are sent to both the Houses at the Centre as well as the State. India has a multi-tier democratic system.

A constituency is a well defined territorial area which is required, at the time of elections, to elect its representative to the apex legislature body of India–Lok Sabha (Union legislature), State legislature body called Vidhan Sabha (legislative assembly) and local bodies like Zila Parishad, Municipal corporation and Gram Panchayat. Hence, every area has a constituency under which it falls. There are separate constituencies for the Assembly elections and Parliamentary elections, the constituencies for the Parliamentary elections being much bigger in size as compared to those for the State Assembly elections.

In India, every constituency is a single-member constituency with only one representative. Most democratic countries have this kind of constituency as it builds closeness between the voters and the elected candidate and follow a simple majority system in declaring the elected candidate. The country is divided into 543 Parliamentary Constituencies, each of which returns one Member of Parliament (MP) to the Lok Sabha, which is the lower house of Parliament. For example, Uttar Pradesh has the largest number of constituencies i.e., 80, and therefore have 80 MPs in the Lok Sabha. While states like Mizoram, Nagaland and Sikkim have one constituency each and thus only one MP each represents these states.

In most European countries, constituencies are drawn as multi-member constituencies, where more than one representative is elected from each constituency. The voter gets as many votes as the number of members in that constituency. However, this style of voting is losing its popularity and is now being replaced by single-member constituency in most countries.

ADVANTAGES AND DISADVANTAGES OF DIRECT AND INDIRECT ELECTIONS

ADVANTAGES

Direct Elections	Indirect Elections
1. It stimulates the interest of the masses in various affairs related to public welfare and the nation.	1. It reduces the role of people as the choice is made by a handful of representatives.
2. The elected representatives are accountable to the voters for their actions.	2. It is more appropriate for elections in extremely large constituencies.
3. Depending upon their judgment, the voters can select as well as reject representatives.	3. It mostly involves low cost campaigns.

DISADVANTAGES

Direct Elections	Indirect Elections
1. The voters may develop partial attitude towards the wrong candidates based on the caste, religion or emotions.	1. This is less democratic as what the people want to say is to be inferred from their representatives.
2. The accurate public opinion that is expressed through the voting ballots may get disfigured as all voters do not vote, out of indifference or due to corrupt practices like threats, rigging or booth capture.	2. As the number of voters is quite low, there are chances of corruption, horse-trading and bribery to secure votes.
3. A huge amount of time, energy and money is involved in direct elections. Moreover, election campaigns may result in disputes, tension and even killings.	3. Some voters may even disobey orders from their party and cast their vote in favour or against a specific representative.

DIFFERENCE BETWEEN DIRECT AND INDIRECT ELECTIONS

Direct Elections	Indirect Elections
1. Representatives are directly chosen by the people through voting.	Officials of the State. 1. Representatives are indirectly elected by the people through an intermediary group who further elect the representatives.
2. Members of the Lok Sabha, Vidhan Sabha or Legislative Assemblies, local bodies like	2. Members of Rajya Sabha, Vidhan Parishad,

Municipal Corporation, Municipalities and Gram Panchayats are directly elected.	Zila Parishad, President and Vice President are indirectly elected.
3. There is a very large body of voters called the electorate.	3. There is a very small voting body generally called electoral college.
4. The age and qualifications of the voters are established and regulated by law for the	4. The elected representatives are not based on qualifications and treated equally.

LIST OF CHIEF ELECTION COMMISSIONERS OF INDIA

No.	Name	Took Office	Office Tenure
1.	Sukumar Sen	21 March 1950	19 December 1958
2.	Kalyan Sundaram	20 December 1958	30 September 1967
3.	SP Sen Verma	1 October 1967	30 September 1972
4.	Nagendra Singh	1 October 1972	6 February 1973
5.	T. Swaminathan	7 February 1973	17 June 1977
6.	S. L. Shakdhar	18 June 1977	17 June 1982
7.	R. K. Trivedi	18 June 1982	31 December 1985
8.	R. V. S. Peri Sastri	1 January 1986	25 November 1990
9.	V. S. Rama Devi	26 November 1990	11 December 1990
10.	T. N. Seshan	12 December 1990	11 December 1996
11.	M. S. Gill	12 December 1996	13 June 2001
12.	J. M. Lyngdoh	14 June 2001	7 February 2004
13.	T. S. Krishnamurthy	8 February 2004	15 May 2005
14.	B. B. Tandon	16 May 2005	29 June 2006
15.	N. Gopalaswami	30 June 2006	20 April 2009
16.	Navin Chawla	21 April 2009	29 July 2010
17.	S. Y. Quraishi	30 July 2010	10 June 2012
18.	V.S. Sampath	11 June 2012	15 January 2015
19.	H. S. Brahma	16 January 2015	18 April 2015
20.	Nasim Zaidi	19 April 2015	5 July 2017
21.	Achal Kumar Jyoti	6 July 2017	22 January 2018
22.	Om Prakash Rawat	23 January 2018	1 December 2018
23.	Sunil Arora	2 December 2018	Incumbent

In Retrospect

- **Election** : Election is a process of choosing the representatives to form the government.
- **Need for Elections** : Elections give common people the right to choose their leader. The government is hence answerable to the common masses.
- **Kinds of Elections** : Direct Election : representatives in the legislatures are directly chosen by the voters; Indirect Election : In case of Indirect Election, an intermediate body is elected by the voters, which ultimately proceeds to elect the President or the representatives, as the case may be.
- **Types of Elections** : General Election, By-Election and Mid-term Elections.
- **The Election Commission** : Elections in India are conducted by the Election Commission of India, President appoints the Chief Election Commissioner and other two Election Commissioners, stays in office till the age of 65 years, can be removed by parliament with two-thirds majority in the Lok Sabha and

ELECTIONS IN INDIA   39

Rajya Sabha, responsible for updating electoral rolls, recognition of political parties, registration of voter identity cards, conduct of free and fair elections, scrutinizing nomination papers and expenses.

◆ *Meaning of Constituency* : *A well defined territorial area that includes a body of residents who select a representative amongst them.*
◆ *Returning officers*: *In each constituency, an afficial deliberates on the process of an election and declares the result. This official is regarded as returning officer.*

EXERCISES

Part-I (Short Questions)

1. What do you mean by the term 'Election' ?
2. What is the need for elections in India ?
3. What are the two kinds of elections in India ?
4. Point out one advantage each of the above kinds of Elections.
5. State two disadvantages of both Direct and Indirect Elections.
6. What are the types of elections? When were the first General Elections held in India ?
7. What do you understand by the term 'By-Election' ?
8. State the differentiate between By-election and Mid-term election.
9. What is an Universal Adult Franchise? Give two reasons why it is adopted in India ?
10. When was the Election Commission established in India ?
11. Who appoints the Chief Election Commissioner of India ?
12. What is the maximum term of office of an Election Commissioner ?
13. Name the first and present Chief Election Commissioner of India.
14. How can the Election Commissioner be removed from office ?
15. What is an Electoral roll ?
16. What is the importance of voter identity cards ?
17. What is the role of the Returning Officers ?
18. Mention two important aspects in the scrutiny of election expenses.
19. What does the term constituency mean ?

Part-II (Structured Questions)

1. What are the border implications of Elections in India ? What are the comparative advantages and disadvantages of Direct and Indirect Elections ?
2. What do you understand by the term 'General' and 'Mid-term' election ? Provide a brief explaination.
3. Elections in India are conducted by the Election Commission of India. In this context, answer the following questions :
    (a) Composition of the Election Commission of India.
    (b) Appointment and tenure of the Election Commissioners.
    (c) Role of the Election Commission in the conduct of free and fair Elections.
4. Summarize the following functions of the Election Commission of India :
    (a) Formation of Electoral rolls
    (b) Voter's Identity Card
    (c) Conduct of Elections
    (d) Scrutiny of nomination papers
    (e) Scrutiny of Expenses.
5. Differentiate between Direct and Indirect Election.

CHAPTER 4

LOCAL SELF-GOVERNMENT—RURAL

♦ Rural : Three-tier system of Panchayati Raj—Gram Panchayat, Panchayat Samiti, Zila Parishad–their Meaning and Functions.

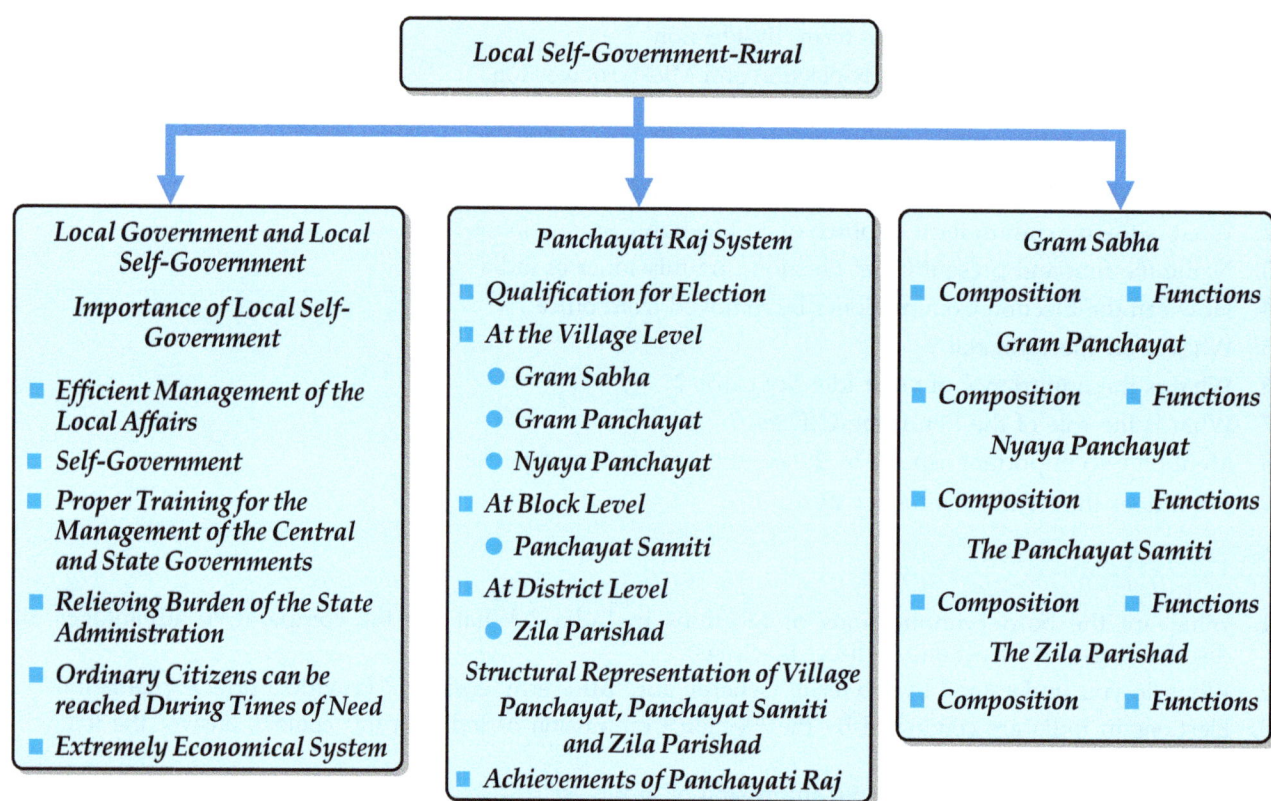

Local Self-Government means *"an elected body that enjoys a certain extent of autonomy and serves as a governmental unit for local affairs."* In India, the democratic structure is divided into three-tiers that look after the governance of the country. At the National level, the Central Government looks after the interests of the entire country; at the State level the State Government takes care of the problems and welfare of the people in the State, while the Local self-government manages the affairs at the grassroots level through the local representatives of that area. Thus, Local-self government forms an integral part of the three-tier system of the Indian government. It looks after the needs and issues of people of a village, a town, a district or a city.

LOCAL GOVERNMENT AND LOCAL SELF-GOVERNMENT

Local self-government can be stated as an institution managed by locally elected representatives who take care of the issues of a locality and provide the people with basic amenities. Such institutions are called **PRIs** or **Panchayati Raj Institutions** in rural areas and **MIs** or **Municipal Institutions** or **Municipal Corporation** or **Municipality** in urban areas. They receive government grants for activities like sanitation, health, providing elementary education, drainage, maintenance of roads, street lighting, setting minor disputes etc. whereas, local government comprises officials appointed by the government to look after the administration of a locality. Such officials include District Magistrate, Deputy Collector etc. These bodies receive grants from the government to take care of works like ensuring basic education, sanitation, buildings, roads etc.

IMPORTANCE OF LOCAL SELF-GOVERNMENT

The various institutions of Local self-government have a significant role to play in the operation of democracy at the local level. The vital role played by these institutions is underlined by the following functions that they are entrusted with to discharge efficiently :

Efficient Management of the Local Affairs

Local people tend to know best about the problems that are related to their areas like water supply, sanitation, education, electricity and other public works. Since the local people have a first-hand understanding of their locality and problems, they are the best judge of what requirements they may have. Thus, getting involved in local self-government, they can smoothly and more effectively cater to their needs.

Self-Government

The beneficial aspect of self-government is that it offers the public the opportunity to govern, which is the true essence of democracy. The local citizens learn to actively participate in administration and taking decisions that affect the lives of the people. In this way, every citizen gets a chance to evaluate the functioning of the elected representatives. Since the local self government institutions acquire the assistance of local communities, they tend to live more peacefully and without any trouble.

Proper Training for the Management of the Central and State Governments

The local institutions act as training grounds to prepare its members to manage State or National affairs in later years. Their experience will guide them to accept bigger challenges at the level of State or Nation. Majority of leaders, notable amongst them being Dadabhai Naoroji, Bal Gangadhar Tilak, Pheroze Shah Mehta, Gopal Krishna Gokhale, Pt. Jawaharlal Nehru and others, started their careers from local self-government bodies to reach higher platforms regionally and nationally.

Relieving Burden of the State Administration

The local institutions are capable of relieving the workload of State as well as Central Government by taking over some of their duties. These local bodies act as the machinery to handle problems locally and assume responsibility for developmental work. With some of these responsibilities taken over by the local bodies, the State administration can have time to look into bigger problems at the State level.

Ordinary Citizens can be reached during times of Need

In times of National Emergency due to foreign aggression, these institutions can reach out to ordinary citizens. The local people can form self-defence committees quickly and smoothly.

Extremely Economical System

The local bodies are generally less expensive to run than the expenses incurred by the officials of State administrations to manage a locality. These local institutions foster the idea of voluntary services and self-help that helps in saving substantial State funds. These saved funds are then used for constructive work of the State itself. Many honorary members join these local institutions that work without the involvement of money so that it doesn't create any economic burden on the people for their wages.

PANCHAYATI RAJ SYSTEM

In 1956, under the directions of the National Development Council, a committee was constituted under the chairmanship of Balwant Rai Mehta to look into the problems of Panchayati Raj. Along with many other recommendations, he recommended a three-tier system of Panchayati Raj. According to this system, besides Gram Panchayats at village level, there shall be a Panchayat Samiti at block level and a Zila Parishad at district level. The report was accepted on 12 January 1958. Rajasthan was the first State to implement the Panchayati Raj system on 2 October 1959 at the village *Nagaav*.

Thus, the three-tier system in the Panchayati Raj comprises :

- At the village level, there are three bodies- *Gram Sabha*, the *Gram Panchayat* and *Nyaya Panchayat*.
- At the block level, there are *Panchayat Samitis* that fall in the middle level.
- At the District level, *Zila Parishads* are set up.

Qualification for Election

In order to become members of the Gram Panchayat, the following criteria have to be fulfilled by the aspiring members :

- As per the Act, a candidate has to attain the prescribed age.
- The name of the candidates must be registered as voters in that particular Panchayat area.
- The candidates must be mentally sound.
- The State Legislatures must not have disqualified the candidates under any law.
- The candidate should not hold any office of Profit under the government.

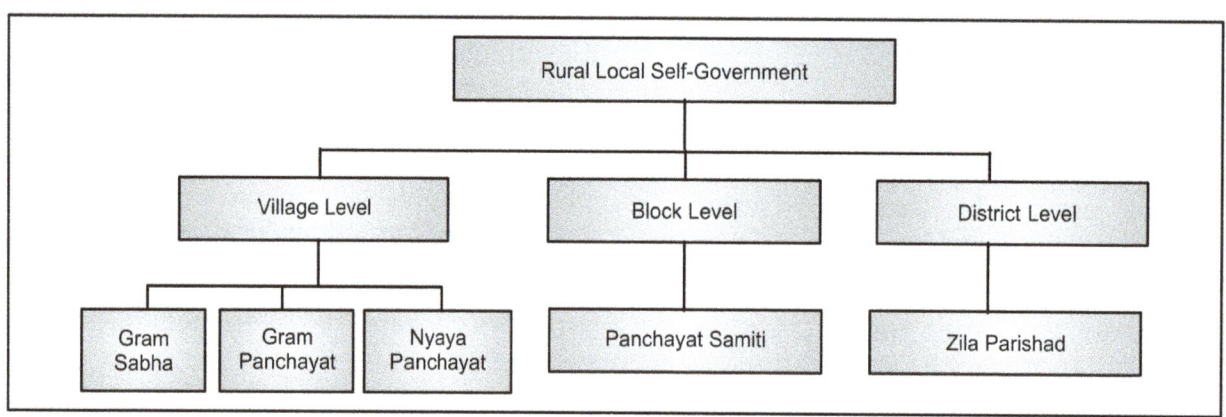

At the Village Level

Three bodies that operate at the village level are- *Gram Sabha, Gram Panchayat* and *Nyaya Panchayat*. The working of these panchayats at village level is discussed below :

Gram Sabha

Gram Sabha is a meeting of all adults who live in the area covered by a Panchayat. Anyone who is 18 years old or more and who has the right to vote is a member of the Gram Sabha. People who are either minors or eccentric or people who have been disqualified for some reason by a Court of Law are not eligible to become members of the Gram Sabha. It is the best example of grass root level organization as the people themselves are directly involved in managing the affairs of the village. Whenever there is a need to discuss a problem, the entire adult population of village meets and discusses the problem. The decisions are taken by majority vote and are binding on the entire population of the village. In case of a tie, the casting vote is cast by the *Sarpanch* (President of Gram Sabha) to resolve the situation. The Sarpanch along with other elected panchas (members) constitute the Gram Panchayat. The sarpanch mediates between government officers and the village clique.

LOCAL SELF-GOVERNMENT–RURAL

Gram Sabha at the Village Level

Composition
- A Gram Sabha consists of all the adult citizens and is constituted in every village with a population of not less than 1500.
- All the adult members of the Gram Sabha elect the *Gram Pradhan* or *Sarpanch* for a period of five years.
- The number of members in Gram Sabha differs from one State to another.
- The State government, depending upon the population of the village determines the number of 'Panchas' in a Sabha. However, the number generally varies between 7-15 members.
- Out of the total seats, one-third is reserved for women, a quota that will soon be raised to 50% of the total number of seats.
- Some of the seats in the Panchayats are also reserved for the Scheduled Castes and Scheduled Tribes in accordance with the total population of the village.

Functions
The main functions of the Gram Sabha are as follows :
- It keeps an eye on the working of Gram Panchayat, which is the administrative body of the Gram Sabha.
- It elects Gram Pradhan (*Sarpanch*) and other members of the Gram Panchayat.
- It prevents the Gram Panchayat from wrong doing and can seek clarifications from the *Sarpanch* and *Panchas* regarding any particular decision, implementation of scheme, income, expenditure etc.
- It approves the annual budget plan after considering the new taxes that Gram Panchayat may like to impose.
- It reviews the annual account statement, administrative report, progress report and audit reports of the Gram Panchayat.
- Implementing governmental schemes related to generation of employment in the village.
- It oversees all the activities of village like the construction and maintenance of water sources, roads, drainage systems, school building etc.

Gram Panchayat

The Gram Panchayat is the executive wing of the Gram Sabha and is derived from the word *'panch'*, a body of five members. The number of *Panchas* or members of Gram Panchayat is no longer five, as was the tradition, but varies from state to state. A gram panchayat is the focal point of a local self-governing institution in India.

Composition
The Gram Sabha is based on the principle of Adult Franchise and elects the members of the

Gram Panchayat from amongst themselves. The Head of the Gram Panchayat is known as the *Sarpanch*, while other members are known as the *panchas*. In some states the Sarpanch is elected directly by the members of Gram Sabha whereas in others, the members of the Gram Panchayat elect the Sarpanch indirectly. From the members of the Gram Panchayat, the Vice-Sarpanch is also elected. The name 'Panchayat' may be a misnomer since it is no longer mandatory for the Panchayat to have only five members. The number of members differs from one State to another. Depending upon the population of the village, the State Government determines the number of *Panchas* for a State; however, it generally varies between 5 – 30 members. According to the new Act some of the Panchayat seats are to be reserved for the Scheduled Castes and Scheduled Tribes in accordance with their total population. one-third of the seats are reserved for women in each Panchayat, which soon will be raised to 50% of the total number of seats.

Functions

To achieve the main objective of the Panchayats, i.e., decentralisation of political power, the Panchayats carry out several functions under two broad categories: Obligatory and Discretionary functions. However, now with the Schedule IX of the Constitution, the Panchayats have been given many other functions besides the two mentioned earlier. These are :

Civic Facilities and Welfare Functions

- Providing safe drinking water that includes measures like building and maintaining wells, tanks and drains for the public.
- Health Care Facilities like setting up of health centres and dispensaries by the Panchayat.
- Maintenance and construction of roads, good drainage, street lights, culverts, footpaths, bridges and cart tracks.
- To look after the well-being of expecting mothers and their children.
- Introducing welfare programmes for youth, children and women.

Developmental Functions

- Undertaking schemes for irrigation and arranging for fertilisers and seeds.
- Preparing and executing various agricultural plans.
- Electrification of the rural areas.
- Provision for education at primary and secondary levels.
- Developing and fostering small scale and cottage industries that include industries related to food processing.
- Housing in the rural areas.
- Introducing schemes for the well-being of the handicapped and weaker sections of society.

Functions Relating to the Regulation and General Administration

- Registering marriages, births and deaths.
- Maintenance of burial grounds for the cremation rites.
- Upkeep of watch and ward services like *Chowkidars*, etc.
- Collecting and maintaining of records and statistics of the villages' purchases, sales, land grants, etc.
- Maintaining public property of the village.
- Extending help to the government in preserving law and order.

Social and Economic Measures

- Building libraries, guest houses, marriage halls, etc.
- Planting trees, gardens, constructing parks and playgrounds for entertainment and leisure.
- Arranging fairs and exhibitions in the village.
- Setting up of fair price shops and societies for cooperative credit.

Nyaya Panchayat

A Nyaya Panchayat is a system of dispute resolution at the village level. Nyaya Panchayats can be entrusted with varied duties based on expansive principles of natural justice. It can remain very simple, as far as procedures are concerned. The Panchayat is responsible for

LOCAL SELF-GOVERNMENT–RURAL

meeting out justice to the villagers in a speedy and economical manner. In some States the Panchayat tends to act as a court, while other States have Nyaya Panchayat as a separate body responsible for securing justice. In the State of Uttar Pradesh, for every group of villages or block, there is a Nyaya Panchayat. Although the authority of the Nyaya Panchayat differs from State to State, it is generally responsible for dealing with petty civil cases dealing with minor offences like petty thefts, assaults, cheating, trespassing, illegal occupation of common places are some of the offences that fall under the jurisdiction of the Nyaya Panchayat.

Composition

In case of Nyaya Panchayat, each village has three representative members. Every member of the Nyaya Panchayat is called the *'Nyaya Panch'*. It is these Nyaya Panches who elect the *Sarpanch* of the Nyaya Panchayat. The *Panchas* in a Nyaya Panchayat are divided into three classes. Panchas in Ist and IInd class can levy a fine of up to ₹ 100 whereas Panchas in class IIIrd can levy a fine up to ₹ 50.

Functions

Some of the main functions of the Nyaya Panchayat are :
- They provide fast justice in an economical manner.
- The maximum amount monetary fine they can impose is ₹ 100.
- They are not entitled to award a sentence of imprisonment.
- Lawyers are not permitted to appeal before these Panchayats.
- If the Nyaya Panchayat has exercised its powers within its jurisdiction, then no further appeal can be made challenging the decision of the Nyaya Panchayat.
- The Nyaya Panchayat is permitted to dispose of minor criminal cases.
- As per the Panchayati Raj Act, the District Sub-Judges and Sub-Divisional Magistrates are entrusted with powers to hear appeals as well.
- It is the State Judicial Service or the State government that decides on the limit of the jurisdiction of these Panchayats.

Thus, in case of a village, the Gram Sabha appears to act as the legislature along with being a general body, the Panchayat acts as the Executive and the Nyaya Panchayat acts as the Judicial Body.

AT THE BLOCK LEVEL

The Panchayat Samiti

The Panchayat Samiti is placed just above the village panchayats. It manages all the activities of all the Gram Panchayats within the block. The Panchayat Samiti forms a liaison between the gram panchayat (village council) and the Zilaparishad (district board). In general, one Community Development Block covers nearly 100 villages and presently, in the entire nation, there exists about 5,900 Panchayat Samitis altogether. The Panchayat Samiti is an intermediate body that is known in different States by different names. In Madhya Pradesh, it is known as *'Janpada Panchayat,'* while in Uttar Pradesh, it is known as *'Kshetra Samiti'*. At the same time, it is known as 'Mandal Praja Parishad' in Andhra Pradesh, 'MandalPanchayat' in Karnataka and 'Taluka Panchayat' in Gujarat.

Composition

The members of the Panchayat Samitis are :
- Presidents or *Sarpanchas* of all the Panchayats within the specified area.
- Members of the Legislative Assembly (MLAs), Legislative Council (MLCs) and Parliament (MPs) belonging to that area.
- Chairman of the Nagar Panchayats or the Town Area Committees of that area.
- The Block Development Officers of an area are also members of the Panchayat Samitis along with the voted members of the Zila Parishad of that block.
- The representatives of women, Co-operative Societies, Scheduled Castes, and Scheduled Tribes.

❏ Provision is made for reserving seats for co-opted members like women, Scheduled Castes and Scheduled Tribes. Currently, reservation for women is limited to one-third of the total number of seats, but this is soon to be raised to 50%. The reservation for the Scheduled Castes and Scheduled Tribes is set in accordance to their proportion in the population.

The tenure of a Panchayat Samiti is five years and its Chairman is chosen via voting among the members of the Samiti. The chief administrative officer of Panchayat Samiti is elected by the State government and is known as the Block Development Officer (BDO). Samiti also accept several Standing Committees that undertakes some special works. The members of these committees can be chosen from outside members as well.

Panchayat Samiti Meeting

Functions

There are many aspects of the broad based programmes of rural development and the functions of the Samiti are divided into three categories:

Developmental Functions and Facilities of the Cities

❏ The Panchayat Samitis are responsible for providing hospitals and health care services with a range of facilities at the block level of the rural community.

❏ It is the duty of the Samitis to provide drinking water in the rural areas, construct and develop rural roads and regulate the markets.

❏ The Samiti is responsible for providing improved quality of agricultural equipment, undertaking small irrigation schemes, provide chemical fertilizers, improved seeds and ensure distribution of pesticides.

❏ In order to increase job opportunities, industries of rural areas like handlooms, handicrafts, etc. are promoted by the Samiti.

❏ Numerous programmes have also been started in order to improve the status of women and children in rural society. For this, *'Anganwadis'* have been established in various villages. In Indian tradition, the term *'Anganwandis'* means 'courtyard shelter'. They were initiated by the government of India in 1975 as part of the Integrated Child Development Services program. The objective of the institution was to resist malnutrition and child hunger.

❏ Various schemes are implemented by the Panchayat Samitis for the social and economic welfare of Scheduled Castes, Scheduled Tribes and other backward classes.

❏ Samiti is also responsible for setting up Higher Secondary Schools or colleges for higher education.

Related to Supervision

❏ The duty of coordinating and supervising the works of Gram Panchayat rests with the Panchayat Samiti.

❏ The Samiti scrutinizes the budget of the Panchayats and proposes necessary changes in it.

Related to Delegations

❏ Through schemes like *Integrated Rural Development Programme* (IRDP), *Sampoorna Gramin Rozgar Yojana, Indira Awaas Yojana*, the Panchayat Samiti works to improve the quality of life in the rural areas.

❏ Additionally, the Panchayat Samitis acts as the link between the Zila Parishad and the Gram Panchayat.

AT THE DISTRICT LEVEL

The Zila Parishad

The apex body of the three-tier Panchayati Raj System consists of the Zila Parishad. This is the unit of local self-government at the level of the districts, which is responsible for administering the activities of numerous Panchayat Samitis. The Panchayat Samitis form the connection between the Zila Parishad and the Gram Panchayat. Similarly, the Zila Parishad forms the connection between the Gram Panchayats and the State Government.

Across the country, the Zila Parishad is known by various names in different States. In Assam, it is called *mahakuma parishad*. In Andhra Pradesh, it is called the *zila praja parishad*, while in the States of Tamil Nadu and Karnataka, it is known as the District Development Council.

Composition

A Zila Parishad generally consists of 40–60 members comprising of the following :

- *Pradhans* or Chairmen of all the Panchayat Samitis in the districts.
- Members of Parliament and members of State Legislative Assemblies within the area of jurisdiction.
- One person to represent each of the Co-operative Societies in that district.
- Representatives of women, Scheduled Castes and Scheduled Tribes.
- Chairmen of Municipalities in the district.
- Deputy Commissioner of the district.
- Supervisor of all Government Departments in the district.

In some States, provision is there for the District Magistrate to attend the assemblies of the Zila Parishad; however, he is not empowered with the right to vote. The Zila Parishads in general have a five year term. Every Zila Parishad is headed by a Chairperson, who is elected by the members of the Parishad amongst themselves. Similarly, the members from amongst themselves also elect a Deputy Chairperson.

Representatives at a Zila Parishad Meeting

The only full time paid employee of the Zila Parishad is its Secretary, who is paid a salary by the State Government.

Functions

Zila Parishad is a recurring functioning body that carries out its functions mostly through different Standing Committees. There are also certain boards of the Districts who direct the functions of the circle Panchayats. Although the functions of the Zila Parishad vary from one State to another, the basic functions are :

Facilities and Functions Catering to the Public.

- Building and conserving public roads, parks, culverts and bridges.
- Introducing and applying new programmes related to agriculture.
- Development of water, land and human resources of a district.
- Setting up of libraries, dispensaries and educational institutions.
- Providing help in situations of drought, distress of any kind and scarcity.
- Upholding the welfare of the weaker sections of the society.

Functions Related to Coordination and Supervision

- The work of the Gram Panchayats and Panchayat Samitis are supervised by the Zila Parishad.
- It is also responsible for probing and approving the accounts of the Panchayat Samitis in States like Assam, Punjab and Bihar.

Functions Catering to the Developmental Plans

❏ The Zila Parishad is responsible for undertaking many developmental functions like poverty eradication programmes, irrigation schemes, rural electrification, public distribution system and more.

❏ The working committee of the Zila Parishad acts as the executive body of the District Board.

Achievements of Panchayti Raj System

❏ Panchayati Raj System ensures effective co-ordination between Government Programmes and those of Voluntary agencies.

❏ It has brought political awakening in the rural parts of India.

❏ It is sucessful in improving the conditions of villages in India, by taking up various welfare activities.

❏ It has increased representation of men and women from Backward classes as well.

STRUCTURAL REPRESENTATION OF VILLAGE PANCHAYAT, PANCHAYAT SAMITI AND ZILA PARISHAD.

Tiers of PRI	Gram Panchayat	Panchayat Samiti	Zila Parishad
Level	Village	Block/Circle	District
Composition	The members are directly elected by the Gram Sabha and comprise of at least 5 members and can maximum go up to 30 members.	The members of this body include the Sarpanchas of the Gram Panchayats, the MPs and MLAs that belong to that area, Block Development Officers and members of the Zila Parishad.	The members here are the Deputy Commissioner, Chairmen of every Panchayat Samitis and BDOs, Heads of the various government departments and MPs and MLAs that belong to that particular district.
President	Sarpanch	Chairman	Chairman
Functions	Offering basic civic amenities. Taking care of issues like sanitation, primary education and offering primary health centres. Arrangements are also done for managing public property.	Harmonizing the operations of the various Panchayats that come under it. Manages schools and colleges, looking after hospitals and other well-being centres and promoting the development of agriculture.	Coordinating the operations of the Panchayat Samitis coming under it. Recommending finances for helping local bodies. Help in the devising of different plans and act as a link between the local bodies and the government.

LOCAL SELF-GOVERNMENT–RURAL

In Retrospect

- **Local Self-Government :** Local Self Government is "an elected body that enjoys certain extent of autonomy and serves as a governmental unit for local affairs."
- **Panchayati Raj Institution and its Organization :**
  - At village level, there are two-bodies- the Gram Sabha and the Gram Panchayats.
  - At the block level that falls in the middle, it is called Panchayat Samiti.
  - At the District level, it is called Zila Parishad.
- **Gram Sabha :** A body with group of people, who are registered in the Panchayat area as voters who are all adults, is stated to be a Gram Sabha. A Gram Sabha is constituted in every village with a population of not less than 1500.
- **Functions of the Gram Sabha :** To Look after the working of Gram Panchayat, To elect Sarpach and other members of the Gram Panchayat, To seek clarifications regarding implementation of scheme, expenditure etc., To approve annual budget plan, To generate employment in the village, To maintain water sources, roads, drainage system, school building etc.
- **Gram Panchayat :** The Gram Panchayat is the executive wing of the Gram Sabha. The Head of the Gram Panchayat is known as Sarpanch. The number of Panchas for a State is determined by the State Government. However, it generally varies between 7-15 members.
- **Functions of the Gram Panchayat**
  - Civic Facilities and Welfare Functions
  - Developmental functions
  - Functions Relating to the Regulation and General Administration
  - Social and Economic Measures
- **Panchayat Samiti :** The Panchayat Samiti is an intermediate body that is known in different States by different names. In Madhya Pradesh, it is known as "Janpada Panchayats," while in Uttar Pradesh, it becomes "Kshetra Samiti.
- **Functions of the Panchayat Samiti**
  - Developmental Functions
  - Functions Related to Supervision
  - Functions Related to Delegations
- **Zila Parishad :** The apex body of the three- tier Panchayati Raj System consists of the Zila Parishad, generally consists of 40–60 members. The Zila Parishad forms the connection between the Gram Panchayats and the State Government.
- **Functions of the Zila Parishad**
  - Facilities and Functions Catering to the Welfare of the Public.
  - Functions Related to Coordination and Supervision.
  - Functions catering to the Developmental Plans.

EXERCISES

Part-I (Short Questions)

1. What do you understand by the term Local Self-Government ?
2. State one reason for the need of Local Self-Government.
3. What is the difference between the Local Government and Local Self-Government ?
4. How does local self-government prove to be beneficial in relieving the burden of state government ?
5. What does three-tier institution of the Panchayati Raj System mean ?

6. Name the local bodies in rural areas that work at– (a) the village level, (b) the block level, and (c) the district level.
7. What is Gram Sabha? State any two functions of the Gram Sabha.
8. What is Gram Panchayat? Mention two qualifications to be elected as member of Gram Panchayat.
9. Give any two Developmental functions of the Gram Panchayat.
10. What is Nyaya Panchayat? Mention its functions.
11. What do you understand by Panchayat Samiti ? State any two functions of it ?
12. State two socio-economic functions of the Gram Panchayat.
13. Name the highest organ of rural Local Self-Government at the district level.
14. Discuss in short the composition of the Zila Parishad.
15. What are the functions of the Zila Parishad with reference to :
    (a) Coordination and Supervision
    (b) Developmental plans
16. Who is the President (or Head) of each of the following :
    (a) Gram Panchayat
    (b) Panchayat Samiti
    (c) Zila Parishad.

Part-II (Structured Questions)

1. The beneficial aspect of Self-Government is that it offers the opportunity to the public to govern, which is the true essence of Democracy. In this context, answer the following questions:
   (a) Meaning of Local Self-Government
   (b) Importance of Local Self-Government
   (c) Difference between Local Government and Local Self-Government.
2. With reference to Gram Panchayat, answer the following :
   (a) Composition of Gram Panchayat
   (b) Functions of Gram Panchayat.
3. Discuss the composition and functions of the Panchayat Samiti.
4. At the apex of the three-tier system there stands the Zila Parishad. In this context, answer the following questions:
   (a) How is Zila Parishad constituted ?
   (b) What are its chief functions ?

CHAPTER 5

LOCAL SELF-GOVERNMENT—URBAN

◆ Urban : Municipal Committees and Municipal Corporations– Meaning and Functions.

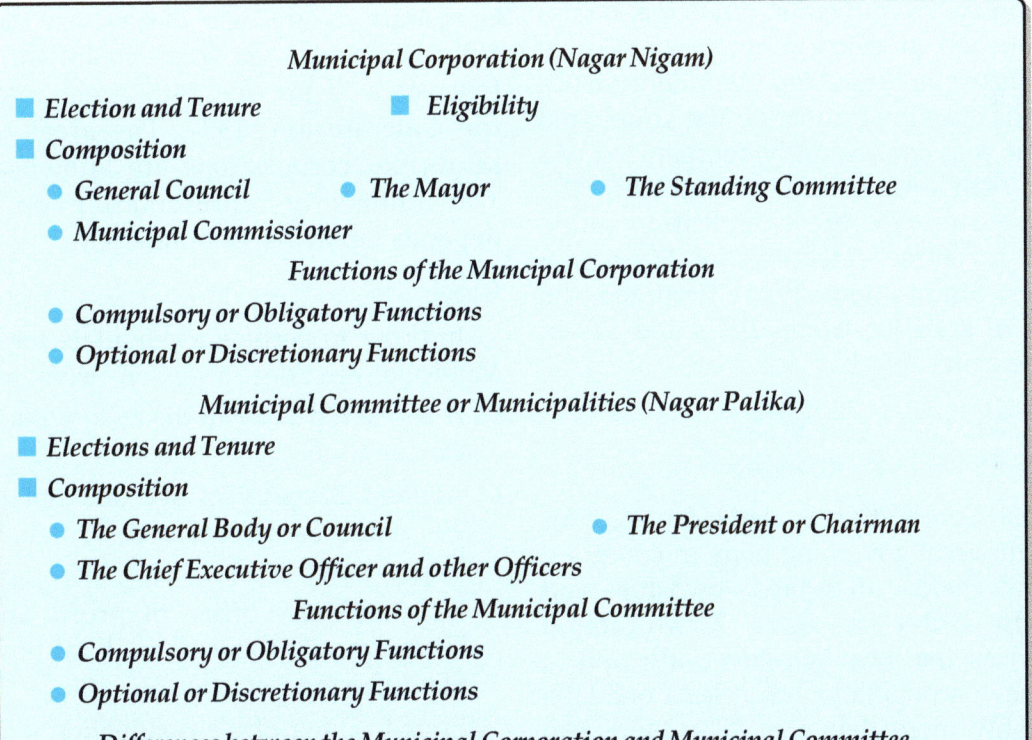

Town and cities are called urban areas and cities with a population of more than 40 lakh are known as metropolitan cities. Local self-government institutions in all urban areas function independently of one another. Local self-government indicates the development of local or regional governing units. It is an inherent part of central or state governments. It is very related to the interest of the local people.

As it is known, it is difficult for the Central and State Governments to fulfill the requirements of local people all the time. Consequently, corporations, municipalities, district and local boards are formed for reviewing the needs and interests of common people in different localities. This system is known as Local Self-Government.

HISTORY OF LOCAL SELF-GOVERNMENT–URBAN

The history of local self-governing institutions in urban areas of India dates back to the 1870s. Lord Ripon is considered the founding father of urban local self-government as he implanted the concept of municipal authorities as units of self-government. His Resolution on local self-government dealt with the constitution of local bodies, their functions, finances and powers laid the foundation of urban local self-government in modern India.

The Presidency Towns of Kolkata, Mumbai and Chennai were the first urban areas to set up Municipal Corporations in the later half of the 19th century. From then on municipal bodies were established in every other town, slowly increasing their numbers. After the independence of India, the administration of the municipal corporations was meticulously reorganized. As per the 74th Amendment Act of the Constitution in 1993, the constitution made provisions for three categories of Municipal institutions. Simultaneously, it finalized the reservation of seats for women, SCs and STs in each Municipality.

MUNICIPAL CORPORATION (NAGAR NIGAMS)

Municipal Corporation is the term used for describing the local governing body in countries, cities, towns, charter townships, townships and villages. In order to have a Municipal Corporation as the local self-governing unit, a city must have a population of at least one lakh and preferably more than that. The Municipal Corporations or *Nagar Nigams* provide essential community services such as housing, health-care, educational facilities and transport services. It is the responsibility of state legislature to pass a special statute and set up a Municipal Corporation in a concerned state whereas in union territories, the Union Parliament sets it up. Presently, there are Municipal Corporations in cities like Delhi, Varanasi, Agra, Kolkata, Lucknow, Patna, Allaha-bad, Mumbai, Kanpur, Bangaluru, Trivandrum, Chennai and others.

The Municipal Corporation building, Kolkata

Elections and Tenure

Like the members of the Legislative Assembly, the members of the Municipal Corporations are also elected on the basis of Adult Franchise via secret ballot for a term of five years as per the 74th Amendment Act of the Constitution, 1992. The areas under the Municipal corporations are known as Wards. The number of representatives in each city depends upon its population.

Eligibility

In order to become a candidate for contesting Municipal elections, a person needs to be :

❏ A registered voter in the area of the Municipal Corporation
❏ At least 21 years of age and not more than 25 years as prescribed under the State Corporation act.
❏ Not hold any office of profit under State Government or any of the local bodies of the State Government.
❏ Prior to filing of his nomination papers, he is expected to resign his current post.

Composition

The management of the Corporation is generally vested in a Council that is elected and the Corporation is known to exercise its powers through a structure that includes :

❏ General Council
❏ The Mayor

LOCAL SELF-GOVERNMENT—URBAN

- The Standing Committee
- Municipal Commissioner

General Council

The General Council is composed of members, known as Municipal Councillors, who are elected directly based on Universal Adult Franchise via secret ballot. Depending on the population of the city, the State government determines the number of seats in the General Council and thus, the size of this Council can vary from one place to another. With respect to the population, a proportion of the seats are also reserved for the SCs and STs and a specific one-third proportion of the total number of seats are reserved for women.

Other than the elected members, there are some chosen Aldermen (respected persons of the city) in the Council who are generally renowned and important personalities of the city and are nominated by the Governor. There are altogether 296 members in the Delhi Municipal Corporation, out of which 272 are elected members. The General Council is responsible for the appointment of most of the officials of the Municipal Corporation except the Municipal Commissioner.

The Mayor

The Mayor is the head of the Municipal Corporation. In cooperation with the Aldermen the Councillors elect the Mayor and the Deputy Mayor from amongst themselves. The Mayor is usually elected for a term of one year and can also be re-elected yearly for the full five-year tenure of the Corporation. Being the 'First Citizen' of the town or city, the Mayor holds an extremely honourable position. The mayor performs various functions, which are as follows :

- Presiding over the meetings of the Corporation and regulating the conduct of business.
- Maintaining discipline and decorum at the meetings.
- Fixing the agenda of discussion for the meetings of the Corporation.
- Receiving foreign guests visiting the city.
- Securing reports of the different programmes and projects from the Municipal Commissioner. This is undertaken by the Corporation.
- Acting as the link of communication between the Corporation and the Union or the State Government.

The Standing Committees

Based on elections, the members of the General Council secure representations in the Standing Committee, through which the General Council carries out its various functions. Each Standing Committee handles a specific area, viz., Finance, Taxation and Budget, Health, Engineering, Transport, Water Supply, Plan for Economic Development, Education Services, Sewage, Schemes etc for the well-being of the weaker sections.

Municipal Commissioner

The Governor of a city or town appoints the Municipal Commissioner, who is the Chief Executive Officer of the Corporation. Although the State Government generally elects him, the Union or Central Government makes his selection in case of Union Territories. He enjoys tenure of five years, but can be dismissed from his office by the Government prior to the scheduled time as well. His functions and responsibilities include :

- Controlling and administering the Corporation and giving guidelines to every officer of the Corporation.
- Putting the various projects and programmes that have been laid out by the General Council into operation.
- Implementing the rules, policies and decisions of the Corporation.
- He acts as the Custodian of all personal files and records of every staff member and of all the properties of the Municipal Corporation.
- Preparing the budget and making estimations that are to be presented before the General Council and similar related financial functions.
- Participating in the deliberations and meetings of the General Council but is neither entitled

to move any resolution nor to vote in any of the meetings. He acts as the Secretary of the Council and keeps a record of all the minute details of the proceed-ings of the Corporation.

Functions of the Municipal Corporation

The unit of local self-government in the city is the Municipal Corporation. It deals with all the grievances of the citizens. The functions of the Municipal Corporation are broadly classified into two categories : (a) Compulsory or Obligatory functions and (b) Optional or Discretionary functions. It depends on the Corporation what discretionary functions it needs to undertake, depending on the resources that are available.

Compulsory or Obligatory Functions

The functions that come under this category are :

Providing Electricity, Water Supply and Sewage Disposal

The Corporation performs basic public services like providing for safe drinking water, building new water works and maintaining the existing ones, proper supply of electricity and sewage disposal on a daily basis.

Services Rendered to Health and Sanitation

This includes measures like establishing and maintaining hospitals, centres for child welfare, maternity homes and dispensaries. It is the duty of the corporation to organize vaccinations and inoculation camps for eradication of infectious diseases. This also includes provision for the safe disposal of garbage.

Provisions Related to Education and Sports

The Corporation is responsible for setting up schools up to primary and secondary levels, along with centres for educating adults, setting up libraries, museums, and night schools. It is the duty of the corporation to ensure that all children below the age of 14 go to schools. They also organise and embark on the promotion of games and sports among young boys and girls.

Various Public Works

Under this category, the duties of the Corporation are :

- Providing buildings, roads, bus-shelters and public urinals for the convenience of the people.
- Preserving and giving names to the various public streets and roads.
- Setting of rules with regard to the building of hotels, restaurants and shopping centres.
- Issuing notices and demolishing various structures and buildings that are in a miserable condition.
- Planting trees.

Keeping Records of Births and Deaths

The account for births and deaths are to be maintained by the Corporation along with the upkeep of the burial and cremation grounds in the city.

Preparing Various Reports

The wide range of projects, programmes and activities of the Corporation are to be stated in the reports of the Corporation. So, one of their compulsory functions includes preparing, publishing and distributing such reports.

Miscellaneous Functions

This includes building crematoriums, maintaining departments like fire brigades, creating disaster management programmes for the rescue of citizens during natural disasters like earthquakes and floods and man-made disasters like fire, riots, terrorist attacks etc. They are also responsible for structuring rules for the auto and taxi drivers etc.

Optional or Discretionary Functions

The discretionary functions of the Corporation entirely depend on the budget available with the corporation. Some of these functions are :

- The Corporation can arrange for a bus service for transportation of people across the city.
- Providing facilities like public housing via organizations that handle housing related issues like housing boards etc.
- Some cultural activities of the Municipal Corporation include funding of museums, libraries, theatres, public parks etc. The Corporation also sets up picnic resorts and *Akharas*.

- The Corporation organizes exhibitions, functions, fairs or *melas* and wrestling events and similar recreational facilities for the entertainment of the citizens.
- The Corporation undertakes numerous programmes like poverty eradication for the welfare of the society. With this motive, they establish and maintain orphanages, night shelters, rest houses and homes for children and the aged.
- Finally, beautification of the city also falls under the responsibility of the Corporation.

MUNICIPAL COMMITTEE OR MUNICIPALITIES (NAGAR PALIKAS)

In cities and towns that have a smaller population ranging between 20,000–300,000, a Municipal Committee is constituted. The minimum population required for setting up Municipal committees in some States is 20000, however, this number varies from State to State. The composition of these Municipal Committees is similar to that of the Municipal Corporation, since it is just a smaller version of the Municipal Corporation.

Elections and Tenure

According to the new Nagar Palika or Municipality Councils Act, 1992, every Municipality will have a uniform tenure of five years. The membership for the municipality depends on the population of the city or town.

Composition of the Municipal Committee

Since this Committee is smaller in size, it has three wings namely.
- The General Body or the Council,
- The President/Chairman
- The Chief Executive Officer and other officers.

The General Body or Council

The members of General body or Council are called Councillors and the adult citizens residing in a particular Municipal ward elect them. Depending on the population of the town or a city, the number of members in the Council is decided. Any adult citizen can participate in the municipal election if he/she :

- Has attained the age of 25 years or more.
- Does not hold any office of profit under the government or Local body.
- Has his name registered in the voter's list of that area.

As per the new Nagarpalika Act, every Municipality has to reserve a certain proportion of seats for the SCs, STs and women. Provision is made for the election of Aldermen by the Councillors.

The President or Chairman

The Councillors of a Municipal Committee directly elect their President, a Senior Vice President and a Junior Vice President from amongst themselves. In some states it is the general voters who directly elect these officials of Municipal Committee. The Chairman or the President is considered to be the presiding officer who enjoys the below mentioned powers and functions :

- He/she presides over all the meetings of the Board and regulates how business is to be conducted in these meetings.
- Acts as the communicating link between the government and the Municipal Board over various matters.
- Acts as the custodian to all the documents and records of the Municipality.
- He/She holds the power to make appointments of lower staff and teachers of primary schools and suspend certain municipal staff except the Executive officer, Health officer or other officers of similar posts who are appointed by State Civil Service.

The Chief Executive Officer and Other Officers

The Chief Executive Officer is responsible for managing the administrative section of the Municipal Committee. In most States, the Municipal Committee appoints their own Chief Executive Officers while in some States the State government appoints them. The various functions performed by the Chief Executive Officer and other officers are as follows :

- He/She looks after Municipal Office and allocates work among all the Municipal Officers.

- The employees of the Municipal Committee have to secure his approval while getting leave sanctioned.
- Preparing the estimates of the Municipality budget each year.
- Responsible for issuing licenses and agreements for different jobs that feature under the rule of Municipal Board.
- Participating in every meeting of the Municipal Board or any of its committees. In these meetings, he/she holds the position of a Secretary.

FUNCTIONS OF A MUNICIPAL COMMITTEE

There are two broad categories under which the functions of the Municipal Committee can be discussed. These are the Obligatory and Optional or Discretionary Functions.

Compulsory or Obligatory Functions

Under this category, the following functions are performed :

Health and Sanitation

It is the responsibility of the Municipality to maintain numerous hospitals and dispensaries in the city or town. Other responsibilities of the Committee that come under this head are cleaning public lanes, putting a stop to the sale of foodstuffs that are rotten and selling of adulterated milk etc.

Providing Electricity and Supply of Water

One of the most important functions of Municipal Committee is to provide electricity and safe drinking water for use in domestic as well as commercial circles.

Provision of Education and Sports Facilities

Setting up primary and secondary schools is another responsibility of the Municipalities. In order to cultivate the aptitude of young boys and girls for sports, this Committee also provides facilities related to games and sports.

Public Works

This largely includes building of roads, community halls and shopping centres.

Registering Births and Deaths

An account of the number of births and deaths in the city is also to be maintained by the Municipal Board.

Optional or Discretionary Functions

The Municipalities and the Municipal Corporations both share the same discretionary functions. These functions range from carrying out activities like funding reading rooms and libraries, arranging exhibitions and fairs, building stadiums for sports activity to providing transport facilities and other services for the welfare and comfort of the people.

The Municipalities are expected to adopt schemes that plan to provide work for weaker sections of the society. For encouraging self-employment to the small artisans, schemes like *Nehru Rozgar Yojana* exist to provide financial help to small artisans. Provisions are also in place to cater to the clearance of the slum areas and various constructive housing programmes.

DIFFERENCES BETWEEN THE MUNICIPAL CORPORATION AND MUNICIPAL COMMITTEE

Municipal Corporation	Municipal Committee
1. Large metropolitan cities with a population of 10 lakh or more are governed by the Municipal Corporations.	1. Smaller cities and towns are governed by the Municipal Committee.
2. It is the Mayor who acts as the head of the Corporation.	2. It is the President or the Chairperson who acts as the head of the Municipal Committee.
3. More funds are required.	3. Less funds are required.
4. The corporations deal directly with the State government.	4. The Municipalities need to work their way through the district government in order to reach the State government.

LOCAL SELF-GOVERNMENT—URBAN

In Retrospect

- ✦ **Urban Local Self Government :** The Constitution has provided for three categories of Municipal Institutions.
  - Municipal corporation (Nagar Nigam)
  - Municipalities (Nagar palikas)
  - Other Urban Bodies (Nagar panchayat)
- ✦ **Municipal Corporation (Nagar Nigam) :** Presently, there are Municipal Corporation in areas like Delhi, Varanasi, Agra, Kolkata, Lucknow, Patna, in cities with a population of at least one lakh and more. These bodies are also known as Nagar Nigam.
- ✦ **Structure of the Municipal Corporation**
  - The General Council
  - The Mayor
  - The Standing Committee
  - A Municipal Commissioner
- ✦ **Functions of the Municipal Corporations**
  - **Obligatory Functions :**
    - Providing Electricity, Water Supply and Sewage disposal.
    - Services Rendered to the Public related to Health and Sanitation.
  - **Discretionary or Optional Functions :**
    - Providing facilities like public housing.
    - Some cultural activities of the Municipal Corporation include founding museums, libraries, theatres, public parks etc.
- ✦ **Municipal Committee or Municipalities (Nagarpalikas) :** In case of cities and towns that have a smaller population ranging between 20,000–3 lakhs, a Municipal Committee is constituted. These bodies are also known as Municipalities or Nagarpalikas or Municipal Boards.
- ✦ **Composition of the Municipal Committee**
  - The General Body or the Council
  - President/Chairman
  - Chief Executive Officer or the Secretary and other officers.
- ✦ **Functions of a Municipal Committee**
  - **Obligatory Functions :**
    - Health and Sanitation of the Public
    - Providing Electricity and Supply of Water
    - Provision of Education and Sports
  - **Discretionary or Optional Functions :** These functions are carrying out activities like founding reading rooms and libraries, arranging exhibitions and fairs, building stadiums for sports activity, offering conveyance facilities and other services for the welfare and comfort of the people.

EXERCISES

Part-I (Short Questions)

1. Name two urban local self-governing institutions.
2. Who elects the members of Municipal Corporation ?
3. Who sets up Municipal Corporation ?
4. Who are Aldermen ?
5. Who is a Mayor and how is he/she elected ?
6. Give any two functions of the Mayor of a Municipal Corporation.

7. What is the role of Municipal Commissioner in a Municipal Corporation ?
8. Give any two important functions of the Municipal Commissioner of a Municipal Corporation.
9. State one obligatory function of a Municipal Corporation with respect to Health and Sanitation.
10. What do you understand by the term 'Municipal Committee' and who heads it ?
11. State the three wings in the administrative set-up of a Municipality.
12. What qualifications are needed to participate in the Municipal Council's election ?
13. State any two functions of the President of a Municipal Committee.
14. Who elects Chief Executive Officer in Municipal Committee ? State two of its functions.
15. State some of the Discretionary Functions of Municipal Committee.
16. State any two points of difference between a Municipal Corporation and Municipal Committee.

Part-II (Structured Questions)

1. With regard to the composition of Municipal Corporation, write short notes on :
   (a) The General Council
   (b) Municipal Commissioner
   (c) The Mayor
   (d) Standing Committee
2. Elucidate the functions of the Municipal Corporation with respect to :
   (a) Education and Sports
   (b) Public Health and Sanitation
   (c) Public Works
   (d) Electricity and Water Supply
   (e) Record of Births and Deaths
3. Explain briefly the working of the municipality mentioning the roles of :
   (a) The General body
   (b) The President
   (c) The Executive Officer.
4. What are the functions of the President and the Chief Executive officer of a Municipal Committee ?
5. Describe some of the Discretionary functions of a Municipal Committee.
6. Differentiate between Municipal Committee and Municipal Corporation.

SECTION-B

HISTORY

CHAPTER 1

THE HARAPPAN CIVILIZATION

- ◆ Sources : Great Bath, Citadel, Seals, Bearded Man, Dancing Girl, Dockyard, Script.
- ◆ Origin, Extent, Urban planning, Trade, Art & Craft, and its Decline.

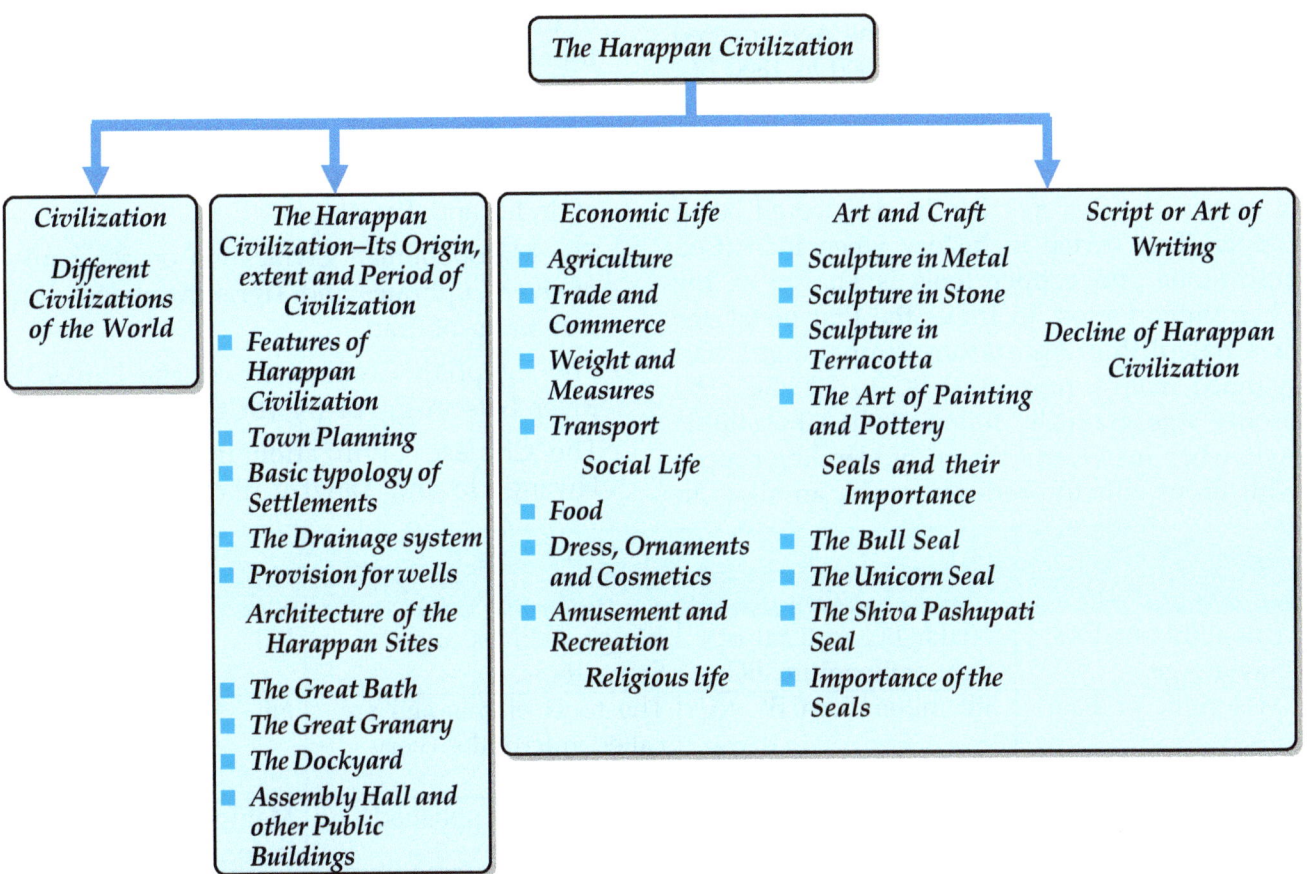

WHAT IS CIVILIZATION?

The word 'civilization' has a vast implication that entails a specific cultural stage pertaining to the development of cities and writing.

The Oxford Dictionary defines civilization as "an advanced stage or system of human social development." With the advent of agriculture (10000 BC), the primitive man transformed from 'food-gatherers' to 'food-producers.' Simultaneously, man started to build permanent shelters and also learnt the art of spinning, weaving and forming a society of farmers, weavers, potters and carpenters. The concept of religion also emerged and the process of gradual evolution started. According to H. A. Davies, "civilization implies settlement in definite territories, the building of cities, the evolution of ordered methods of government, the development of trade and commerce and a capacity for progress which is unrestricted."

Some of the important characteristics of civilization are as follows :
- Settlement in definite territories.
- Rise of towns and cities.
- Development of trade.
- Evolution of kingship and government.

DIFFERENT CIVILIZATIONS OF THE WORLD

Neolithic Age or the New Stone Age covered the period approximately from 4000 to 1800 BC. The primitive men used stone tools and implements in this period. The Neolithic Age was followed by the period when men learnt the use of metals, the first metal to be discovered being copper. This period in history when man used both stone and copper tools is known as the Chalcolithic Period. In India, the first metal age or Chalcolithic Age (stone-copper age) had spanned mainly from 2000 BC to 700 BC. The Bronze Age gradually followed the Chalcolithic Age, when man learnt the art of blending copper with tin or zinc to produce bronze, an alloy. In the Indian sub-continent, the Bronze Age commenced around 3000 BCE. In the end, it gave rise to the Indus Valley Civilization and its mature phase spanned from 2500 BCE to 1900 BCE. The Bronze Age is a distinct historical period that is marked by the usage of bronze tools, proto-writing and other fledgling aspects of urbanization.

- Sequentially, the Bronze Age is the second significant period of the three-phased Stone-Bronze-Iron system. This theory is posited by Christian Jirgensen Thomsen in modern times. The first civilizations that flourished around the world during this period are known as Bronze Age civilizations, so called due to the important role played by bronze in their growth. By about 2500 BC, four great Bronze Age civilizations had evolved. These were :

- The Indus Valley or The Harappan Civilization in the northern and western parts of India and Pakistan.
- The Mesopotamian Civilization on the banks of river Euphrates and Tigris in modern Iraq and parts of Iran.
- The Egyptian Civilization on the banks of River Nile in Egypt (North East Africa).
- The Chinese Civilization in the Valley of Hwang Ho and Yangtze rivers (East Asia).

Period	Time-Frame (Global Context)	Features	Civilization
Paleolithic or Old Stone Age	3 lakh BC to 8000 or eight millennium BC	Rough pebbles and Stone tools.	Nil
Mesolithic or Late	8th millennium BC to	The tools of this age are called microliths (very small tools).	Nil
Stone Age	4th millennium BC	The usage of polished stone tools.	Mehrgarh Civilization is located in Kaachi
Neolithic Age (New Stone Age)	4000 to 1800 BC	Domestication of animals and agriculture	Plain of Baluchistan in Pakistan.
Bronze Age	3000 to 500 BC	The transitory period between Neolithic and Chalcolithic age. The usage of Bronze, proto writing. Features of urbanization were in vogue.	Mesopotamian Civilization of West Asia, Egyptian civilization in Egypt, Central Asia and Harappa and Mohenjo-Daro in India.

Chalcolithic age or Stone-Copper Age	1800 to 1000 or 800 BC	The period saw the usage of copper (the first metal to be used in India) as well as stone.

THE HARAPPAN CIVILIZATION–ITS ORIGIN, EXTENT AND PERIOD OF CIVILIZATION

The Discovery

The 'Indus Valley Civilization' or 'Harappan Civilization' developed during the Chalcolithic or Bronze Age, as copper and bronze implements were discovered at various sites in the vast topographic spread. The 'Indus Valley Civilization' or 'Harappan Civilization' broadly falls within the *Proto-history period*. (During this period, inscriptions were written on seals, pots and parchment but they could not be deciphered till date. The age appeared prior to the Vedic Age and is considered Proto-History in India).

Approximately, 1400 Harappan sites have been explored in the sub-continent. The Harappan sites belong to early, mature and late phases of the Harappan culture. The phenomenal sites are Harappa (in the Montgomery district of West Punjab) discovered by Daya Ram Sahni, in 1921, Mohenjo-Daro (in the Larkana district of Sindh in Pakistan) in 1922, by R.D Banerjee in 1922, Dholavira (West Gujarat) discovered by J.P Joshi and R.S Bisht in 1990-91, Kalibangan (Rajasthan) by Dr. A. Ghosh, Lothal (Gujarat) in 1955-63, Chanhu-daro (Sind) discovered by Dr. Ernest Mackey and Banawali (Haryana) in 1975-77. Prior to this discovery, it was believed that the history of India began with the Aryans from 1000 BC, Historians named it as Indus Valley Civilization, because the ruins of these early sites were found in the valley of the River Indus and its tributaries. However, modern historians prefer to term it as the Harappan Civilization, as

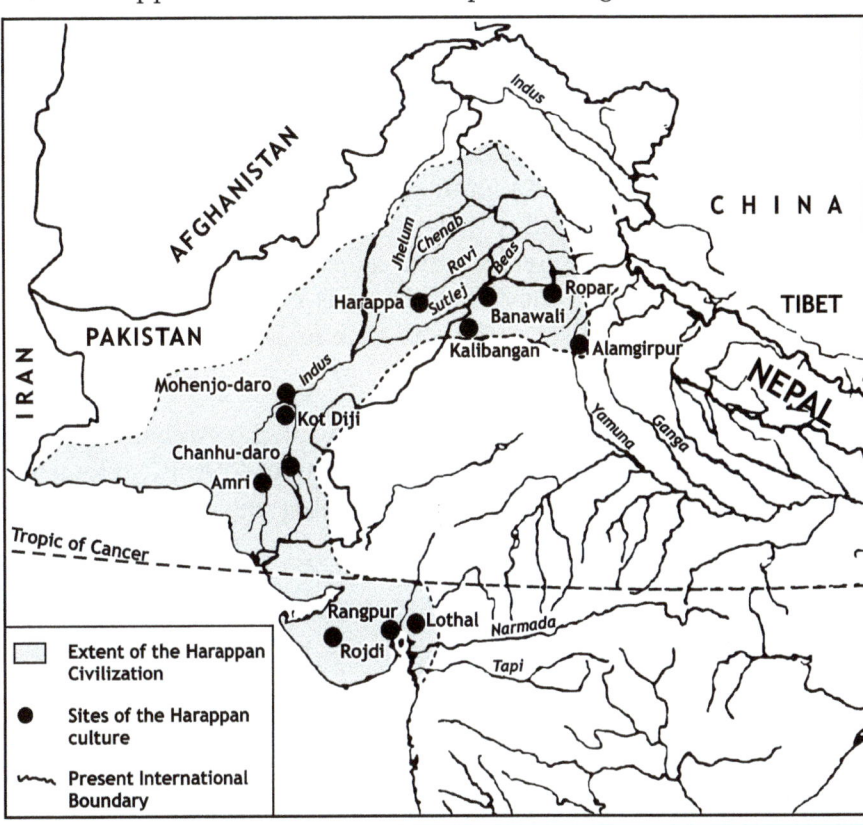

The extent of Indus Valley Civilization

Harappa was the first site to be discovered and it flourished much beyond the Indus valley civilization.

The Origin

There are several theories regarding the origin of the Harappan Civilization. According to one group of historians, the Harappan civilization was the handiwork of the Indo-Europeans. Others believe that the Urban Harappan Civilization was only an extension of the village culture of Mehrgarh (6000 BC). Prior to Harappa or Indus Valley Civilization, village culture developed in the interior parts of India at popular sites in

Baluchistan, Sindh, Punjab, Haryana and Rajasthan. The oldest vestiges of the village culture have been discovered around 7000 B C at Mehrgarh in Baluchistan. In this particular site, clay-pottery was along with copper in some areas. Other remarkable sites of the Mehrgarh culture are Gomal Valley, Jabalpur (Punjab), Amri and Kotdiji (Sind), Kalibangan (Rajasthan) and Banwali (Hisar, Haryana).

The Extent

The 'Indus Valley Civilization' or 'Harappan Civilization' covered the area from the valley of the Saraswati-Sutlej along the Indus and Saurashtra belt. The whole area of the Harappan Civilization, acknowledged as the largest ancient civilization, features a triangular shape and spans an area of about 1,299,600 sq. km. The site of Harappan civilization covered portions of Punjab, Haryana, Gujarat, Rajasthan, Sindh, Baluchistan and the border of Western Uttar Pradesh. Presently, the prime centers of the civilization, including Harappa, Mohenjo-daro, Chanhu-daro and Suktagendor are in Pakistan. Some of the centers of the Harappan Civilization located in India are Banawali (in Haryana), Manda, Kalibangan (in Rajasthan), Alamgirpur (in Uttar Pradesh) and Rupar (in Punjab). However, of late, a number of extensions of this civilization have been discovered in Punjab and Gujarat. The most important among them are Lothal, Rangpur, Gola, Dhoro, Rojdi and Dholavira (all in Gujarat). According to Mortimer Wheeler, the 'Indus Valley Civilization' or 'Harappan Civilization' is the most expansive pre-classical civilization. The civilization is called the 'Indus Valley Civilization'. However, it went far beyond the jurisdiction of the valley. In India, it is extended to the Ganga-Yamuna doab in the East and to Gujarat in the South-West. It is a distance of 1600 KM from the Sutlej.

Period of the Civilization

Sir John Marshall, the Director General of the Archaeological Survey of India, dated the period of Harappan civilization to be around 3250 BC–2750 BC. However, the radio carbon dating process differs from this estimate and indicates that the Harappan Civilization flourished between 2500-1700 BC.

FEATURES OF THE HARAPPAN CIVILIZATION

Town Planning

Town-Planning at Mohenjo-daro

The most remarkable feature of the Indus Valley Civilization was the brilliant town-planning and excellent architecture. The Indus Civilization comprised all the elements of an urban civilization. Mohenjo-Daro was the oldest planned city of the world. Buildings were made of baked bricks, some double-storied or even three. Houses were constructed by following a sequence and most houses had a well-patterned bathroom. There was a proper drainage system in every household and even in public areas. The main features of the Harappan town planning are as follows :

❑ The ruins of the cities of Harappa and Mohenjo-daro indicate that each city had two divisions: The raised area called the 'Citadel' and the 'Lower Town.' In most cities, a wall separated the raised citadel area from the lower town. Public buildings like assembly hall, the granaries, and the workshops were located on the citadel, whereas the lower town housed the residential buildings where people lived and carried on their occupations.

- Unlike the Sumerian cities, which developed in a circular pattern centering the temple, the cities of the Harappan Civilization followed a grid pattern.
- The entire city was divided into rectangular or square blocks by streets and each block was further sub-divided by a number of lanes. The main road in Mohenjo-daro was 800 meters long and 10.5 meters wide.
- All the roads and streets were straight, running from north to south, or from east to west, cutting each other at right angles. The Harappan people used fire-burnt bricks for paving the streets.
- The corners of the streets were rounded to make the movement of heavy carts easy. Houses were not allowed to encroach upon the streets.
- The houses varied greatly in size and were constructed on raised platforms to safeguard the buildings against the danger of floods. They were generally double storied and made of burnt bricks and had paved floors, which were usually earthen or 'Kuccha'.
- The residential buildings had well-sized rooms, bathrooms, solid staircases and water wells. The rooms of the house were built around an open courtyard, and the kitchen was positioned in a corner of the courtyard. The houses had storerooms, private baths, and well chambers. Each house was constructed with doors, windows and ventilators.
- Every house had a wastewater drain, which emptied into the main street drains. The house drains were provided with covers and were linked to the main underground drains of the street.

> **SOURCES TO RECONSTRUCT THE HARAPPAN CIVILIZATION**
>
> There are many sources to reconstruct the Harappan civilization.
> - The archeological remains of Mohenjo-daro and Harappa with the Great Bath, Assembly Hall, and other public buildings reveal a great deal about the town planning of the civilization.
> - The Indus valley seals offer much information about the religious beliefs and also about the physical features, dresses, and ornaments of the people.
> - The bronze statue of the dancing girl, the terracotta figurine of Mother Goddess, and the bust of the bearded man provide great information.
> - The beaded necklaces and other ornaments of gold and ivory reveal information about the metallurgical advancements.
> - The coins and other objects of Mesopotamian origin found in the Indus cities reflect trade relations with the Fertile Crescent at such an early age.

Basic typology of Settlements
- The early settlements like Mohenjo-Daro, Harappa and Kalibangan had the twin mounds, which were enclosed separately.
- The settlement like Surkotada in Western Gujarat was an imitation of the western sector at Kalibangan.
- Lothal had a single enclosed complex that housed public buildings and other residential structures.
- Mohenjo-Daro was 18 times bigger than Lothal. However, the two sites shared similar features like burnt brick houses, drains and granary. Kalibangan, which was more than double the size of Lothal, had a relatively inferior infrastructure.
- There were small but remarkable urban settlements like Ahladino and Hulas. These sites had no internal divisions and enclosing walls.

The Drainage System

The salient aspect of the 'Indus Valley Civilization' or 'Harappan Civilization' was the extensive usage of burnt-brick drainage system. The drainage system had extensively been used by the larger settlements like Mohenjo-Daro and Lothal. The width and profundity fluctuated from regions to regions.

The Drainage System

The features of the drainage system are as follows :

❑ The floors of kitchen and bathroom were water-tight and had a slight slope towards one corner, to allow the water to drain out into the narrow drain situated alongside.

❑ The house drains were linked to the underground sewers in the streets, which carried the waste to the large wells located outside the city.

❑ The streets of the Harappan cities were equipped with a brick-lined drainage channel, flowing alongside the street. They were provided with manholes and soak-pits for facilitating proper inspection and cleaning.

The presence of such an organized drainage system in every Harappan city indicates that the Harappan people were highly concerned about cleanliness and valued hygiene.

Provision for Wells

According to historians, a large number of burnt-brick wells have been excavated at the archaeological sites. Burnt-brick wells formed an important feature of Harappan civic planning. At Mohenjo-Daro, at least 700 wells had been excavated. The interior diameter of the wells fluctuated between 2 ft and 7 ft 6 inches. However, the average size was 2 ft 2 inches. The wells were found at other sites as well but they were hardly found at Kalibangan.

ARCHITECTURE OF HARAPPAN SITES

In addition to numerous dwelling houses, there were a few spacious buildings of elaborate structure and design, which are discussed below :

The Great Bath

The Great Bath is one of the largest and most important public buildings of Mohenjo-daro. It was a large open quadrangle (four-sided building) surrounded by galleries and rooms on all sides. The site features a huge swimming enclosure, which measures 39 feet long, 28 feet wide and 8 feet deep.

The Great Bath at Mohenjo-daro

The floors and walls of the pool were made with burnt bricks. However, to make the walls of the pool watertight, specially made burnt bricks were used with gypsum, mortar and bitumen. The pool was connected to a well, built nearby to supply water to the pool. The water from the swimming pool could be disposed into a drain, which was linked to the main drain of the street. The bath was surrounded with porticos and sets of rooms and a stairway leading to an upper storey. According to some historians, these rooms were utilized for religious activities but some believe that the rooms were built for changing clothes.

The Great Granary

The Great Granary formed an important part of the civic planning of the civilization. Two rows of six granaries have been discovered at Harappa, where each granary measured 15.23 × 6.09 meters. The granaries were utilized for storing grains. They were also equipped with ventilation to keep the grains fresh. Towards the south of the granaries, working floors were arranged in rows and built with circular bricks, have been discovered, which were probably used for threshing grains, as traces of barley and wheat

THE HARAPPAN CIVILIZATION

The Great Granary at Harappa

have been found there. In addition to this, two-roomed barracks for accommodating the laborers were also found. The granaries at Harappa were built on a raised platform to safeguard them from floods.

A large granary has also been unearthed at Mohenjo-daro, measuring 45.71 meters in length and 15.23 meters in breadth.

The presence of the Great Granary indicates the prevalence of a centralized tax collecting unit.

The Dockyard

The brick-built dockyard had a seemingly rectangular structure, with the longer axis running from north to south. It was encompassed by a massive brick wall, which protected the structure from massive flood. The great Dockyard at Lothal, discovered in 1954, is a proof of the long distance trade connection of the Indus Valley cities with Mesopotamian and Egyptian cities. Lothal's dock—the world's earliest known port, connected the city to an ancient course of the Sabarmati river on the trade route between Harappan cities in Sindh and the peninsula of Saurashtra, when the presently surrounding Kutch desert, was a part of the Arabian Sea. It was a vital and thriving trade center in ancient times, with its trade of beads, gems and valuable ornaments, reaching the far corners of West Asia and Africa.

The Assembly Hall and other Public Buildings

A pillared hall, made up of thick walls was discovered at Harappa. The hall was built with long corridors and low benches. It is believed that the hall was possibly used as an Assembly Hall for ceremonial or administrative functions. The other public buildings found at the site were a market place and a group of cottages.

At Mohenjo-Daro, an oblong multi-pillared structure was excavated, which can be construed as an assembly hall by the historians. The assembly hall was a public building that served the purpose of governance.

THE ECONOMIC LIFE OF HARAPPAN PEOPLE

Agriculture

Agriculture was the main occupation of the Harappan people and was the backbone of their economic life. Crops such as wheat, barley, peas, dates, bananas and melons were cultivated. The recovery of a wooden plough and granaries, indicates that the Harappans produced food grains in surplus. According to Dr. B. Lal, Kalibangan in Rajasthan bears testimony to the earliest ploughed agriculture field (2800 BC). It is believed that Harappans possibly used wooden ploughshare, drawn by men, and oxen to plough the land. According to archaeologists, the Harappan people sowed seeds in flood plains in the month of November and were the first to produce cotton. Specimens of mustard and sesame plants have also been found at both Harappa and Mohenjo-daro, indicating that it might have been grown for the production of oil. At Rangpur and Lothal, rice husks were also discovered, embedded in clay and pottery. Traces of canals found at Shortughai in Afghanistan indicate the need of irrigation for agriculture. Moreover, the discovery of a water reservoir at Dholavira in Gujarat also shows that water was possibly supplied by the wells, for irrigation purposes.

Trade and Commerce

The Harappans maintained trade relationships not only with different parts of India, but also with Mesopotamia and Egypt. Gold was imported from North Karnataka and Afghanistan; Copper from South India, Rajasthan, Arabia and Baluchistan and Lead from either East or South India. The exchanges were done through barter system.

Cities like Harappa, Mohenjo-daro and Lothal were prime hubs for metallurgy, producing tools and weapons, along with the kitchenware and other objects for wide distribution. There is an evidence which indicates that rice was imported in Punjab from Gujarat. Chanhu-daro and Balakot were the prime locations for bangle-making and shell works. Again, beads of carnelian were mainly produced from Lothal and Chanhu-daro.

Besides thriving in internal trade, the Harappans also maintained strong commercial relationships with their western neighbors. Surkotada, Lothal and Balakot were some of the prime trading coastal towns, which linked them to Mesopotamia and other West Asian sites. Articles of Sumerian origin were found at the Indus cities indicate that trade relations were also maintained between these countries.

Trade was carried on by both, sea and land routes. The discovery of a seal representing a mast-less ship, indicates the popularity of the sea-routes among the traders.

Weight and Measures

A number of stone weights have been excavated from the sites of Harappan civilization. The excavated stone weights indicate that commercial exchanges were quite common during this period. The Harappan people used the sets of cubical stone weights and the basic unit of the stone weights was 16. The larger weights were multiples of 16 like 32, 48, 64 and so on. Whereas the smaller weights were all fractions of 16. The decimal system was also known to them.

Transport

Discovery of a number of seals with pictures of ships engraved on them indicate the use of ships during the Harappan civilization. A terracotta model of a ship has also been excavated from Lothal. The Harappan people also used boats. The most popular means of transport within the cities were bullock carts. Copper or bronze models of carts with seated drivers have also been excavated at Harappa and Chanhu-daro. Skeleton remains of camels have also been excavated from the site of Kalibangan in Rajasthan. This proves that camel was also an important mode of transport.

THE SOCIAL LIFE OF HARAPPAN PEOPLE

Food

Wheat and barley formed the staple diet of the people of Harappa. Rice, fish, poultry, milk and mutton were also common in their diet. They also preferred to eat date palms.

Dress, Ornaments and Cosmetics

The people of the Harappan Civilization wore dresses made from Cotton fabric. The men usually wore two-piece dresses, which included the upper garment and a lower garment. The upper garment was a shawl worn round the shoulder whereas the lower garment resembled somewhat a contemporary *dhoti*. The women wore a loin cloth bound by a girdle and used to cover their upper portion with a cloak. Their heads remained covered with a scarf. Presently, a number of spinning wheels and needles of the Harappan age have also been discovered. Since remains of a large number of spindles have been found in the houses of the Harappan people, it can be concluded that spinning of wool and cotton was common among the Indus Valley people. Spindle whorls or spindles were made of porcelain or terracotta. Moreover, the unearthing of a dyer's vat on the site also suggests that the Harappan people were familiar with the art of dyeing clothes.

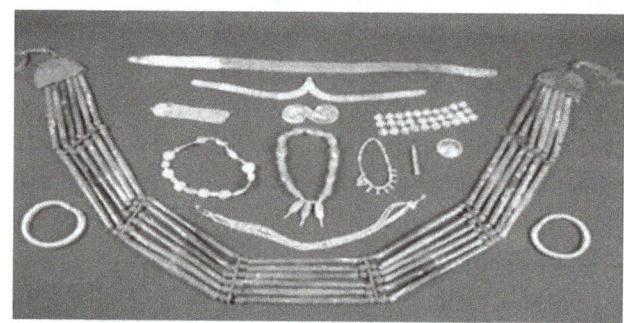

Ornaments of Mohenjo-daro Women

Both men and women were fond of wearing ornaments of gold, silver, copper and precious stones like Jade, Carnelian, Agate, Chalcedony and Lapis lazulli. Ornaments of various designs such as armlets, finger rings and necklaces have been discovered. Women of Mohenjo-daro were quite stylish and aware of the use of cosmetics. A number of fixtures made of ivory and metal for holding and applying cosmetics excavated at the site suggest that the women were aware of the practice of face painting and collieries. The other evidences are combs of various shapes, oval bronze mirrors and small dressing tables that have been found during excavation.

Amusement and Recreation

Recreation through indoor games was an important part of Harappan civilization. Dicing was a popular game preferred by the Harappan people. Men were also fond of fishing and hunting. The Harappan people were also inclined towards music and dance. A large number of clay models of men, women, animals, dolls, carts, whistles in the shape of birds and rattles have been excavated from the sites, indicating their use as toys in daily life.

Terracotta toys or clay models excavated from the various Harappan Sites

RELIGIOUS LIFE

A large number of figurines have been excavated from the major sites of the civilization. However, the scholars have suggested that the Harappan people worshipped a mother goddess indicating fertility. Some Indus Valley seals showed swastika or other mythical symbols, which were pervasive in religions conceptualised later and mythologies, particularly in Hinduism, Buddhism and Jainism. The early vestiges of Hinduism have been unearthed from the Harappan period. According to Frederick. J. Simoons, the phallic symbols representing Hindu Shiva Lingam have been excavated from the Harappan sites.

ART AND CRAFT

The Art of Sculpture

Sculpture in Metal

The Harappan artists were great sculptors and metal sculptures during the Harappan civilization were made by using a special wax process. In Harappan civilization or Indus Valley Civilization, metal casting was popular at the major excavated sites. For example, the bull from Kalibangan, copper bird and dog from Lothal and the anthropomorphic figures of copper and bronze discovered from Harappa and Mohenjo-daro. The most extraordinary metal work of the age was the bronze figure of a 'dancing girl', which was the symbol of vitality, variety and originality. The bronze statue of 'Dancing Girl' has been excavated form Mohenjo-daro. The right hand of the girl rested on her back and her left hand is fully covered with bangles made of ivory or bones. The statue holds a small ball against her left leg. She also wore necklaces and her hair was neatly tied in a bun. Beside the dancing girl, a number of bronze figures of buffalo and humped bull have also been discovered from the sites of excavation. People were accustomed to using gold, silver, bronze and copper objects. They did not know the use of iron. Copper was used in manufacturing of weapons, tools and implements, domestic utensils, daggers, knives and axes.

Dancing Girl

Sculpture in Stone

The stone figures excavated at Mohenjo-daro and Harappa indicate the outstanding skill of the sculptors belonging to the Harappan civilization. One of the most remarkable stone images excavated

Priest King

from the sites of Mohenjo-daro was of a nobleman or a 'priest king', draped in a shawl over the left shoulder and the right arm. It also featured a well-trimmed beard and half-closed eyes. Therefore, some of the scholars hold that it is a statue of a *yogi*. The other excavated figure is a beautiful sculpture of a male torso in red stone with socket holes in the neck and shoulders for the attachment of head and arms.

Sculpture in Terracotta

Terracotta Figurine

Terracotta sculpting was an important craft of the Harappan civilization. The most notable work of terracotta sculpture excavated at Mohenjo-daro was the terracotta figurine of the Mother Goddess. The sculpture of Mother Goddess with a punched nose and artistic ornamentation on the body shows it as the symbol of fertility and prosperity. The other exquisite pieces of terracotta sculpture include figures of human beings, birds, animals, bullock carts and ploughs, cattle–both humped and humpless bulls.

The Art of Painting and Pottery

The artistic skills of the Harappan people were also evident from the various exquisite designs and figures of men, birds and animals painted on earthenware with geometrical patterns, using a wide range of colors. The highly efficient Harappan potters used to make various types of jars, pots and vases of different shapes and sizes on a potter's wheel. The pots meant for daily use were plain and simple whereas, the valuable pots were made glossy and shining.

Remains of Harappan Pottery

SEALS AND THEIR IMPORTANCE

Around 2000 different types of seals have been unearthed from the various sites of the civilization. Most of these were rectangular or square shaped, though some circular seals have also been discovered. The seals were made of steatite, ivory, etc., while traders and merchants used terracotta and agate to stamp their commodities. Most of the seals are engraved with images of real animals (buffalo, rhinoceros, elephant, tiger, antelope and bison) while a few were engraved with the most common mythical animal (unicorn). Some seals with knobs at the back, through which runs a hole have also been found. Scholars believe that these were probably worn by people as amulets to protect them from evil spirits.

The Bull Seal

The Bull Seal

The bull seal depicts the figure of a humped bull of great vigour. The figure shows the artistic skill of Harappans and their good knowledge of animal anatomy.

The Unicorn Seal

The unicorn seal reflects the mythical beliefs of the Harappan people. It is engraved with the figure of the mythical animal unicorn, featuring a single protruding horn. It is believed that the designs on the seal are of religious character.

The Shiva Pashupati Seal

Seal of Pashupati

The most notable seal was that of the *Pashupati*, which portrayed a three-faced deity, resting in a yogic posture, surrounded by animals like a rhinoceros, a buffalo, an elephant and a tiger. Under his throne are two deer and a pair of horns crowns his head. He has been identified as *Shiva*, who is considered as the lord of animals and is worshipped even today. Seals of Pashupati signify the belief of Harappan people in religion and idol worship.

Importance of the Seals

- ❏ The seals of the Indus Valley civilization are the authentic sources of information about the culture and civilization of the Harappan people.
- ❏ The figures engraved on the seals provide information about the physical features, ornaments, dresses and hairstyles of the Indus people.
- ❏ The seals also explain the religious faith and beliefs of the Harappan people.
- ❏ The seals also offer ideas about the commercial activities of the people.
- ❏ They reflect the outstanding skill of the artists and the scripts prevalent in those days.

SCRIPT OR ART OF WRITING

The Harappan people are credited for developing the art of writing using a form of pictographic script. No regular documents on stone or baked clay tablets have been found but numerous seals unearthed at Harappa and Mohenjo-daro were engraved with some form of pictorial writing and other objects have also been found which gives us an idea that the people had a language of their own. Some historians are of the view that the scripts found on the seals are similar to the ones used in Egypt, Sumeria and other countries of Western Asia. However, the pictorial script has remained undeciphered till date, even though there are nearly four hundred inscriptions.

There are debates regarding the pattern and direction of the script. The writing was generally from left to right, but in some cases it was right to left in the first line and left to right in the second. Dr. S. R. Rao in his book, *The Decipherment of the Indus Script*, holds that Harappan people used the phonetic script in the beginning that later evolved as alphabetic pattern. However, the script continues to be a puzzle for the historians, and still remains to be deciphered.

S. R. Rao and Krishna Rao have claimed that the Indus script is connected with the Brahmni Script. On the contrary, scholars like Iravatham Mahadevan, Kamil Zvalebil and Asko Parpola have argued that the Indus script has Dravidian root.

DECLINE OF THE HARAPPAN CIVILIZATION

The Harappan Civilization declined sometime around 1800 BC. However, no exact cause has been cited as the reason behind this decline. Some of the speculative causes for the decline of the civilization are as follows:

- ❏ The climate change in the Indus region might have had an adverse impact on cultivation and stock breeding which led to the decline of the Harappan civilization.
- ❏ Excessive use of natural resources and vegetation might have turned the fertile area of the Indus region into totally unfertile land and thus depopulated the cities.
- ❏ The sinking of the land due to continuous floods may have led to the break down of the Harappan civilization.
- ❏ Sudden earthquakes and epidemics might have altered the course of the Indus River, causing immense damage to the cities.
- ❏ The excessive use of wood to bake bricks, to produce jewelry, to make pottery, stoneware and to manufacture furniture and boats could have caused deforestation leading to climatic changes in the area thereby causing the decline of the civilization.
- ❏ Some historians like Mortimer Wheeler, believe that possibly the invasion of the Aryans brought destruction to the Harappan Civilization. The discovery of the skeletons of 13 males and females along with one child lying in a room also support this cause.

Thus, even though the exact and specific causes for the decline and disappearance of the Harappan civilization are still shrouded in mystery, it can be concluded that in spite of the fact that this remarkable civilization ended abruptly it succeeded in leaving the mark of its philosophy and religion on its successors.

In Retrospect

- **Civilization :** Civilization means human settlements in cities within distinct areas and development of trade and commerce in those settlements.
- **Different Structures of Civilization :** The four civilizations to be studied are Harappan, Mesopotamian, Chinese and Egyptian. These Civilizations evolved due to the fertility of the soil in the vast river valleys and its rivers which acted as useful means of transport.
- **Foundation and Extent of the Harappan Civilization :** On the banks of the River Ravi, Harappa was located and Mohenjo-daro was located in the Larkana district of Sind. Other sites were Lothal, Chanhudaro, Banawali, Ropar.
- **Phase of the Civilization :** The Harappan Civilization existed from 2500–1700 BC as per radiocarbon dating techniques. Although the overall time frame might be between 3250–2750 BC.
- **Sources that help in reconstructing Harappan Civilization :** Mainly the relics of both the towns of Harappa and Mohenjo-daro helped in recreating the past the figure of a Dancing girl in Bronze. Seals—model of Mother Goddess, Statue of a Bearded Man in Stone, Utilization of cotton, Ivory and Gold Ornaments, stone cubes that were used as weights, they all provided essential informations.
- **Chief Features of the Harappan Civilization :** Planning of the Town keeping the chief streets straight and wide-planned system of drainage. Dwellings like the Great Granary, the Great Bath, Citadel, Assembly Hall and other buildings of public importance.
- **Social Life of the People of Harappa :** Their food items were made of barley, wheat, mutton, poultry and milk. They used to wear simple clothes, men and women both wore ornaments, they were interested in a variety of games and sports–used cosmetics.
- **Economic Life of the People of Harappa :** Basic occupation of the people was agriculture, other engagements were taming animals, relations of trade and commerce were maintained with Kashmir, eastern and southern India as well as other nations of Asia, trade relations were extended up to the Sumerians and Egyptians.
- **Art and Craft :** Harappans possessed brilliant crafting skill–sculpting in stones, terracotta and metal. They used special clay and potter's wheel to create pottery of different sizes and shapes that had figures of men, animals and birds, painting using vibrant colours, wool and cotton were spun commonly, metal crafting flourished around this time, development of the art of writing.
- **Use of Seals :** Copper, terracotta and soapstone were used to produce Animal Seals like that of bull, Unicorn Seals, Seals of the Shiva Pasupati. The seals highlighted the people's beliefs, script, artistic skill, commercial contacts, their physical features, ornaments, dresses, etc.
- **Religious life :** A large number of figurines have been excavated from the major sites of the civilization. However, the scholars have suggested that the Harappan people worshipped a mother goddess indicating fertility. Some Indus Valley seals showed swastika or other mythical symbols, which were pervasive in later religions and mythologies, particularly in Hinduism, Buddhism and Jainism. The early vestiges of Hinduism have been unearthed from the Harappan period. According to Frederick. J. Simoons, the phallic symbols representing Hindu Shiva Lingam have been excavated from the Harappan sites.
- **Downfall of the Civilization :** No basic evidence stating the reason for the end of the Civilization, flood and earthquake, exhaustion of natural resources due to overusing, might have destroyed the cities, attack from outsiders might have cause destruction.

EXERCISES

Part-I (Short Questions)

1. Name the different Bronze Age civilizations that developed across the world.
2. Who was Sir John Marshall ?
3. Who discovered the city of Harappa and when ?
4. Name four sites of the Harappan Civilization. What was the period of Civilization ?

THE HARAPPAN CIVILIZATION   73

5. Besides which river did Harappa flourish ?
6. State any two important features of the Great Bath.
7. What was the purpose of the rooms surrounding the Great Bath ?
8. Where was the Great Granary discovered? What was its purpose ?
9. Name any two occupations followed by the Harappan people.
10. Name the Agricultural crops raised by Harappans.
11. Write a short note on the dietary patterns of the Harappan people.
12. Name the ornaments worn by the people of Harappan civilization.
13. Enlist two important features of 'Dancing girl' and 'Priest King'.
14. Name any two important seals. What were these made of ?
15. What is the importance of seals excavated at various Harappan Sites ?
16. What was the style and pattern of script during Harappan period ?
17. What are the reasons for the decline of Harappan Civilization ?

Part-II (Structured Questions)

1. Briefly describe the extent of the Indus Valley Civilization?
2. In respect to Indus valley Civilizations, write short notes on :
   (a) Town Planning   (b) The Drainage system   (c) Citadel   (d) The Great Bath   (e) The Granaries
3. Provide evidence in each case to prove that the Indus people excelled in the art of sculpture:
   (a) In metal   (b) In stone   (c) In terracotta.
4. With reference to the economic life of the Harappan Civilization, discuss the following :
   (a) Trade and Commerce   (b) Agriculture
5. With reference to the Seals, explain the following :
   (a) Importance of Seals
   (b) Different Kinds of Seals unearthed at various sites of the Harappan Civilization.
   (c) In what ways the Harappan seals were relevant to the culture ?
6. What are the probable causes behind the decline of the Harappan Civilization ?

CHAPTER 2

EMERGENCE OF VEDIC INDIA

- Sources : Vedas and Epics (Brief mention); Iron Artifacts and Pottery.
- Brief Comparative study of Early and Later Vedic Society and Economy.

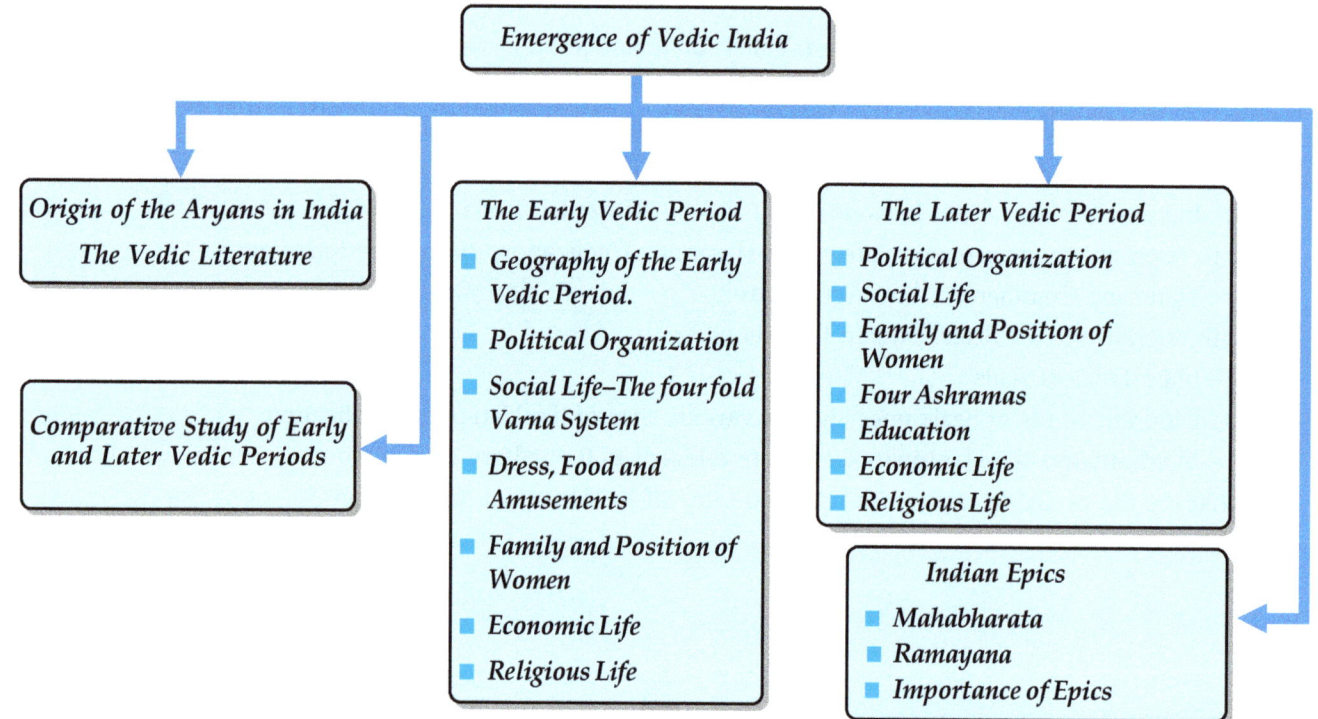

ORIGIN OF THE ARYANS IN INDIA

The Vedic civilization succeeded the Harappan civilization in ancient India, but there is conflicting historical evidences about its origins. One of the most controversial issues of ancient Indian history is the origin of Aryans. Scholars are making tireless efforts for finding out the original homeland of the Aryans. Around 1583, Filippo Sassetti visited Goa for the purpose of trade and commerce. He was the first person to find similarities between his own language Italian (developed from Latin) and the indigenous language Sanskrit. Joseph Schalligar (1542 to 1609), a scholar of the 'Renaissance' period wrote a book where he divided the European languages into four branches. In 1767, James Parsons wrote a book, entitled *Remains of the Japhet: Being historical enquiries into the affinity and origin of the European languages.* Parsons tried to highlight the language used by the Biblical family of Noah and his son Japhet. During the last half of the 18th century, William Jones discovered that Sanskrit, Greek and Indo-Iranian languages were similar. He stated that the Aryans had their original homeland in Central Asia or Eastern Europe and they belonged to similar human species. The theory propounded by Lokmanya Tilak suggests the Polar region as the regional homeland of Aryans. This theory has met with criticism, as the historians argue over the vast differences of culture between the Harappans and the Aryans. However, the most accepted theory was put forward by Max Muller, a German Indologist, who believed that the Aryans came from the Caspian Sea region or Central Asia, and migrated to various parts of Europe and Asia. For a long time, the Aryans lived in the *Sapta Sindhu* region of India. It is also known as the land of seven rivers, which were River Sindhu (*Indus*), River Chenab (*Asikni*), River Beas (*Vipas*), River Jhelum (*Vitasta*), River Ravi (*Parusni*), River Satluj (*Satadru*) and River Saraswati. It covers the present areas of Punjab, Eastern Afghanistan and parts of Western Uttar Pradesh. At this place, the hymns of '*Rig Veda*' were composed that provided references to both the popular rivers of India, Ganga and Yamuna.

The term Aryan is derived from the Sanskrit word '*arya*', meaning civilized or noble. It should be mentioned that the word 'Aryan' literally signifies a language and not a race. They first settled in India between 1500 to 1000 BC and this period is known as the Early Vedic Period or Rig Vedic Period. The period from 1000 BC to 500 BC is known as the Later Vedic Period. During this period, the Aryans discovered iron and used iron tools to clear the forests. They followed the course of the Ganga and Yamuna Rivers, and moved in south-eastward and eastward directions. Slowly, the nomadic and tribal Aryans began settling down in the Gangetic valley.

The discovery of the Painted Greyware (900-500 BC) from the sites in the Indo-Ganga divide, upper Ganga Valley and the Ganga-Yamuna doab bear testimony to the archaic vestiges that supplemented the literary data of the Vedic corpus, particularly the later Vedic texts.

THE VEDIC LITERATURE

The term '*Vedic literature*' simply means literature based on or derived from the *Vedas*. There are mainly four vedas—the *Rig Veda*, the *Yajur Veda*, the *Sam Veda* and the *Atharva Veda*. The *Rig Veda*, *Sam Veda* and *Yajur Veda* are collectively known as *Vedatrayi*, while *Atharva Veda* is considered a later addition.

Rig Veda Manuscript

Vedic Texts

Etymology :

The term '*Veda*' comes from the root *Vid* that indicates 'knowledge par excellence'. The hymns were addressed to gods such as Indra, Agni, etc and were recited during the sacrificial rites.

The Rig Veda (Veda of praise) comprises 1028 hymns (*suktas*), backed by 11 other books called *valakhilyas*. It is dissected into ten books or *mandalas*. The oldest hymns are encapsulated in mandalas II to VII (these are known as the 'Family Books', as their composition is attributed to certain family of sages, such as *Visvamitra, Vamadeva, Atri, Bharadvaja, Vasishtha and Gritsamada*). The Rig Veda is the oldest and most important of all the Samhitas. In Mandala III, we find the reference of the famous *Gayatri mantra*, composed by the sage Vishvamitra. The Gayatri mantra is dedicated to the solar deity *Savitri*.

The Sama Veda (the name comes from the word 'Saman', indicating a song or rhyme) comprises 1603 hymns chanted by the *udgatri priests* during the *soma* sacrifice.

The Yajur Veda (Veda of Yajus or magical formulae) comprises 2086 hymns chanted during the sacrifices. The two royal sacrifices of rajasuya and vajapeya are first highlighted in this text book.

The Atharva Veda (Veda of the atharvans or the ken of magical spells) comprises 731 or 760 hymns dissected into 20 popular books. The book contains magical formulae that would extinguish diseases and evil practices.

Another classification of the Vedic Literature is *Shruti* and *Smriti*. *Shruti* literature refers to the revelations by God to the sages that had been orally passed on by them from generation to generation. The literature that was composed by the *Rishis* is known as *Smriti* literature. It is to be remembered that except the *Rig Veda*, which is considered the earliest literary work to be possessed by humanity, all the other three *Vedas* were composed in the Later Vedic Period. The texts which constitute the Vedic literature are *Vedas*, divided into four parts i.e., *Samhitas, Brahmanas, Aranyakas* and the *Upanishads*.

❏ *Samhita* is a collection of *mantras* or hymns, which are concerned with nature and deities. Each *Veda* has its own *Samhita*.

❏ Similarly, each *Veda* has its own *Brahmana* which explain the hymns of the Vedas. They are written in prose, and elaborately describe the various sacrifices and rituals, along with their mystic meanings.

❏ The word *Aranyaka* means 'the forest' and these were written mainly for the hermits and students living in the jungles. They offer a bridge between *Karma marga* (way of deeds) and the *jnana marga* (way of knowledge) which was the sole concern of the *Brahmanas* and *Upanishads* respectively.

Knowledge imparted by Guru to his Students

❏ The word *Upanishad* has been derived from the root *Upanisad*, meaning 'to sit down near someone'. It denotes a student sitting at the feet of his guru to learn. *Upanishads* are also called *Vedanta* (the end of the Veda), firstly because they denote the last phase of the Vedic period and secondly, because they reveal the final aim of the Veda.

❏ The *Upanishads* comprise philosophical texts that actively deal with topics like the universal soul, the absolute, the individual soul, the inception of the universe and the accult powers. The *Upanishads* indicate the glimmering advent of rational thinking. They highly denounce the rituals and put an emphasis on the right knowledge and beliefs. According to the *Upanishads*, there are two distinct factors : the higher and the lower. The higher knowledge deals with the impregnable Brahman. At the same time the lower can be extracted from the four *Vedangas* (Limbs of *Vedas*).

The philosophical principles of Sankara, Ramanuja, Ramakrishna Paramhans, Aurobindo and others are derived from *Upanishads*. In fact, the entire later Indian philosophy is rooted in *Upanishads*.

THE EARLY VEDIC PERIOD

Geography of the Early Vedic Period

The Rig Vedic text is the principal source that reflects on the geographic spread of the Early Vedic Period (1500-1000 BC). The Aryans were domiciled in the area that is regarded as *Saptasindhu* region (Land of the seven rivers). They gained the occupation of more and more land in the Eastern and Northern parts of the country. They named it *'Aryavarta'* or the 'Abode of the Aryans'. The region includes modern day Eastern Afghanistan, Punjab (both Indian and Pakistani) and parts of Western U.P. Max Muller claims that these seven rivers are the life-line rivers of the region. from the Rig Veda, we derive references of many rivers, such as Krumu (Kurram), Kubha (Kabul in present time), Gomati (Gumal), Sindhu (Indus) and its five tributaries (Vitsae or Jhelum, Askini or Chenab,

EMERGENCE OF VEDIC INDIA

Vipas or Beas, Sutudri or Sutlej, Parushni or Ravi) and Ganga, Yamuna, Sarasvati, Ghaggar (Drishadvati), Sarayu and many more.

The Rig Veda also points out the word *Samudra* that signified an assemblage of water bodies and not sea in that period. The *'Himavat'* or Himalayan mountain range is mentioned in the Rig Vedic source. A lofty peak of the Himalaya mountain range is known as *'Mujavant'* that indicated the incepting point of *soma juice*. According to Rig Veda, the historical battle of ten kings or *Dasarajna* was fought along the bank of Parushni (Ravi) river.

Political Organization

The *grama* (village), *vis* and *jana* were political units of the early Vedic Aryans. A number

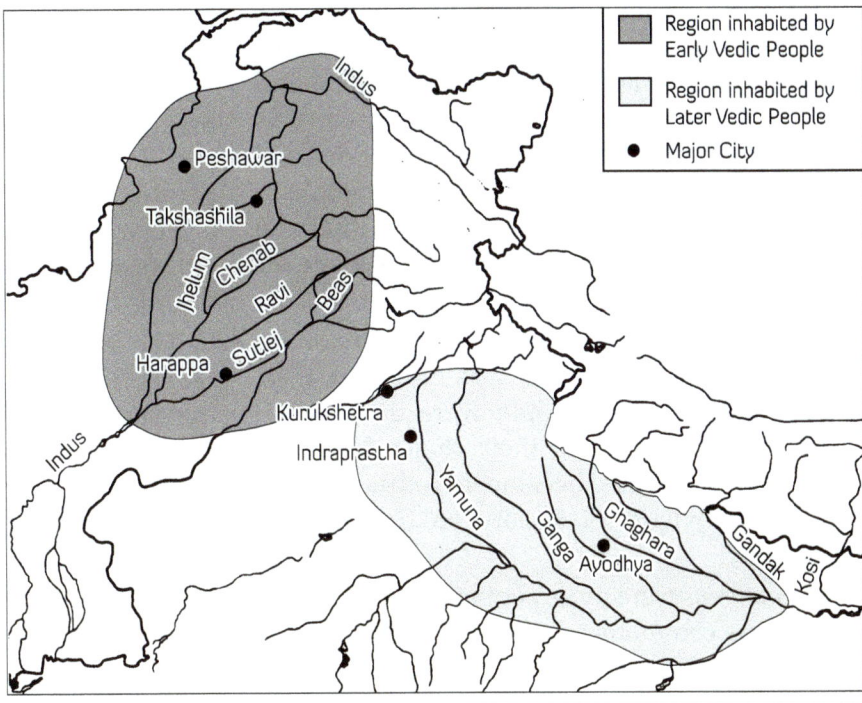

Extent of Aryans in Early and Later Vedic Period

of families *(kulas)* formed the village (grama). The headman or leader of a grama was called *gramani* and that of a vis was called *vishpati*. Several vis together formed a tribe (jana) under a king. The *rashtra* (state) was governed by a *rajan* (king). Monarchy was the system of government that prevailed in the Rig Vedic age. The term *'Rajan'* or 'king' is frequently mentioned in the Rig Veda. Vedic monarchy was the culmination of the circumstances surrounding the Aryans.

Fourfold division of Early Vedic Society based on Occupation

The king is often referred to as *gopa* (protector) and *samrat* (supreme ruler). He was elected by the tribe and he governed his tribesmen with their consent and approval. The main duty of the king was to protect the tribe from internal trouble and external dangers. In running he administration, he was aided by two functionaries, the *Purohita* (chief priest) and the *senani* (army chief). The king employed *spasa* (spies) and *dutas* (messengers). He often got a ceremonial gift called *bali* from the people. There were four councils, viz. *Sabha, Samiti, Vidhata* and *Gana* of which the former two were popular ones. Both Sabha and Samiti not only gave advice to the King but also practiced spells and charms for success in war. Women were allowed to attend sabha and vidhata only.

Soldiers on foot *(pattis)* and on chariots *(rathins)*, armed with bows and arrows were common. This suggests that early Aryans maintained a high standard of warfare.

Social Life – The Four-fold Varna System

The Purusha Sukta, found in the tenth mandala of the Rig Veda, gives reference to the four-fold caste system. The Rig Vedic society comprised four-fold castes, namely the Brahmana, Kshatriya, Vaishyas and Shudras.

The Aryans belonging to the Early Vedic Period did not mix with the local inhabitants and called them *Dasyus*. It is said that the priests and tribal chiefs acquired a large share of the booty and became rich at the expense of their kinsmen. This created social inequalities and society got divided into three groups - priests, warriors and people. It was only in the late *Rig Vedic* Period that the fourth division, called the *Shudras*, was included in the class division.

In the Early Vedic Period, the division of society into different classes was based on their professions. Initially, people were allowed to choose any profession of their choice but with time, the professions became hereditary. This resulted in division of society on the basis of occupation.

The *Brahmins* were those people who performed the religious ceremonies and explained the Vedic texts. Those belonging to the ruling class were called the *Kshatriyas*. They were warriors, who fought wars and defend the country. The *Vaisyas* were the common people engaged in trade, agriculture and industry. The labourers and servants who served the upper classes were known as the *Shudras*.

At that time, interclass marriages were prevalent and there was no restriction regarding the intake of food cooked by *Shudras*. Later, the class system became the caste system. During the Later Vedic Period, the caste system became rigid. The *Brahmins* and *Kshatriyas* enjoyed a number of privileges. Inter-caste marriages were also not prevalent during the later Vedic period.

Dress, Food and Amusements

The dress worn by the Aryans normally consisted of two or three garments. An upper piece or shirt called *Vasa*, an undergarment called *Dhoti* or *Nivi* and an over garment or loose piece of cloth called *Adhivasa* were part of their attire. These garments were usually made of cotton, wool or silk and were of different colours. During that time, men had long hair and used to wear turbans. There was also the custom of wearing animal skins. Some of the *sadhus* used *Mrigchhal*, or deer skin. Both men and women used to wear ornaments that were made of gold, precious stones, ivory and silver. Common items of jewellery included rings, earrings, bracelets, anklets and necklaces.

The early Aryans ate both vegetarian and non-vegetarian food. Barley or *yava* was the main cereal that was produced by them. They also domesticated cows and used milk and milk products like butter, curd and ghee. Their popular drinks were *Soma* and *Sura*. *Soma* was an intoxicating drink which was consumed during the religious ceremonies and festivals.

The main means of amusement were horse races, chariot races, singing, dancing and hunting. Gambling, however, was regarded as evil. Music, both vocal and instrumental was known. *Flute*, *drum* and *mridang* were the chief musical instruments used at that time. The Aryans also participated in festivals, competitive sports and gambling.

Family and Position of Women

In the Early Vedic Period, the Aryans used to live in villages and their houses were built of reed or wood. The family was the basic unit of the simple social structure. At that time, the society was patriarchal and the joint family system was prevalent. The oldest male family member was the master of the house and he was referred to as *Grihapati* or *Kulapati*. After his death, his eldest son had to take the responsibility of the family.

Women were also respected and treated as equal during that period. They were educated and some were well versed in the sacred scriptures. The *Rig Veda* and *Upanishads* mention several women sages like Maitreyi and Gargi. The women of Early Vedic Period attended all social gatherings and functions and participated in all religious rites. The marriageable age for women in this period was 16 or 17 years. They had the freedom of choosing their husbands through *swayamvar sabha* and the system of widow remarriage was also prevalent. The system of *sati*, child marriage and *purdah* was non-existent.

Economic Life

In the early Vedic Period, agriculture was conducted with the help of bulls and oxen. The ploughed land was called *Urvara Kshetra*. They reared cattles, sheeps, oxes, goats and horses for purposes of milk, meat and hides. Cattle rearing, however, was their main occupation, and was considered as the most important economic activity of the Rig vedic Aryans.

The cows were considered as providers of everything. They were given to the priests as gifts for performing sacrifices. A wealthy person was known as *gomat* and his wealth was measured in terms of number of cows he owned. Prayers were offered for an increase in the number of cattle. The early Aryans had knowledge of agriculture and practiced it to supplement their food requirements. There are references of producing *yava* (jau or barley), during that period.

Apart from cattle rearing and small-scale cultivation, people were engaged in many other economic activities such as hunting, carpentry, tanning, pottery, weaving, chariot making, fishery, etc. Women were also engaged in crafts like weaving, dyeing, spinning and knitting. The products of these activities were exchanged through barter system. However, bullocks and horses were the most favoured medium to carry goods from one place to another.

Religious Life

Religion in Early Vedic Period revolved around crude forms of worshipping, which basically included nature worship. They worshipped different forms of nature as god, which were predominantly male, like *Indra* (the God of Rain), *Varuna* (the God of Sky), *Surya* (the God of Sun), *Pusan* (the God of Roads, Herdsmen and Cattle) and *Agni* (the God of Fire). Since there were no scientific explanations for natural phenomena like rain, thunder, wind, etc., people feared them and thus worshipped them. Chanting of prayers and hymns were a common practice to invoke the Gods and it was normal to sacrifice animals in the name of religion. There were no temples and no idol worship in this period. Some female dieties like *Aditi* and *Usha* were also mentioned, but they were not as important as the male gods.

There is an allusion to abstract deities such as Shraddha or faith and Manyu or wrath. There were minor deities or demigods, such as Gandharvas or aerial spirits, Ribhus or aerial elves and Apsaras or water-nymphs. The Rig Vedic people had complete faith in life after death in the world regulated by Yama (the God of Death).

The Rig Vedic people offered oblation to the deities in the hope of receiving boons or favor. An extensive procedure was followed for performing sacrifices and various sorts of priests participated in the process. These priests were Hotri (chant mantras and incantation), Adhvaryu (responsible for the physical details of the sacrifices) and Udgatri (chanter of hymns).

THE LATER VEDIC PERIOD

The Aryans moved towards east in the Later Vedic Period. The information on the later Vedic Civilization can be extracted from the *Samveda Samhita, Yajurveda Samhita, Atharvaveda Samhita,* the *Brahmanas*, the *Aranyakas* and the *Upanishads*. The *Satapatha Brahmana* refers to the expansion of Aryans to the eastern Gangetic plains. Several Kingdoms such as Kosala, Videha and Kashi emerged as powerful centres.

Political Organization

In later Vedic times, the *vidatha* completely disappeared and larger kingdoms were formed. The *sabha* and *samiti* continued to hold their ground, but their importance withered away. Women were no longer permitted to sit in the *sabha* and it was now dominated by nobles and *Brahmanas*. The formation of wider kingdoms made the king more powerful. Tribal authority tended to become territorial. The term *rashtra*, which indicates territory, first appears in this period. The King performed various rituals and sacrifices to strengthen his position. They include *Rajasuya* (consecration ceremony), *Asvamedha* (horse sacrifice) and *Vajapeya* (chariot race), in which the royal chariot was made to win the race against his kinsmen. The Kings also assumed titles like *Rajavisvajanan, Ahilabhuvanapathi* (lord of all earth), *Ekrat* and *Samrat* (sole ruler). Even the king did not possess a standing army. Tribal units were mustered in times of war and, according to one ritual for success in war, the king had to eat along with his people from the same plate.

During this period, a large number of new officials were involved in administration in addition to *purohita, senani* and *gramani*. They include *sangrihitri* (treasury officer) and *bhagadugha* (tax collector).

Social Life

The caste system became very rigid. Birth determined the caste of a person and it was difficult to change one's caste. The four divisions of society (*Brahmans, Kshatriyas, Vaishyas* and *Shudras*) were thoroughly established. *Brahmana* and *Kshatriya* emerged as the most important classes. They enjoyed privileges that were denied to *vaishyas* and *Shudras*. Shudras were considered untouchables and the lowest among the four castes. Many sub-castes on the basis of their occupation appeared in this period. According to *Satapatha*, Kshatriyas and Brahmans could marry women from the Vaishyas and Shudras but the Vaishyas and Shudras could not marry Brahmana and Kshatriya women.

Family and Position of Women

According to the Satapatha Brahmana, A man was considered incomplete without his wife. She had full control over her family members. In practice, her social status declined considerably and she could not participate in assemblies or *yajnas*. They lost the right to property and the freedom to choose their husbands. She was considered subordinate to their male counterparts. According to Aitareya Brahmana, daughter has been described as a source of misery. The condition of women relegated to the background in the later Vedic period. However, there was a ray of hope in the dismal picture. Women like Gargi and Maitreyi had set a paradigm in the sphere of education and culture. Gargi was one of the learned persons summoned by King Janaka and she attended the conference organized by him. The Upanishads allude to an intellectual conversation between Maitreyi and her husband, Yajnavalkya. In the later Vedic period, there were many learned women, referred to as Brahmavadins. However, they were receded to the background and eventually lost their rights to attend many religious ceremonies.

Four Ashramas

In the Later Vedic Period, the life span of an Aryan was divided into four stages. Each stage of life comprised of 25 years and the stages were known as *ashramas*. The four ashramas were *Brahmacharya, Grihastha, Vanaprastha* and *Sanyasa*. These ashramas were meant only for the upper castes of society.

- The period of *Brahmacharya Ashrama* (till the age of 25 years) was for the pupil to observe strict discipline and obtain knowledge from his guru in the *gurukul* or school.
- The second period was *Grihastha Ashrama* (25 to 50 years), during which a man was supposed to marry and raise a family. As a householder, he had to take full responsibility of maintaining the family.
- The *Vanaprastha Ashrama* (50 to 75 years) is the third period in which Aryan man was to retire from worldly life, in order to achieve philosophical and spiritual knowledge.
- The *Sanyasa Ashrama* (75 to 100 years) was the last period and stage of the life of an Aryan man. During this period of renunciation, he had to leave everything and meditate to attain salvation or *moksha*.

Education (The Gurukul System)

In the Vedic Period, education was imparted through gurukuls. The residence of the *guru* or the teacher was called *gurukul*, meaning the 'family of the *guru*' and was considered to be the most sacred institution. The students had to live in the *gurukuls* that were usually located in forests or on the outskirts of the village.

The Gurukul System

The Aitareya Brahmana first mentioned about the ashrama system. However, the Chandogya Upanishad gave a clear indication of three ashramas. In the Jabala Upanishad, Yajnavalkya explicated the four ashramas. Therefore, the four-fold ashrama system belonged to the later Vedic period. Each stage of life consisted of 25 years and the stages were known as ashramas. The four-fold ashrama system comprised four distinct stages, like brahmacharin or student life, grihastha or life of the domestic house-owner, vanaprastha or partial retirement and sannyasin (yati) or complete recluse (adoption of ascetic life). The SatapathaBrahmana gave a detailed explanation of the system of Upanayana, which was a significant form of sacrament (samskara). Most of the education was imparted orally. Subjects taught at the *gurukul* included the *Vedas*, *Puranas*, Mathematics, Logic, Ethics, Grammar and Military Science. The main object of such education was to bring about physical, spritual and mental development in pupils.

The *gurus* were greatly revered and respected by their pupils. In turn, the guru treated the students like his own children. The students also had to do household work for their *guru*. They had to get up early in the morning, take a bath and chant the *Vedic mantras*. At the completion of their education, the custom was that the students had to give *guru dakshina* or a present to the *guru*.

Economic Life

The discovery and use of iron was considered to be the other important event of this period. It helped them to invent new tools which enabled the people to clear forests and bring new lands under cultivation. Agriculture grew in importance and metal tools and iron ploughshares were used instead of the wooden ones. Besides barley, rice and wheat were grown. With the discovery of iron, metal and leather work, carpentry and pottery made great progress which gave rise to trade and enabled exchange of goods in the markets. In addition to internal trade, foreign trade also became extensive. The later Vedic people were familiar with the sea and therefore, traded their goods through the inland rivers. A class of hereditary merchants *(vaniya)* also came into existence. *Vaishyas* also carried on trade and commerce. Besides *nishka* of the Rig vedic period, gold and silver coins like *satamana* and *krishnala* were used as media of exchange. The trade also led to the development of markets and the markets led to the development of cities and towns. Thus, trade was considered to be the pivot around which the whole city and town life moved.

Religious Life

Gods of the Early Vedic period like *Indra* and *Agni* lost their importance. Religious practices were refined and worship of Gods in the form of idols gained importance. *Prajapathi* (the creator), *Vishnu* (the protector) and *Rudra* (the destroyer) became prominent. Priesthood became a profession and hereditary. Animal sacrifices increased during this period and the rituals connected with them become more elaborate. Therefore, towards the end of this period there was a strong reaction against priestly domination, sacrifices and rituals. The rise of Buddhism and Jainism was the direct result of these elaborate sacrifices.

INDIAN EPICS

The Vedic literature comprises mainly the *Vedas* and the two great epics of India – the *Ramayana* and the *Mahabharata*. All these books are in Sanskrit and throw great light on all spheres of life of the Aryans during the Later Vedic Period.

Mahabharata

This epic was believed to be written by sage Vyasa in Sanskrit language. Originally, it comprised of 8800 verses and was known as *Jaya* or the collection of verses that dealt with victory. Later, the verses were raised to 24,000 and were known as *Bharata* as it contained the stories of the descendants of *Bharata*, one of the earliest Vedic tribes. The final compilation came to be known as *Mahabharata* and contained 100,000 verses. A part of Mahabharata called Bhagawad Gita is still considered to be one of the most sacred and popular religious texts of India.

Ramayana

Maharishi Valmiki who lived in 3rd century BC composed the *Ramayana*. The epic was originally composed in Sanskrit language.

Importance of Epics

These epics are important for a number of reasons such as :

- These epics are the best literary works of the ancient period and are highly praised for their philosophical and literary value.
- They serve as the primary source of information regarding the political institutions and the cultural and social organisations of the Epic Age. These epics have also revealed the high ideals of the family life of Aryans.
- These epics provide information about various Aryan kingdoms, their armies and weapons. In fact, the depictions of the great heroes in these epics have had an immense impact on successive generations.
- Certain religious aspects like immortality of soul and the philosophy of *Karma* have also been upheld by a part of the *Mahabharata* epic called *Bhagawad Gita*.

COMPARATIVE STUDY OF THE EARLY AND LATER VEDIC PERIODS

Points of Comparison	Early Vedic Period	Later Vedic Period
Vedic Literature	Religion *Rig Veda*	*Sama Veda, Yajur Veda* and *Atharva Veda. Brahmanas, Upanishads, Aranyakas, Vedangas, Sutras,* Epics, etc.
Political Organization	**King** : A tribal leader who was elected by his tribe and his position was not heriditary. *Sabha* and *samiti* acted as checks on the king's power. His position was not ritualised. King received voluntary gifts i.e., *bali* from his tribesmen	**King** : Became associated with territory and his position became hereditary. *Sabha* and *samiti* lost their importance. A number of rituals and sacrifices were conducted to strengthen the position of the king. For the collection of revenue from the people officials were appointed by the king.
Society	**Family** : The basic unit of the society; patriarchal in nature; prevalence of joint family **Women** : They had equal status as men; could participate in assemblies; widow remarriage was allowed and they could also receive education. **Caste system** : It was not rigid; the fourfold division was made primarily on the basis of occupation. **Food items** : It included barley, milk, vegetable, fruit, rice and meat.	**Family** : Became more patriarchal in nature; the status of father had increased. **Women** : The position of women declined; they were considered as a source of misery; were not allowed to participate in assemblies or *yajnas*; widow remarriage was looked down upon; education for fewer women. **Caste system** : It became more rigid; birth became the basis of one's caste; each class had a distinct role; four *ashrams* developed. **Food items** : Consumption of meat was reduced.

EMERGENCE OF VEDIC INDIA

| Economy | **Pastoral :** The primary occupation of Cattle rearing was the important source of wealth.
Agriculture : It was conducted with the help of bulls and oxen domestication of animals was done.

Trade : Barter system prevailed and was carried out in terms of bullocks and horses. Many people were engaged in commerce and trade.

Other economic activities : Hunting, carpentry, tanning, pottery, weaving, chariot-making, fishery, embroidery, dyeing, weaving, etc., were known.

Worship : They worshipped natural forces as male Gods such as *Agni*, *Indra*, *Pushan* and *Surya*; female goddesses like *Aditi* and *Usha* were also worshipped.
Chief mode of worship : Chanting of prayers and animal sacrifices were common. | **Pastoral :** Cattle rearing continued.

Agriculture : It became an important source of economy and large tracts of forests were cleared for it. The important source of wealth was the land.
Trade : It continued in barter and currency; silver coins were the media of exchange; foreign trade became extensive; vaishyas also carried on trade and commerce.
Other economic activities : Metal work, leather work, jewellery making, carpentry and pottery made great progress

Worship : *Indra* and *Agni* lost their importance. *Vishnu* and *Rudra* became prominent.

Chief mode of worship : Animal sacrifices increased during this period; Priesthood became prominent. |

In Retrospect

- **Aryans: origin and settlement** : Most historians believe that the Aryans came from the Caspian Sea region or Central Asia and migrated to India between 1500 to 1000 BC (Early Vedic Age).
- **Vedic Literature** : Two distinct types–(a) Early Vedic (b) Later Vedic. Early Vedic Literature developed between 1500 BC to 1000 BC. The Rig Veda was composed during this period. Later Vedic Literature was composed between 1000 BC to 500 BC. During this period, the remaining Vedas– Sama Veda, Yajur Veda and Atharva Veda with Samhitas, Brahmanas, Aranyakas and Upanishads were written.
- **Vedic Society** : Family and Position of Women : Society was patriarchal during the Early Vedic Period but women were respected and treated as equals. However, in the Later Vedic Period the status of women suffered a significant decline.
- **Social Divisions** : The Four fold Varna System : The four Varnas were Brahmins. (Men of Scriptures), Kshatriyas (Men of Arms), Vaishyas (Farmers) and Shudras (labour and servant class). Interclass marriages were prevalent in the Early Vedic times but during the Later Vedic Period, the caste system became rigid.
- **Four Ashramas** : The life span of an Aryan was divided into four stages. Each stage of life comprised of 25 years and the stages were known as ashramas. The four ashramas were Brahmacharya, Grihastha, Vanaprastha and Sanyasa.
- **Vedic Economy Agriculture** : The Rig Vedic economy was primarily agrarian. In the Later Vedic Age, agriculture grew in importance with the advent of iron.
- **Trade** : The main items of trade were leather goods and cloth. Barter system was still predominant. The cow was considered to be the standard unit of value.
- **Epics** : The Mahabharata and the Ramayana are the two important epics of India. Mahabharata is believed to be written by sage Vyasa in Sanskrit around 1000 BC. The Ramayana was written by Maharishi Valmiki who lived in the 3rd century BC the epic was originally composed in Sanskrit.

EXERCISES

Part-I (Short Questions)

1. When did Aryans settle in India?
2. What do you understand by *Sapta Sindhu* ?
3. What does the word *'Veda'* means ?
4. Name the four Vedas.
5. How many hymns are there in the *Rig Veda* ?
6. What were the important duties of *Rajan* in the Early Vedic Period ?
7. Who were *Purohita* and *Senani* ?
8. What were the main occupations of the Aryan people in the Early Vedic Period ?
9. Mention the important Gods of the early Aryans.
10. Mention the four important kingdoms of the Later Vedic Period.
11. Mention three important sacrifices performed by the king to strengthen his position during the later Vedic Period.
12. Who was *sangrihitri* and *bhagadugha* ?
13. Name the four *Ashramas* and discuss its implications for the Vedic life.
14. What is the difference between *Brahmanas* and *Aranyakas* ?
15. What do you mean by the *Gurukul* system? Which subjects were taught ?
16. Name the three important Gods of the Later Vedic Period.
17. Compare the position of women in Early and Later Vedic Period.
18. Name the two epics of Later Vedic Period ?
19. State one point of difference between the Early Vedic Period and the Later Vedic Period.

Part-II (Structured Questions)

1. With reference to Vedic India, answer the following :
   (a) Vedic literature.
   (b) Which is the oldest Vedas among all ?
   (c) Features of Rig Veda.
2. State the political institutions of the Rig Vedic Age that exercised a check on the powers of the King.
3. Discuss the following in the Early as well as Later Vedic Period:
   (a) Social Life
   (b) Position of women
4. How did the discovery of iron play an important role in the Later Vedic Period?
5. Describe briefly the four Ashramas practised by the Aryans during the Later Vedic Period.
6. Who were the important officers who looked after the administration of the kingdom during the Later Vedic Period ?
7. Compare the changes between the Early Vedic Period and Later Vedic Period in the following areas :
   (a) Political Organization
   (b) Society
   (c) Economy
   (d) Religion

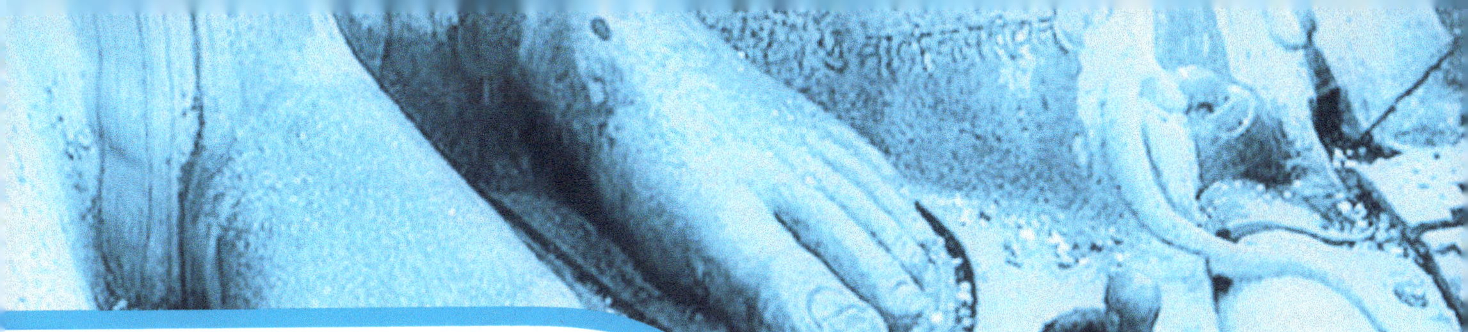

CHAPTER 3

JAINISM AND BUDDHISM

- ◆ Sources : Angas, Tripitakas and Jatakas.
- ◆ Causes for their rise in the 6th century BC; Doctrines.

Jainism and Buddhism

Causes for the Rise of Jainism and Buddhism in India
- Rigid and Expensive Ritualism
- Supremacy of the Brahman Priests
- Animal Sacrifices
- Rigidity of the Caste System
- Difficult Vedic Language
- Faith in Magic and Charms
- Political Circumstances
- Religious Reformers' Efforts

Vardhamana Mahavira and Jainism
Doctrines of Jainism
- The five Vows
- Nirvana or Salvation
- Karma
- No Belief in God
- Refusal of Vedic rituals and Sacrifices
- Equality of People and Universal Brotherhood
- Belief in Penance
- Non-Violence

Sects of Jainism
- Svetambaras
- Digambaras

Spread of Jainism

Impact of Jainism on Indian Culture
- Vernacular Languages and Literature
- Religion
- Political Life
- Society
- Art and Architecture

Decline of Jainism

Gautama Buddha and Buddhism
- The Four Great Sights

Teachings of Buddhism
- The Four Noble Truths
- The Eightfold Path
- Attitude Towards God
- The Karma Theory
- Nirvana
- Ahimsa
- No Faith in Caste System
- No Belief in Rituals and Sacrifices
- Stress on Moral Character
- Code of Conduct

The Buddhist Literature

Sects of Buddhism

Spread of Buddhism

Impact of Buddhism on Indian Culture
- Ahimsa
- Social Life
- Culture
- Education
- Religious Life
- Politics
- Language and Literature
- Art and Architecture

Decline of Buddhism

Similarities and Dissimilarities between Jainism and Buddhism

The 6th century BC was a turning point in Indian history, as this period witnessed immense political, social, religious and economic upheavals. *Solasa Mahajanapadas* or sixteen states, began to dominate the political scene. Among these some important Republics were the Sakyas of Kapilavastu and the Lichhavis of Vaishali while others like Kaushambi (Vatsa), Magadha, Panchala, Kamboja, Kosala, Gandhara, Kuruand, Avanti were monarchies. Prof. Rhys Davis in his book *"Buddhist India"* provided detailed insights into the prevalence of 16 *Mahajanapadas* or states. Magadha was the most eminent state, which covered the modern districts of Patna and Gaya. Magadha emerged victorious after defeating other weak states. The rise of these Mahajanapadas and their conflicts led to widespread unrest and an underlying discontent against the tyranny of the priests, the ritualistic forms of religion, the brutality of the caste-system, the dominance of Brahmanical society, etc. giving rise to new philosophical principles and religious ideas. This led to the emergence of two new sects of religion, which were anti-brahmanical in nature and influenced our culture and society greatly– Jainism and Buddhism.

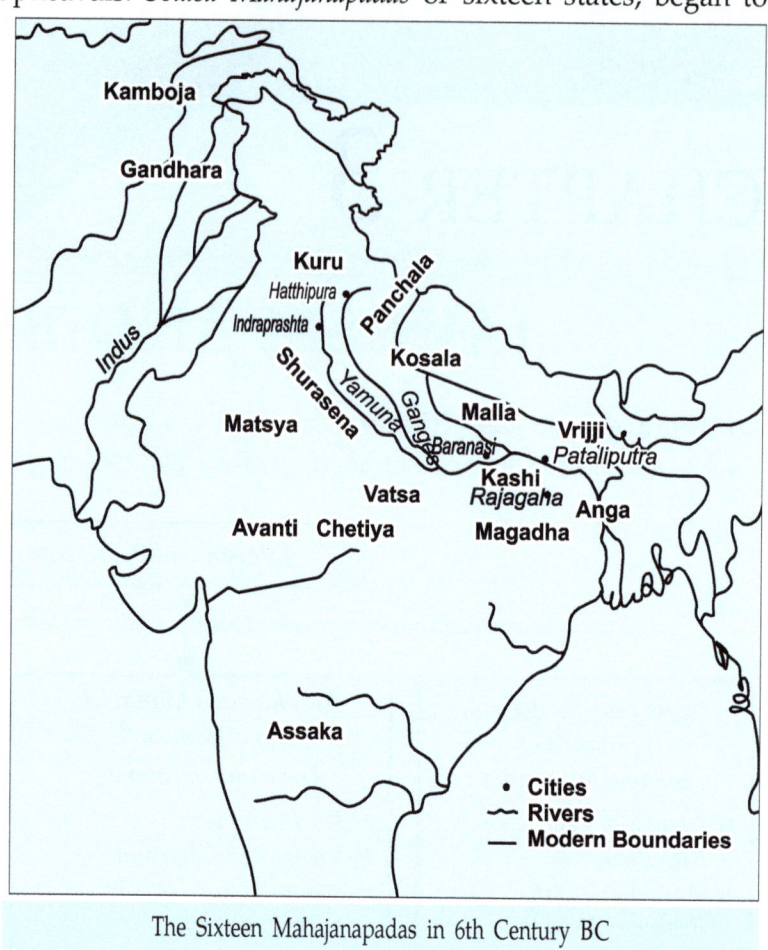

The Sixteen Mahajanapadas in 6th Century BC

CAUSES FOR THE RISE OF JAINISM AND BUDDHISM IN INDIA

During the 6th and 5th century BC; the society was rifed with intellectual unrest and inequalities in the economic and social sectors. The ordinary people desperately wanted change in the society and religion. In this context, we have to understand the chief causes, which centributed to the rise of the two religious sects of Jainism and Buddhism in 6 century BC in India..

Rigid and Expensive Ritualism

In the 5th-6th century BC., the simplicity of Vedic religion was eclipsed by the elaborate sacrificial rites and cumbrous festivities. The *rishis* of the Upanishads criticized sacrificial rites and the practice of idolatry. They believed that the *effects of Karma* governed the life-cycle of a man. Honest work and purity of life could free human beings from the cycle of life and death. These teachings had set a new paradigm in sphere of religious thinking. As a matter of fact, common men lost faith in the rigor of Brahminical tradition. Historian Richard E. Oldenburg says, "For hundreds of years, before Buddha's time, various movements which prepared the way for Buddhism".

Kshatriya rulers and *vaishya* businessmen were staunchly against such practices and the common man also felt the same. The universal truth and purity of heart vanished, which led the people in the 6th century to crave for a simpler religion.

Supremacy of the Brahman Priests

The seeds of the protest movement lay in the Vedic society. The Vedic society was divided into four distinct classes or *varnas*: Brahmans, Kshatriyas, Vaishyas and Shudras. The social status of the first two *varnas* increased and the prestige of Vaishyas diminished. The Shudras occupied the lowest order in the society. They were considered 'untouchable' or 'outcast' stocks. This grave social discrimination gave rise to social crises and tensions. At the same time, the predominance of the Brahmans was very much resented by the Kshatriyas. From the later Vedic period, the Brahman-Kshatriya feud surfaced and the question of supremacy loomed large in the background. In this context, it should be mentioned that both Gautama Buddha and Mahavira were Kshatriya by caste. Dr. Dinesh Chandra Sarkar says that Gautama Buddha was first to rise in protest against the power and rituals of the Brahmans.

Animal Sacrifices

The sacrifice of animals in the form of *yajnas* was an important part of Brahminical rituals in Rig-Vedic period. People resented the practice of 'animal slaughtering' that was needed to appease the Gods. The absurd rituals put the common public on the threshold of financial crisis. They took recourse to *'heterodox sects'* that would be much easier for them. Both Jainism and Buddhism were prominent religions, which fought against the practice of animal sacrifice and violence.

Rigidity of the Caste System

The *Varna* or fourfold division of the early Vedic age became extremely rigid with time. It bound society into watertight compartments, where social mobility was impossible. The earlier notion of caste division according to profession was changed to caste according to birth. Moreover, people of higher castes ill-treated the people of lower castes and interchanging between castes was not allowed. The *shudras* were considered to be untouchables and strict restrictions were imposed upon them on the grounds of marriage, food and drinks. Both Buddhism and Jainism rejected caste distinctions and gave a call for equality.

Difficult Vedic Language

The Vedic literature was mostly in Sanskrit, a language beyond the understanding of the common people. The priestly class were the only segment of society who could read and understand these texts. This encouraged the common people to look for a religion whose verses they could understand. Both Jainism and Buddhism were propagated through people-friendly languages like Pali and Prakit.

Faith in Magic and Charms

The early Vedic religion lost its purity and simplicity and the people began to believe in charms, spells and magic. But many progressive thinkers did not believe in such practices blindly. They gradually lost faith in such a religion and craved for a simpler religion which could rid them of such evils.

Political Circumstances

Tolerant and broad-minded rulers like Bimbisara and Ajatasatru who ruled Magadha during the 6th century BC, were free from the influence of Brahmans and criticised some social practises in their kingdoms. Thus, when Jainism and Buddhism reform movements began, they supported them fully.

Religious Reformers' Efforts

Due to the unrest created by the evils prevailing in society at that time and the strict codes of Vedic religion, many questioned the value of the hollow rites and the superiority of the priestly class. As an alternative to the established notions of complicated Vedic religion, people who felt oppressed by the orders of the Brahmans welcomed the teachings of social reformers like Gautama Buddha and Vardhamana Mahavira and looked upon them as a means of liberation from the Brahmans.

VARDHAMANA MAHAVIRA AND JAINISM

Vardhamana Mahavira is known as the reformer and founder of Jainism. In the Jain belief, there have been 24 *Tirthankaras* (*acharyas* or saints or spiritual gurus); he was the twenty-fourth and last of the *Tirthankaras* in the history of Jainism.

Mahavira was born in a Kshatriya family in Kunda-grama, a suburb of the town Vaishali near Patna in 599 BC. He was a kshatriya prince and received the education befitting a prince.

He married a princess named Yashoda and at the age of 30, he renounced all worldly pleasures, including his clothes, and led a life of severe penance and intense meditation for 12 years, enduring all hardships silently. In the 13th year, he gained supreme knowledge or *Kaivalya*. He came to be known as *Jina*, which means one who has conquered self, curbing all desires. His disciples in due course came to be known as *Jinas* or *Jains*. He organized his followers into a four-fold order, namely monk (*Sadhu*), nun (*Sadhvi*), layman (*Shravak*) and laywoman (*Shravika*). This order is known as *Jain Sangh*. After he became a *Jina*, Mahavira spent his life travelling far and wide to preach his principles. Mahavira delivered his first sermon at Rajgriha, Magadha's capital at Mount Vipul. He also travelled to Anga, Kosala, Mithila and various parts of northern India. At the age of 72, Lord Mahavira attained *Nirvana* or salvation in Pavapuri (presently Rajgir) in the Patna District of Bihar. When Mahavira died, he had roughly 14,000 disciples.

Lord Mahavira

Doctrines of Jainism

The five vows

According to Jainism, the head of a Jain household has to take these five vows :

- *Ahimsa* (Non-injury or Non-violence) - not to cause harm to any living being.
- *Satya* (Truthfulness) - to speak the harmless truth only.
- *Asteya* (Non-stealing) - not to take anything not properly given.
- *Aparigraha* (Non-possession) – complete detach-ment from people, places and material things.
- *Brahmacharya* (chastity) – to practise celibacy or to lead a virtuous life.

Tirthankara (name) with symbols :
1. Rishaba : bull
2. Ajita : elephant
3. Parsvanath : hooded serpent, and
4. Mahavira : lion

Parsvanath, who was the twenty-third Tirthan kara, established the first four vows, while Mahavira added the fifth vow. To observe absolute *chastity* he asked his followers to abandon all pleasures of material life even to the extent of shedding their clothes.

Nirvana or Salvation

Mahavira preached that the supreme goal in a man's life is to achieve *nirvana* or salvation and freedom from the material bonds of this world. This could be achieved through the three gems or *tri-ratnas*- Right faith, Right knowledge and Right conduct. These *tri-ratnas* encourage a Jain to lead a severe life based on self-denial and non-violence.

Karma

Mahavira believed in the theory of Karma which suggests that an individual must be responsible for his/her own actions or *Karma*. According to him, the soul or *atma* is immortal and it is the body that dies and not the soul. Each cycle of birth is accompanied with attachment, aversion, anger, deception, greed, etc. The karma get accumulated with repeated cycles of birth and death. To attain liberation or *moksha* from the cycle of birth and death, it is good deeds that count a lot.

No Belief in God

Mahavira had no faith in God's existence or in the concept that God is a creator, protector and destroyer of the universe. He believed that every object whether living or non-living has a soul. He denounced the worshipping of gods and goddesses as a means of material gains and personal benefits. According to him, man unlike God is responsible for his own fate. Getting freedom from suffering doesn't depend upon any external force. Rather to save oneself from suffering and misery, the only way is to lead a life of abstinence.

Refusal of Vedic Rituals and Sacrifices

Mahavira denounced the yajnas, animal sacrifices and other rituals preached by the Brahmans as it involved violence and killing. He considered these rituals and the accompanying sacrifices to be worthless.

Equality of People and Universal Brotherhood

According to Mahavira, every man and woman is equal and each one of them has the right to achieve *nirvana* by living a pure life. He believed in universal brotherhood, where everyone is equal and no distinctions on the grounds of caste, creed or sex can be accepted. He also encouraged and supported the idea of freedom for women and urged them to join *Jain Sangha*. He said all living beings should be dealt with compassion, from the smallest insect to the most superior form of life.

Belief in Penance

Jains supported the idea of penance as they directed all followers to lead a severe life. The idea of starving oneself to death or *santhara* was considered highly virtuous. They laid so much stress on leading an austere life that for most people it became difficult to practice such austerity.

Non-Violence (*ahimsa*)

The central theme of Jain philosophy is to practice non-violence. Jains are supposed to cause no harm or injury to any living being like humans, plants, animals or insects. Mahavira opposed the practice of three kinds of violence :
- Physical violence–inflicting pain, injury or killing.
- Verbal violence–causing pain by usage of harsh language.
- Mental violence–by thinking ill about people. Every living being's right is to live and the purity of life is the ultimate thing in which Jains believed.

Sects of Jainism

Differences had cropped up between the Jains of the South and the Jains of Magadha, to sort out which, a council was called upon in 300 BC at Pataliputra. In this council, decisions taken by either of the groups were not acceptable to both and as a result of these differences, Jainism got split into the two sects, i.e., *Svetambara* and *Digambara*.

Svetambara

These were the white clad Jains who followed *Sthulabhadra* and stayed at Magadha. They wore white clothes and covered their mouth and nose with a small piece of white cloth. This is because they wanted to prevent killing even the smallest of living beings or even germs that could possibly enter their noses while breathing. They believed in fasting but not in severe penance and a life of austerity.

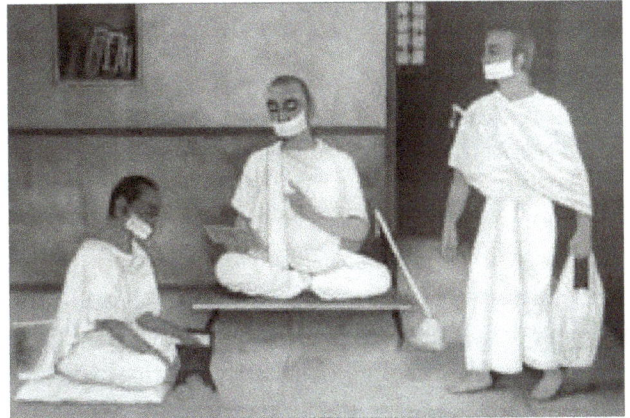

Svetambara Jain

Digambaras

These were the sky clad jains who followed Bhadra-bahu and didn't believe in wearing any clothes. The Digambaras believed that nature is the best cover for the body and living without any clothes implied renunciation of all the pleasures of the world. Members of this Jain sect were the orthodox supporters of Mahavira, who kept long fasts and lived in austere conditions.

Digambara Jain

Spread of Jainism

Mahavira organised the *sangha* to spread his teachings of Jainsim. Both men and women were admitted to the *sangha*. It was the dedicated work of *sangha*, which helped him to spread his teachings to regions like Magadha, Kosala,

Champa, Mithila and many other places. By the 1st century BC, Jainism had spread to areas of Orissa, Rajasthan and large parts of Gujarat. The Jain monks established monasteries at all these places. The Mauryan emperor, Chadragupta Maurya and the royal dynasties of South India such as the Gangas, the Kadambas, the Chalukyas and the Rashtrakutas patronized Jainism. Shravanabelagola in Karnataka became a major pilgrimage centre for Jains in the 7th century AD. In his old age Chandragupta came to Shravanabelagola where he died of starving and penance. Soon merchants and businessmen became the patrons of Jainism in Royal courts of India.

IMPACT OF JAINISM ON INDIAN CULTURE

Jainism with its pragmatic approach and spirit of equality and accommodation attracted people from all walks of life, rich and poor, kings and commoners, men and women, princes and priests, touchable and untouchables. It had a strong impact on the social and political lives of the people. Some of these are described below :

Impact on Vernacular Languages and Culture

With the rise of Jainism, the vernacular language of Prakit received a boost. The original teachings of Mahavira can be found in the 14 books called *Purvas*, which were later transformed to 12 new books called *Angas* and *Upangas* written after the Purvas. The 12 *Angas* were written in Ardha - Magadhi, which was the mixed dialect used by Mahavira to preach to the people. Works of Jain Scholars like Jinasena's *Mahapurana*, Bhadrabahu's compilation of *Kalpasutra*, *Amoghavarsha*, the Rashtrakuta ruler's *Ratna Malika* and many more profoundly influenced the Jain literature in 6th-4th century.

Impact on Religion

Jainism had a great impact on the evil practices of Hindu religion that existed in the Vedic society. It professed *ahimsa* and therefore, the Yajnas and rites involving sacrifices of animals in the Vedic religion came to a halt. It denounced the empty rituals, superstitions and rigid caste system that existed in Hindu society.

Thus, non-violence and universal brotherhood as a rule of life was first set by the Jains, which had a positive effect on the lives of people.

Impact on Political Life

The main doctrine of Jainism was non-violence or *Ahimsa*. They created a political environment based on the tenets of ahimsa. When the Kshatriyas accepted the faith, they gradually lost their fighting spirit and became docile. This made the country vulnerable to foreign invasions and this had an adverse impact on political life. This religion also produced several eminent and efficient monarchs, ministers and generals. Jain saints were responsible for the foundation of the Ganga kingdom in the 2nd century AD and the Hoysala kingdom in the 11th century AD

Impact on Society

Jainism did a meritorious job by removing the evil of the Varna system or the caste system. The Jains did not believe in inequality among men, mean ingless ceremonies, rituals and superstitions associated with Hinduism. Jainism promoted and preached feelings of social unity and social equality. Members of different castes were accepted in their religious fold, thus breaking the barriers of caste and class. Besides, their faith in non-violence and the motivation of doing good to others filled them with the zeal of service to all.

Art and Architecture

Jains propagated their religious principles through art and architecture. Jain architecture has made commendable contribution to the architecture of India. By the 2nd century BC,

Chittor Jain temple, Rajasthan

they had created *stupas* that were made of stone to honour their sages, which they decked with pillars, gateways and railings. They constructed monasteries and cave temples carved out of rock. Some classic examples of Jain architecture are the renowned Ellora caves in Maharashtra and caves of Udaygiri and Khanda-giri in Orissa. A few more famous structures constructed by the Jains are the huge statue of Bahubali or Gomteshwara at Karkala and Shravanabelagola in Karnataka, the Dilwara Jain temples at Mt. Abu, Ranakpur close to Jodhpur and Chittor's Jain Tower in Rajasthan. Palitana in Gujarat is considered holy by the Jains, as there are more than 800 Jain temples in this area.

Palitana– Jain Holy Place in Gujarat

FACTORS RESPONSIBLE FOR THE DECLINE OF JAINISM

With the passage of time, many followers of Jainism grew tired of the spiritual outlook of this religion and stopped propagating it. The major factors that led to the decline of Jainism are :

- ❑ The main preaching of Jainism about leading an austere life was something that the common people found very difficult to follow. Its rigid principles prevented people from embracing Jainism. The rise of Jainism coincided with that of Buddhism.
- ❑ Jainism was restricted to India and didn't spread to foreign countries mainly due to lack of efforts by missionaries in spreading the religion far and wide.
- ❑ With the change in dynasties, Jainism failed to get the support of contemporary rulers. On the other hand, Buddhism got huge support from kings like Kanishka, Ashoka and Harsha.
- ❑ Although Jainism preached equality of men, it couldn't eradicate the low and high positions in society.
- ❑ With the division of the Jain sect into Digambaras and Svetambaras, definite social or religious work was not done properly in the society.

GAUTAMA BUDDHA AND BUDDHISM

The 6th century BC saw the birth of a potent religious movement in India i.e., Buddhism. According to popular legends, Gautama or Siddhartha, founder of Buddhism, took birth in 563 BC in Lumbini (at present, Nepal) in the Sakya (Kshatriya clan) of Kapila-vastu. His father, Suddhodana was

Gautam Buddha

the chief of Kapilavastu's Sakya clan. His mother, Maya, a princess of the Koliyas clan died after the child-birth. As a child, Siddhartha was reared by his aunt and step-mother, Prajapati Gautami. His other relatives were Yasodhara (wife), Rahula (son) and Devadatta (cousin). Like Mahavira, Gautama Buddha showed interest in the formality of court marriage. This legendary native site is characterized by the famous Rummindei Pillar of Ashoka.

The Four Great Sights

One day Siddhartha, riding across town in his chariot, witnessed four different sights which left an indelible mark on him and had a great impact on his future life. The sight of first an old man, then a sick man, and finally a corpse left him shocked and horrified. The fourth and final sight that shook him was of an ascetic, seeking salvation. It is these 'Four Great Sights' that sparked his spiritual journey and compelled him to forsake his family at the young age of 29. He surrendered all worldly attractions and became an ascetic, searching for the ultimate truth of life. This event is known as the **Great Renunciation**. For the next six years, Siddhartha lived the life of an ascetic studying, meditating, enduring pain, fasting nearly to starvation and even refusing water but yet he could not reach the spiritual truth he sought. Finally, he decided to give up the ascetic life and encouraged people to follow a path of balance instead of one characterized by extremism. He called this path the Middle Way. At the age of 35, he meditated under a Pipal tree (known as Bodhi tree), located in Bihar's Bodh Gaya. Here he attained spiritual enlightenment and came to be known as **Buddha** or the '**Enlightened One**'.

After his enlightenment, he preached his first sermon in the Deer Park at Sarnathin, where he explained the Four Noble Truths and the Eight fold Path, which later became the pillars of Buddhism. This event is known as the **Dharma Chakra Pravartan** (or setting in Motion the Wheel of *Dharma*). For the remainder of his 80 years, he preached his teachings and led the foundation of *sangha*s or community of monks. He left this world at the age of 80 at Kusinagar in the district of Gorakhpur in 483 BC. This event was called *parinirvana* or Full Nirvana.

Five legendary episodes of the life of Buddha and their motifs:
- Birth : lotus and bull
- Great Renunciation : horse
- Nirvana : bodhi tree
- First sermon : dharmachakra or wheel
- Parinirvana or death : stupa

Teachings of Buddhism

Buddha led a simple life and encouraged people to do the same. All his teachings can be found in *Sutta Pitaka*, from where it is mostly reconstructed. The main teachings of Buddha emphasised on the four Noble Truths and the Eight-Fold Path, which is supposed to hold the key for attaining salvation.

The Four Noble Truths

Buddhism's basic essence lies in the Four Noble Truths that state :

- Sorrows and sufferings surround the entire world.
- Every suffering has a cause.
- The chief reason behind this suffering is *Trishna* or man's desire for worldly possession and sensual pleasure.
- One can be free from suffering, if desires can be banished from one's life. This can be achieved by following the Eightfold Path

The Eightfold Path

In Buddhism, the way that leads to *Nirvana* is known as the *Ashtangika Marg* or the Eightfold Path. These paths are the 'Middle-Path,' which shows the way without indulging in any form of extremes. Buddha suggested a way of neither too much attachment to earthly pleasures and luxuries nor too much hard self-denial. Thus the 'Middle Path' suggested :

- Right faith or belief, that is to give up all desires in daily life.
- Right action, that is to stay away from theft, violence and luxuries.
- Right living, not to deal dishonestly with people.
- Right speech, that is to speak the truth and not to think bad of others.
- Right effort, that is to work towards liberating oneself from sin and for the welfare of others.
- Right aspiration, to stay away from earthly evils and meaningless rituals.
- Right meditation, that is to focus on only that which is right.
- Right recollection, that is to think only of sacred things.

Attitude towards God

Unlike Mahavira, Buddha didn't profess the non-existence of God. Rather he believed that the entire universe works following *Dharma*, the universal law. Though he never formally denied the existence of God, Buddha brushed aside the mechanical worship of Gods and he attempted to implement an ethical code of high order to raise the religion's status.

The Karma Theory

Buddha believed in the theory of *Karma*. The condition in which a man lives his present life and the deeds he performs, might decide the course of his life in the next birth and he has to face the consequence of his actions. Buddha believed that man is master of his own destiny and he also believed in the theory of rebirth. Since all ill deeds of man can be punished, it is better to take the middle path in life and decide upon the course of one's birth in the next life.

Nirvana

The final goal in people's life is to achieve nirvana, i.e, eternal bliss and peace. This state of Nirvana is free from sorrow, disease and desires and liberates a person from the cycle of birth, death and re-birth. To attain this, one has to follow the Eightfold Path.

Ahimsa

Buddha, like Mahavira attached great importance to Ahimsa or non-violence. He opposed the idea of harming any living being. Thus non-violence was one of his main principles of morality.

No Faith in Caste System

Buddha believed in equality and universal brotherhood. He believed in distinctions on the basis of caste or class should not exist in society and invited people from various sections of society to join Buddhism. This was one of the major attractions in Buddhism as they strongly opposed casteism.

No Belief in Rituals and Sacrifices

Buddha had no faith in the supremacy of the Vedas or the Brahmanas. According to him, rituals, yajnas and sacrifices were meaningless ceremonies, which were not capable of changing the destiny of man.

Stress on Moral Character

Buddha preached about a life led on the basis of good actions and encouraged people to develop a strong moral character. He stressed more on morality of character than on worship. He urged people to remain true in speech, show kindness to all living beings and show love and compassion to his fellow human beings. Buddhism urged people to remain obedient to parents, show respect towards elders, maintain purity and abstain from intoxicating drinks.

Code of Conduct

The Code of Conduct that Buddha formulated for his disciples consisted of the following :
- Not to lie
- Not to commit violence
- Not to possess property
- Not to participate in corrupt practices
- Not to drink alcohol

The Buddhist Literature

The holy Buddhist scriptures are universally known as *Tripitakas*, which means the "Three fold books or baskets". The three books, namely, *Vinaya Pitaka*, *Abhidhamma Pitaka* and *Sutta Pitaka*, were written in languages of Pali, Sanskrit and mixed Sanskrit.

Tripitakas—Sacred book of Buddhism

The *Jatakas* tales refer to a huge number of folklore written in Pali, related to the previous many births of Buddha. These 547 tales form an important part of Buddhist literature, relating the various incarnations of Buddha, in the form of a bird, an animal, a lotus and at times human being too. In these tales, Buddha as *Bodhisattva* teaches kindness and values like morality, self-sacrifice and honesty.

Sects of Buddhism

List of Buddhist Councils :
- First Buddhist Council : It took place around 400 BC at Rajgriha in Bihar.
- Second Buddhist Council : It occurred around 4th century BC at Vaisali in Bihar
- Third Buddhist Council : It took place around 251 BC at Pataliputra in Bihar.

❑ **Fourth Buddhist Council :** It occurred around 1st century BC in Kashmir.

At the time of the 4th Buddhist council, Buddhism suffered a split into two sects i.e., *Mahayana* (The Great Vehicle) and *Hinayana* (The Lesser Vehicle). The *Mahayana* Buddhists followed the more powerful and reformed Buddhism. They worshipped idols and had faith in Buddha being God. The main practices of a Mahayanist are summarized in the six perfections : the perfection of giving, ethics, patience, joyous effort, concentration and wisdom. Instead of keeping to the original goal of liberation from cyclic existence (*nirvana*), they made their goal to attain *swarga* or heaven through complex rituals and ceremonies. Their teachings were mainly written in Sanskrit, and are now called as the *Mahayana Sutras*. The Mahayana tradition mainly developed in North India, and spread further to the North-western parts of India, China and Tibet. However, the Hinayana Buddhists were the ones who followed the less strong but original form of Buddhism. They did not idolise Buddha as incarnation of God and did not support idol worship. Their main goal is to attain the state of liberation for oneself (*nirvana*) because Buddhahood is considered practically unachievable for nearly everyone within this aeon. The eight-fold path was the only route to attain salvation. Their teachings were originally written in Pali language. The main countries where this sect is currently alive are Sri Lanka, Thailand, Burma, Cambodia and Laos.

Spread of Buddhism

Numerous people joined Buddhism due to the simple teachings of Buddha. The teachings of Buddha were quite plain. He vehemently opposed all complicated rites and ceremonies, class and caste distinctions and any form of sacrifice. Buddha and his disciples kept the mode of communication simple. They used the local dialects, which were popular among the common people. Buddhism enjoyed the support of great rulers like Ashoka, Harsha and Kanishka. These rulers embraced and declared Buddhism as the religion of the state and popularised it. Buddhist missionaries from these states were sent to many countries like China, Sri Lanka, Japan, Myanmar and Korea, Nepal and Tibet to spread Buddhism. King Ashoka, a great propagator of Buddhism even sent his son Mahendra and daughter Sanghamitra to Sri Lanka to promote Buddhism. It was the enthusiasm of these people that lead to spread of this religion. The Universities of Gaya, Taxila and Nalanda were turned into Buddhist education centres. Even foreign students were attracted to these universities. These universities produced scholars who contributed greatly to the spread of Buddhism.

IMPACT OF BUDDHISM ON INDIAN CULTURE

Buddhism had profound influence on Indian art, culture, religion, literature and philosophy.

Ahimsa

The principle of Ahimsa acted as a weapon against the evils of society. With the rise of Buddhism, protecting animals became a novel culture.

Impact on Religious Life

With the arrival of Buddhism, people got an alternative to Hinduism that was barren of any complicated ceremonies involving meaningless rituals. Buddha preached a simple religion with practical and simple principles. Taking this to be the cue, Hindus also started reforming their religion. The Mahayana Buddhists brought change in adopting the practice of idol worship of Buddha and *Bodhisattvas*. They erected many idols and temples in honour of Buddha and Bodhisattvas. Following this, Hindus also started constructing gorgeous temples for worshipping their Gods and Goddesses.

Impact on Social Life

Buddhism exposed society's weaknesses and promoted intellectual tradition. They were very concerned about the deprived sections of society who had suffered social injustice. Buddhism aimed at the upliftment and betterment of the down-trodden people of society.

Impact on Politics

Buddhism had reached out to the emperors like Chandragupta and Ashoka, who gave up their lives of war and bloodshed.

JAINISM AND BUDDHISM

Impact on Culture

Buddhism propagated to far flung places like China, South-East Asia and Sri Lanka. This helped in building ties between various countries and India and between various cultures and also helped in boosting India's prestige.

Impact on Language and Literature

Buddhism had contributed mostly in the field of Language and Literature, providing a rich variety of literature based on religion in the popular language of the masses, Pali. All the teachings of Buddha were compiled and made into *Tripitakas*. Apart from these, the *Jatakas* also form a good literary source of Buddhism that deals with Buddha's previous births. Other books written in Pali language that give a glimpse of the political and social conditions of the common people around 4th and 3rd century BC are *Deepavamsha* and *Mahavamsha*. Some books written in Sanskrit in those days, which had greatly contributed to the Indian literature are *Divyavadana, Saundaranand, Lalitvistara* and *Buddhacharita*.

Impact on Education

Buddhist contribution is most notable in the arena of education. The Buddhist monasteries were converted into vital centres of learning. A number of scholars of these monasteries taught about Buddhist scriptures, philosophy, logic, astronomy and medicine. Gradually these centres of education developed and changed into renowned universities in Taxila, Nalanda and Vikramasila. These universities drew the attention of many students from abroad.

The Dhamek Stupa at Sarnath, India, Established by Ashoka (in 249 BCE).

Impact on Art and Architecture

In the field of art and architecture, Buddhism had contributed immensely. Buddhists came to be known for their beautiful carvings in their temples, *Viharas* and monuments. They were also famous for their rock-cut cave temples, which had amazing frescoes. *Dhamek Stupa* at Sarnath is the oldest stupa and is the place where Buddha gave his first sermon. Stupa at Sanchi with its railings and gateways was decorated with various sculptures. The *stupas* at Amravati and Bharhut are some of the other wonderful specimens of art and architecture that have survived till this time. After the Christian era, constructing statues of Buddha became rampant and it was during this period that several schools of art and architecture like the Gandhara Art emerged.

Amravati Maha Stupa, which is also known as Dhanyakataka/Dharanikota

DECLINE OF BUDDHISM

The causes for decline of Buddhism are given below :

Split in Buddhism

During the rule of Kanishka, Buddhism split into two major sects- Hinayana and Mahayana. They lost their spirit of togetherness and quarreled among themselves. This division affected the prestige and popularity of Buddhism. Slowly, Hinduism started absorbing Buddhism, which was another cause of its downfall.

Idol Worship

Buddhism opposed idol worship and blind faith and this was a major reason for its popularity. But with the split in Buddhism, one sect of Buddhists began to make idols of the

Buddha and started worshipping him. Common people now began to think that there was no difference between Hinduism and Buddhism. Moreover, the Hindus had accepted Buddha as one of their own gods. Gradually it got merged within Hinduism and lost its identity as a distinct and powerful religion.

Revival of Hinduism

With the rise of Jainism and Buddhism, reform movements started in Hinduism with full vigour. With the sincere efforts of *Bramhin* scholars like Kumarila Bhatta and Shankaracharya, Hinduism started reviving again. This led to decline of Buddhism.

Loss of Royal Patronage

With the beginning of the Gupta period, the royal patronage shifted to Hinduism from Buddhism. This is specifically because the Guptas were strong supporters of Hinduism. Moreover, Buddhism preached Ahimsa, which was not a policy that Rajputs (who were the new occupiers of political power) encouraged.

Adoption of Sanskrit

Buddha preached his sermons and teachings in Pali or Prakrit, which was the language of the masses. Later Buddhists adopted many doctrines of Hindu thought which made their simple religion complex. Their scriptures also started following Sanskrit language, which was the language of the learned upper class. The difficult language and the complex rituals ceased to attract the common people and hence people moved away from Buddhism.

Corruption in Buddhist Sangha

As time passed Buddhist monks and nuns gave up their disciplined lives and started living a life of luxury. Monks and nuns craved wealth for their personal comforts and thus started living a life associated with worldly pleasures. This moral corruption was another vital cause for the decline of this religion.

The Muslim Invasions

With the invasion of the muslims in around the 8th century AD, many Buddhist monasteries and temples that had massive wealth were looted. The universities of Takshila and Nalanda were looted and plundered. Many Buddhist monks were killed, some accepted conversion to Islam and the vast majority were forced to escape to countries like Tibet and Nepal. All these together marked the decline of Buddhism.

Rise of the Rajputs

The Rajput rulers were most powerful in Northern India from the 7th to the 11th centuries. They were warriors who could never reconcile with the doctrine of *ahimsa*. When they gained power, the Buddhist monks left India to cross into other lands. As such, Buddhists became extinct in India.

SIMILARITIES BETWEEN JAINISM AND BUDDHISM

- Mahavira and Gautam Buddha, the founders of Jainism and Buddhism respectively, share similar backgrounds. Both belonged to clans of princely Kshatriya families and not to priestly families.
- Both denied the existence of God.
- Both religions believed in the theory of *Karma* and aimed at attaining *moksha* or *nirvana* to escape from the cycle of births, deaths and re-births.
- Both opposed the authority of the Vedas and the necessity of performing animal sacrifices and rituals.
- Both religions admitted disciples from all castes and from both sexes.
- *Ahimsa* or non-violence is the prominent principle of both religions.
- Both these religions came as a reform of Hindu religion. They put stress on right conduct and right knowledge and not on religious ceremonies and rituals as the way to obtain salvation.
- Both the Religions were later divided into two sects. Buddhism was divided into Mahayana and Hinayana. Jainism was divided into Svetambara and Digambara.
- Both had their own three gems or *Tri-Ratnas*. Tri Ratna of Jainism were Right faith, Right knowledge and Right conduct. The Tri-Ratna of Buddhism were Budhha, Dhamma and Sangha.

- Both had three main religious texts. *Vinaya pitaka*, *Sutta pitaka* and *Abidhamma pitaka* were the three religious texts of Buddhism, whereas *Anga*, *Upanga* and *Mulgrajitha* were those of Jainism.
- Both religions demanded that their monks and nuns renounce family life and the entire world, which were quite opposite in case of the Brahmins in Hinduism.

DISSIMILARITIES BETWEEN JAINISM AND BUDDHISM

JAINISM	BUDDHISM
1. The foundations of Jainism had been laid even before Mahavira, who was the 24th and last of the Jain *Tirthankaras*, appeared.	1. Buddhism was founded by Buddha around 6th century BC, which was a religion then.
2. Jainism promoted fasts and harsh penance for attainment of *moksha*. This was difficult for the common people to follow.	2. Buddhism, on the other hand, was not strict on severe penance for attainment of moksha. They followed a middle path which was more acceptable and easier for the ordinary people to follow.
3. Jainism believes in the existence of soul in every living being.	3. Buddhists do not believe in the existence of soul.
4. Jainism was more rigid about the principle of *ahimsa* or non-violence.	4. Buddhists believed that *ahimsa* or non-violence against all living beings is important, but they were not rigid in this regard.
5. Most of the Jain texts are in Sanskrit and Prakrit.	5. Buddhist text is in Pali.
6. Jainism remained restricted within the Indian sub-continent.	6. Buddhism extended its reach far and wide beyond the boundaries of India.
7. Jainism never received strong royal support and Patronage. It was mostly patronised by merchants.	7. Buddhism received the royal support and patronage of kings like Ashoka and Kanishka.

In Retrospect

- ♦ *Factors that caused the rise of Jainism and Buddhism* : Domination of the Priestly class, costly rituals of Vedic Religion, animal slaughtering for performing sacrifices, tough Vedic language, inflexible Caste system etc.
- ♦ *Jainism* :
  - (a) **24 Tirthankaras** : *The first one was Rishabha and the last was Mahavira. In 599 BC, Mahavira was born in Kundagrama and in 527 BC he died, Mahavira became Jina after achieving true knowledge, his supporters acquired the name Jains.*
  - (b) **Doctrines and teachings of Jainism** : *There are Five Vows of Jainism like Ahimsa, Satya, Asteya, Aparigraha, Brahmacharya. Nirvana, No Belief in God, Karma, Believing in Penance, Denial of Sacrifices and Rituals, Collective Brotherhood, Non-violence, Opposition towards caste system.*
  - (c) **Reasons that contributed in the Growth of Jainism** : *Use of local popular language, simple doctrines of Jainism, benefaction of the royalty, zeal of the saints, effective order in religion.*
  - (d) **Two sects in Jainism** : *Digambaras and Svetambaras–Main Difference between them is Digambar saints are ascetics who remain nude and Svetambar saints remain dressed in white robes.*
  - (e) **Impact of Jainism on the Cultural life of India** : *Development and popularising vernacular languages, impact on religion, Indian art, growth of the principle of Ahimsa, reduced fighting spirit, paying services for the welfare of mankind, rejection of caste system and meaningless rituals, introduced many reforms in the society.*

- **Buddhism :**
  - (a) **Gautama Buddha** : Born in 563 BC, The Great Renunciation, The Four Sights, The Enlightenment in 537 BC, Dharmachakra Pravartana, First Sermon at Sarnath, Attainment of Nirvana in 486 BC.
  - (b) **His Teachings** : Four Noble Truths, Eightfold Path, Silence about God's Existence, Nirvana, Theory of Karma and Ahimsa, anti–caste system, no belief in sacrifice and rituals, importance given to morality and character.
  - (c) **Literature of Buddhism** : Jatakas, relating stories about the earlier births of Buddha–Tripitakas.
  - (d) **Sects within Buddhism** : Hinayana Buddhism followed the original principles of Buddhism and were the orthodox sect, Hinyana Buddhists used Pali as their medium of communication, lesser in number and their main goal is to attain Nirvana.
  - (e) **Impact of Buddhism** : Widespread acceptance of non-violence and equality, impact on religion that caused the revival of Hinduism, impact on literature like Jatakas and Tripitakas, impact on education which led to the opening of Buddhist centres of learning, impact on architecture and art, the philosophies of Buddhism were greatly followed by Tagore and Mahatma Gandhi.

EXERCISES

Part-I (Short Questions)

1. State two causes responsible for the rise of Jainism and Buddhism.
2. Where was Lord Mahavira born ?
3. Why was Lord Mahavira known as *Jina* ?
4. What is *Jain Sangha* ?
5. What are the five vows that every Jain has to take ?
6. What do you understand by the term *Tri-ratnas* ?
7. Name two sects of Jainism. How do they differ from each other ?
8. Name the language in which majority of Jain books are written.
9. Why is the place *Shrvanabelagola* important to Jains ?
10. What was the adverse effect of Jainism on the political life of the people ?
11. How did the Jainism affect the social life of people ?
12. State five reasons for the decline of Jainism ?
13. Where was Gautama Buddha born ?
14. Name the 'Four Great Sights'. How did they influence Gautama ?
15. Why was Buddha's teaching called the Middle Path ?
16. State Four Noble Truths of Buddha teachings.
17. What is *ashtaangika marga* in Buddhism ?
18. In which language was the early Buddhist literature written ?
19. What are *Tripitakas* ?
20. What are the *Jatakas*? What is their importance ?
21. Name two sects in which Buddhism was divided. State the important points of difference between them.
22. Discuss three reasons for the spread of Buddhism.
23. How Buddhism affected emperors such as Chandragupta and Ashoka ?
24. Mention two reasons for the decline of Buddhism in India
25. State two points of similarity and dissimilarity between Jainism and Buddhism.
26. What was the reason for the rise of Buddhism and Jainism during the end of later Vedic period ?

JAINISM AND BUDDHISM

Part-II (Structured Questions)

1. The dominance of Brahmanical society led to the emergence of two new sects of religion- Jainism and Buddhism. In this context, Explain :
   (a) Supremacy of the *Brahman* Priest
   (b) Rigid Caste System
   (c) Expensive Rituals of Brahmans

2. Explain the following with reference to Jainism:
   (a) Teachings of Jainism
   (b) *Svetambara* and *Digambaras* sects
   (c) Spread of Jainism

3. Jainism had a strong impact on the social and political lives of the people, in this context discuss:
   (a) Impact on Religious life
   (b) Impact on Social life
   (c) Impact on Political life

4. Discuss the various reasons for the decline of Jainism.

5. With reference to the journey of Siddhartha to Gautama Buddha, explain:
   (a) The 'Four Great Sights'
   (b) The Great Renunciation
   (c) The Middle way
   (d) The Enlightenment
   (e) *Dharma Chakra Pravartana*
   (f) *Parinirvana*

6. Explain the following with reference to Buddhism :
   (a) The Four Noble Truths
   (b) Eightfold Path of Buddhism
   (c) The *Hinayana* and the *Mahayana* sects

7. Discuss the impact of Buddhism on the Indian culture with reference to the following:
   (a) Impact on Religious Life
   (b) Impact on Education
   (c) Impact on Language and Literature

8. Discuss in detail the reasons behind the decline of Buddhism in India.

9. Mention the special contribution of Buddhism and Jainism to sculpture and architecture in India.

10. Discuss the points of similarities and dissimilarities between Jainism and Buddhism ?

CHAPTER 4

THE MAURYAN EMPIRE

- Sources : Arthashastra, Indika, Ashokan Edicts, Sanchi Stupa.
- Political history and Administration (Chandragupta Murya and Ashoka); Ashoka's Dhamma.

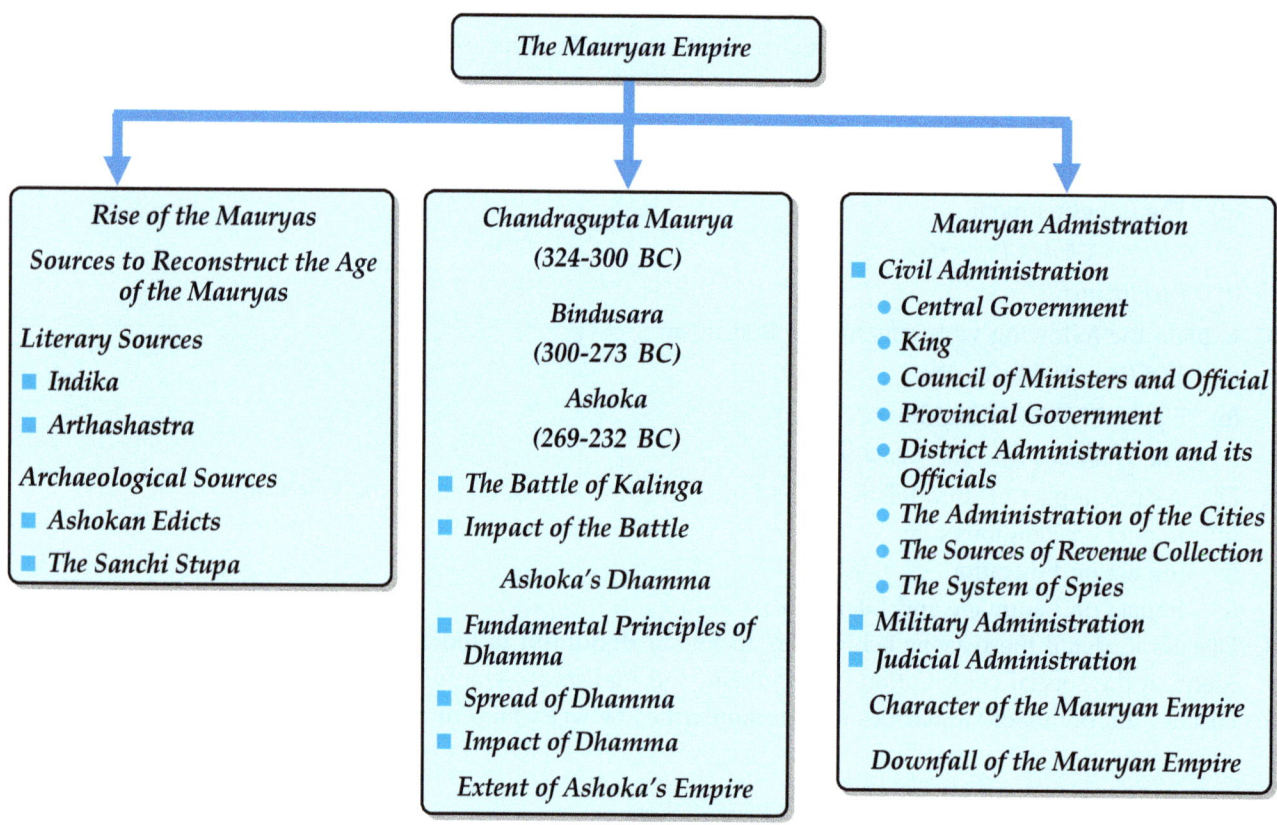

ALEXANDER'S INVASION : RISE OF THE MAURYAS

The invasion of India by The Great Alexander, introduced a new chapter in Indian history. In 326 BC he captured Taxila, without much resistance. He then proceeded beyond the River Jhelum and defeated King Paurava or Porus in 326 BC. He had plans to cross the rivers Ravi, Chenab and Beas but retreated, as his troops rebelled. In 325 BC, Alexander left India and died in Babylon.

It was at this juncture that Chandragupta Maurya founded one of the biggest and most powerful empires in India– The Mauryan Empire in 324 BC by removing the Nandas from the power of Magadha. He not only laid the foundation of a huge empire but also raised and

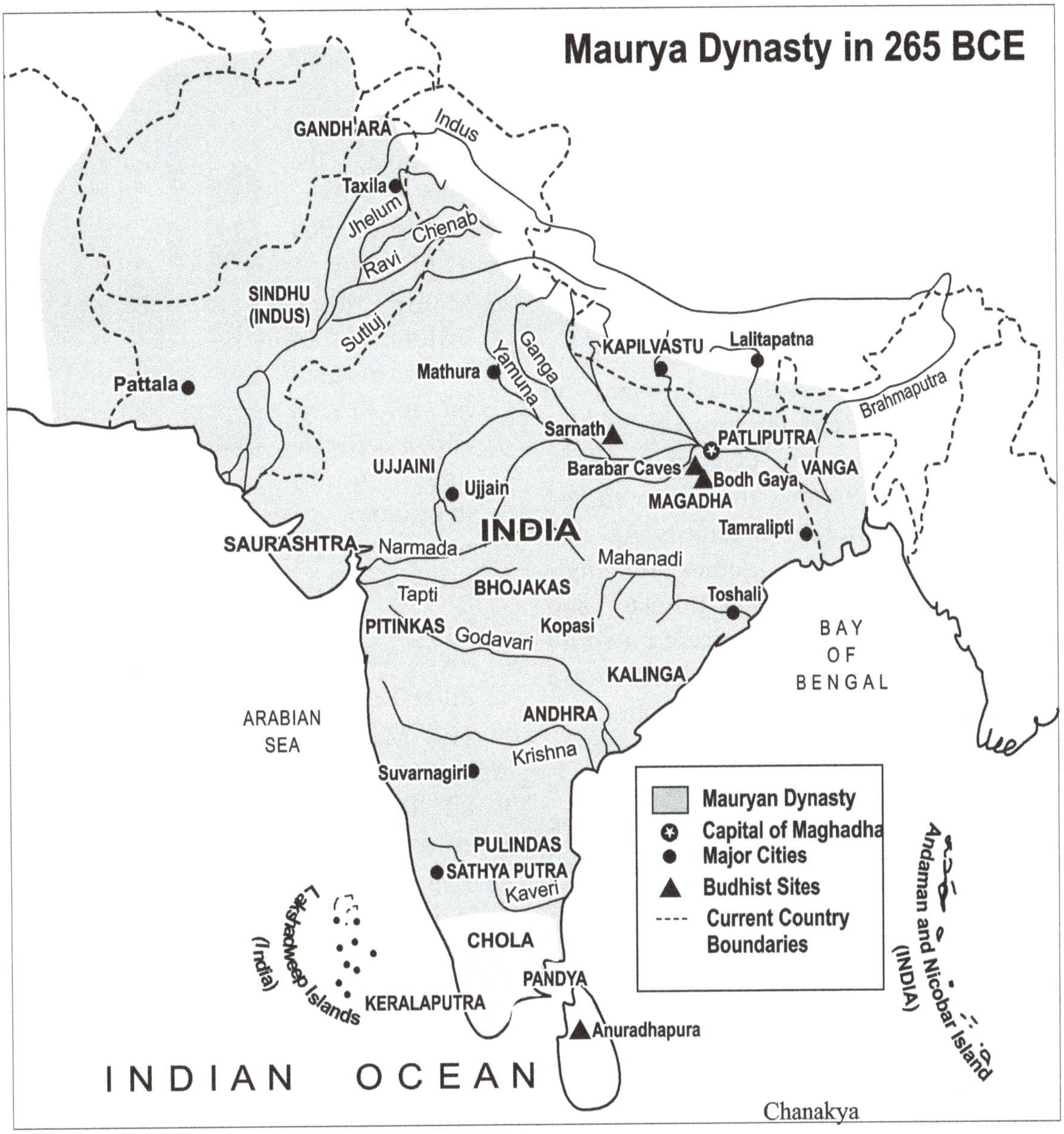

THE MAURYAN EMPIRE

Maurya Dynasty in 265 BCE

Mauryan Dynasty in 265 BC

deployed a large and powerful army. The glory of the Mauryan empire, established by Chandragupta Maurya was maintained and preserved by his successor Bindusara. However, it was Bindusara's son Ashoka, who brought about the brightest period in the Mauryan Empire and Indian history.

SOURCES TO RECONSTRUCT THE AGE OF THE MAURYAS

Literary Sources

Megasthenes and Kautilya are two most important authors whose writings threw a flood of light on the Mauryan era :

Indika

This Greek account 'Indika' by Megasthenes, a Greek ambassador of Seleucus Nicator in the court of Chadragupta Maurya, is one of the authentic sources for knowing the history of Mauryan dynasty. In his book *Indika*, he has described different aspects of Indian life including administration of the state, local administration, life of the King etc. in the 4th century BC. The book also described the seven different classes of Indian society, viz., philosophers, overseers, councillors, cultivators, artisans and traders, herdsmen and soldiers. Though the book *Indika* itself has not survived, its fragments are preserved in later Greek and Latin works and the texts correspond with the Kautilyan text at many places.

Arthashastra

The manuscript 'Arthashastra' by Kautilya (also known as Vishnugupta or Chanakya) is an extremely sophisticated and detailed treatise on statecraft. The ancient monograph was composed in 1st millenium BCE in Sanskrit. According to Dr. Trautmann, the text assumed its present shape in around 3rd century AD and can not be ascribed to a single author and single period. Kautilya, Chandragupta's minister and advisor, in his book has given a detailed account of the contemporary social, political and economic conditions prevailing in the country at that time. The book is divided into 15 segments, 180 subjects and about 6000 *shlokas*. Kautilya also gave a wealth of information regarding duties of the king and ministers, his foreign policy, organization of spies, civil and criminal laws, guilds and corporations, military organizations etc. It further enunciates the principles of interstate relations and suggests methods to win wars. Thus, *Arthashastra* is not only a treatise on economy but also a treatise on political science, *Dandaniti*.

Besides these the *Vayu Purana*, the *Matsya Purana*, Vishakhadatta's *Mudrarakshasa* throw immense light on the Mauryan period.

Archeological Sources

There are two major archaeological sources that help us to rebuild the Mauryan past :

Ashokan Edicts

The Ashokan Rock Edicts are a collection of 33 inscriptions on the Pillars of Ashoka. These are the most reliable source of information about Ashoka's reign. The inscriptions on these edicts in *Prakrit* lan-guage describe Ashoka's ideals and his belief in the Buddhist concept of *dharma* and his efforts to develop the dharma throughout his kingdom. Throughout the country, these edicts are divided into :

Ashokan Pillar, at Vaishali, Bihar

The Ashoka lions at Sarnath, Uttar Pradesh

- Major Rock Edicts: 14 Edicts (termed Ist to XIVth) and 2 separate ones found in Orissa.
- Minor Rock Edicts: The Queen's Edict, Barabar cave inscriptions and the Kandahar bilingual inscriptions.
- Pillar Edicts : 7 Pillar Edicts.

The Major Rock Edict II mentions that Ashoka's neighbours were Pandyas while Rock Edict III shows the roles of provincial administrators in propagating *Dhamma* or *dharma* and the concept of *Dhammavijaya*. The Rock Edicts XII and XIII prescribe non-violence, truthfulness, obedience, respect and the transformation of Ashoka after the conquest of Kalinga. The Barabar Cave Inscription suggests the religious tolerance of emperor Ashoka whereas, The Queen's Edict describes the sacred donations of Ashoka's wife to Buddhist *Sangha*. The Pillar Edict VII describes various administrative actions taken for public welfare. These Pillars are found in various parts of south India like Sanchi, Rampurva, Lumbini, Lauriya, Nandangarh, Vaishali and Lion capital of Sarnath. These are the best examples of these sources.

The most remarkable evidence of the period could be gleaned from Ashoka's edicts in Greek, Aramic and Graeco-Aramic (bilingual language and Scripts) discovered from Afghanistan and Taxila in Pakistan.

The discovery of the Aramic and Greek edicts from Afghanistan and Taxila bears testimony to the fact that Ashoka wielded control over

Arachosia, Paropanisade and Gedrosia. These vast stretches of North-Western part had been ceded to the Mauryan ruler, Chandragupta by seleucus in 301 BC.

The Sanchi Stupa

The 'Great Stupa' at Sanchi, Madhya Pradesh is the oldest stone structure built by emperor Ashoka in the 3rd century BC, in a bid to preserve the ruins of Buddha. Its nucleus was a simple hemispherical brick structure which was circled by a railing made of wood that was replaced later by a huge stone railing. The four gateways that were added later on the four sides of this stupa depict scenes from the life of Buddha and several tales from the *Jatakas*. Buddha had been represented in the form of a symbol, like a wheel or throne placed under a *pipal* tree or a lotus. They are the magnificent existing specimens that reveal the development in the technical and artistic skills of the people during the Mauryan period.

The Great Stupa at Sanchi, India, established by Ashoka (4th–1st century BCE)

CHANDRAGUPTA MAURYA
(324–300 BC)

Chandragupta Maurya founded the Mauryan Empire. Before he came to power, Magadha was ruled by the Nandas. Dhanananda, the last Nanda ruler possessed a mighty army and a great treasury but was extremely unpopular among his subjects. It is said that the Nandas had dismissed Kautilya or Vishnugupta from the service. Kautilya, the learned Brahmin of Taxila met young Chandragupta, who belonged to the East Indian clan of Maurya on the maternal side. Chanakya identified the capabilities of Chandragupta. He took him to Taxila and taught him the art of warfare and governance, so that together they could destroy the Nandas.

Chandragupta Maurya

The North–Western part of India was for a long time under the rule of the Greek ruler Alexander, which Chandragupta had repeatedly tried to capture. After Alexander's departure, with the growing instability in the state of Punjab, opportunity was provided to Chandragupta to occupy Punjab in the year 322 BC. Soon he brought Sindh and West Punjab under his control as well. With Punjab in his hands, Chandragupta aimed at Magadha and in 321 BC he defeated the last king of the Nanda dynasty and gained control over the powerful kingdom of Magadha and declared Pataliputra to be his capital.

One of Alexander's successors, Seleucus Nicator invaded India in the year 305 BC and moved across Punjab. However, he could not proceed further as his troops were severely defeated and beaten by Chandragupta Maurya's mighty army. After this severe defeat, he was compelled to enter a treaty with Chandragupta. In lieu of 500 elephants, Seleucus surrendered the control of the provinces of Herat, Kabul, Baluchistan and Kandahar to Chandragupta. The Greek diplomat of Seleucus called Megasthenes visited India during his reign and later wrote the treatise *Indika*.

The first remarkable and historical Emperor of India, Chandragupta's empire was a vast one. It stretched up to Kandahar and Kabul in the North-west to Mysore towards the South and from Western Saurashtra to the Eastern region of Bengal. After his reign of 24 years, he embraced Jainism and handed over his throne to his son Bindusara. According to Taranath, the Tibetan Buddhist Monk who visited India in the 16th century, Bindusara conquered 16 states that formed the 'Land between the two seas', indicating Arabian sea and the Bay of Bengal.

In the religious domain, Bindusara was more oriented towards Ajivika sect. He reposed his faith in Ajivika Monk, Pingalavatsa, who anticipated the 'monarchical fortune' of Ashoka during his childhood.

BINDUSARA (300-273 BC)

Chandragupta's son Bindusara succeeded his father to the throne and continued to rule for 27 years till 273 BC. He is known to have followed in the footsteps of his father and was even termed by Athenacus, a Greek historian to be the 'slayer of foes (*Amitrochates*).' As per Greek historians, Bindusara is known to have maintained congenial relations with the Greeks. During his reign the Mauryan court received the new ambassador Deimachos, who replaced Megasthenes. Egypt's Ptolemy Philladelphus also sent Dionysius to Bindusara's court. According to the Jaina tradition, 'Parisista parvan', Chandragupta joined the company of Bhadrabahu and many other Jaina monks. He visited Sravana Belegola near Mysore in Karnataka during the last days of his life. At Belegola, he followed the Jaina custom of Sallekhana (starving oneself to death) and breathed his last in 273 BC.

ASHOKA (269–232 BC)

Ashoka the Great, was the third and the most popular of the Mauryan kings; he ruled the Indian subcontinent from 269 BC to 232 BC. He succeeded to the throne after his father's (Bindusara) death in 273 BC, but his coronation ceremony took place only in 269 BC. This delay of four years was due to the war of succession among the sons of Bindusara. On finally ascending the throne, Ashoka took the titles of '*Priyadarshi*' or '*Piyadasi*,' which means 'The Beautiful One' and '*Devanamapriya*' which means 'The Beloved of the Gods.'

Emperor Ashoka

Ashoka's achievements started from an early age, when he served as governor of Ujjain and Taxila. During Bindusara's rule, he crushed a revolt in Taxila. On account of his ability, he was chosen to be the *Yuvraj* or the Crown Prince, eligible for the Imperial throne among all the sons of Bindusara.

The Battle of Kalinga (261 BC)

After acquiring power, Ashoka lead a lavish life of a monarch till 261 BC. During this period he fought the most important battle of his life, the Kalinga War. The main reasons that led Ashoka to fight for Kalinga were :

❏ It was the only Kingdom which was not under Mauryan control. It was controlled by the Nandas.

❏ It was important from military view point, as it controlled the land and sea routes to South India and South-east Asia.

Thus, Ashoka attacked Kalinga and conquered it after a fierce battle. However, the war caused huge losses on both sides, a fact that is inscribed in Rock Edict XIII. It was declared in the Edict that in this epic battle around 1,50,000 people were taken captive, 1,00,000 were killed and innumerable people suffered due to famine and other accompanying misfortunes.

Impact

Though, Ashoka won an immense victory in the Kalinga War, it marked a major turning point in his life. The post war developments and its effects had a profound impact on Ashoka which changed his views on life itself. These are summarized below :

❏ The conquest brought about a significant change in the imperialistic policy of Ashoka. He was immensely moved by the sufferings of people and this made him surrender the violent way of conquest forever. He started following the path of *dharma* and *ahimsa*.

❏ Ashoka, who was a worshipper of lord Shiva before this war, embraced Buddhism and became an ardent follower of Lord Buddha. He took keen interest in Buddhist literature and utilized his resources and power to spread the teachings of Buddhism throughout the country and abroad.

- After embracing Buddhism, he went on pilgrimages to various holy spots of the Buddhists and built about 84,000 stupas and monasteries across the length and breadth of India. He enforced the unity of the Buddhist sangha and became a *bhikshu*.
- A great change in the system of administration was brought about. He adopted a paternal attitude towards his people and devoted himself fully for their welfare. The prosperity of his people became his ultimate the goal in life.

Ashoka's Dhamma

The war of Kalinga filled the heart of Ashoka with remorse and regret. Now his main objective was to promote Dhamma (Sanskrit word, means *dharma*) to far and wide corners of the world. 'Dig Vijay' was replaced by 'Dhamma Vijay'. Ashoka's Dhamma was free from the narrow feelings of sectarianism. His Dhamma did not contain any particular religion or a religious system. Rather it is an "Ethical Order", "Common Code of Conduct" and a "Moral Law" that deals with ideas like virtue, justice, morality and law and duty. It contained the essence of all religions and acted as a meeting ground for every religion.

Fundamental Principles of Dhamma

According to Rock Edict XIII, and several other edicts of Ashoka, the fundamental principles or Code of Duties of Dhamma are :

- *Susrusa* : Obedience towards elders and parents.
- *Anarhan to Bhutaanam* : Refrain from killing of living beings.
- *Avihimsa Bhutaanam* : Non-violence and no harming of all living creatures.
- *Apichiti* : Respect towards teachers.
- *Satyam* : Truthfulness.
- *Bhava-shuddhi* : Purification of heart.
- *Danam* : Being liberal towards all.
- *Sampratipatti* : Appropriate treatment of ascetics, tolerance towards other religions.
- *Dhamma-Rati* : Remaining attached to morality.
- *Apa-vyayata apa-bhandata cha* : Practising saving and spending moderately.
- Good *Karma* or deeds would bring contentment to people in their next birth.
- Disapproval of empty rituals.

Spread of Dhamma

Ashoka adopted various measures to spread his Dhamma, some of which are as follows :

- As a part of propagating Dhamma, Ashoka inscribed the principles of Dhamma on the rock edicts that can be found at various significant places. These rock edicts stating the principles of Dhamma were called *Dhamma lipis* and *Dhamma stambhas* (pillars).
- He used common man's language i.e., Pali to carry his message to all corners of his empire.
- He appointed officers called the *Dhamma Mahamatras* whose duty was to promote Dhamma and take care of the happiness and welfare of the entire population.
- He himself visited holy places and undertook royal tours (*dhamma yatra*) to preach the principles of Dhamma.
- He sent monks to preach the religion of the Buddha to far-off countries. His own son, Mahendra, and his daughter, Sanghmitra, went to Sri Lanka to propagate Buddhism.

Impact of Dhamma on the Imperial Policy of Ashoka

- **Moral Values :** Under the influence of Dhamma, people started leading a moral life.
- **Unity among Religions :** People adopted the policy of religious tolerance propagated by their Emperor, and this unified them religiously.
- **Public Welfare :** With the establishment of the policy of Dhamma, the continuous wars and conquests ended. This paved the way for officials to pay attention to the schemes and welfare measures taken for the good of the common public. This helped people to enjoy a peaceful life, which led to the ultimate prosperity of the nation.
- **End of Crimes :** There was a huge impact on the morality of people as they started

following the *Ahimsa* policy. Because of this, crimes like theft and various illegal activities nearly came to an end in the kingdom.

Salient features of Dhamma : From the major rock edicts, we get important information about Ashoka's attitude towards his kingdom.

- MRE 1 : Prohibition of animal sacrifices and withhold of festivities.
- MRE IX : Shunning costly and absurd rituals in ceremonies.
- MRE XI : Manifestation of secularism of Dhamma.
- MRE VI : Effective arrangement of administration.
- MRE II : Emphasis on Social welfare
- MRE IV : Observance of non-violent activities showing courtesy to relations.
- MRE III : Adopting liberal attitude towards Brahmins, Sramanas etc.
- MRE V : It indicates the appointment of Dhamma Mahamattas. Exposition of humane treatment of servents by lords
- MRE VII and XII : Tolerance among all sects.
- MRE XII : The polices of Bherighosa (sound of war drums) should be replaced by dhammaghosa (sound of peace).
- MRE III : Establishment of constant liaison with the rural people through the system of dhamma yatras.
- MRE : stands for Major Rock Edicts.

Extent of Ashoka's Empire

The Ashokan inscriptions testify that the extent of the Mauryan Empire under Ashoka extended from the North Western Mountains of Hindukush that includes Kashmir, parts of Indus Valley, the whole Gangetic delta and the foothills of Nepal, to the Southern river Pennar of Mysore. A very important part of the empire was Tamralipti, the modern day Tamluk, which was an important port on the coast of Bengal that connected Sri Lanka and Burma or Myanmar to India via ships. Outside India, the provinces of Kabul, Herat and Kandhar were also included in the Ashokan Empire.

The Mauryas also shared close and cordial relations with Central Asia's Khotan Empire. Ashoka maintained friendly relations with the kingdoms of Southern India namely the Pandyas, Cholas and the Keralaputras. He sent delegations to the neighbouring nations of Sri Lanka, West Asia and Myanmar. Under the reign of Ashoka, Mauryan Empire had a Sub-continental or Pan-Indian character.

MAURYAN ADMINISTRATION

The foundations of the highly structured system of Mauryan administration were laid down by Chandragupta Maurya, guided by Chanakya and his book *Arthashastra*. This system was retained by his son Bindusara and some minor changes were made by Ashoka after he underwent a change of heart after the Kalinga War. There were three main divisions in the Mauryan administration - Civil Administration, Military Administration and Judicial Administration.

Civil Administration

Central Government

A centralised bureaucratic set up existed within the Mauryan government that was handled by groups of officers of various ranks.

King

The supreme authority of this government was the King, whose throne passed on to the next in line successor by heredity. He was not only the Head of State but also the Head of the Judiciary and Military administration and had sweeping Executive powers. He was the supreme judge and the power to enact new laws and amend old one's lay with him. Megasthenes mentions that the King had to stay throughout the day in the Court to ensure the transaction of the public business.

Council of Ministers and Officials

A Council of Ministers or *Mantri Parishad* used to act like an advisory body to the king. The Prime Minister was the head of this council. For each department, a separate minister was appointed. The Mantri Parishad comprised a *Purohit*, the Chief Priest of the State, a *Senapati*, who was assigned with the duty of advising the

THE MAURYAN EMPIRE

king on matters of war and peace, a tax expert called the *Samaharta* and the supreme treasurer of the council was *Sannidhata*. Besides the Purohit and Senapati, there are references also to officials like *Pulsias* and *Prativedaka*. The *Pulsias* were like modern public relation officers who kept the emperor updated about public opinion about his rule. The *Prativedakas*, on the other hand were special reporters of the king and had direct access to him.

A superintendent or *Adhyakhsha* used to act as the head of each of these departments. Both the departments of civil and military administration had an *Adhyakhsha* appointed for them. Some other notable posts were Accountant General, Superinten-dent of mines, Superintendent of ports, Controller of Commerce and others.

Provincial Government

The vast empire of Chandragupta Maurya was divided into four provinces–Magadha, Avanti, Gandhara and the Southern Province. During the rule of Ashoka, the new province of Kalinga was added with Tosali as its capital. According to Ashokan inscriptions, governors were appointed to the capitals of Taxila to manage the Gandhara province, Suvarnagiri to manage the Southern Province, Tosali to manage the Kalinga Province and Ujjain to manage the Avanti Province. The heads of these provinces were known as *Aryaputra* or *Kumar* and generally princes were appointed to these positions. Within the provinces, there existed smaller provinces which were under the control of *Pradeshikas*.

District Administration and its Officials

The huge provinces were subdivided into districts called *Janpadas*, which made administration of these regions easy. In the case of a district, there were four major officials who looked after its administration-*Pradeshikas, Mahamatras, Yuktas* and *Rajukas*. The *Yuktas* were in-charge of accounting, collection of revenue and secretarial work. The *Pradeshikas* were responsible for touring the entire district to check whether everything is running smoothly or not. *Rajukas* were responsible for scrutinising and evaluating the land. *Mahamatras* or governors acted as incharges of the provinces.

The Administration of the Cities

All the major cities and capitals of the various Mauryan provinces had a separate local administrative system with a centralised main administrative system of the centre. In *Arthashastra*, it is mentioned that the *Nagaraka* or City Superintendent was entrusted with the duties of maintaining public roads and buildings, to look after the water supply for the entire population of the cities, inspection of city towers and city walls and taking safety measures against fire. The Nagaraks also used to work as the Census Officers of the city as they maintaining the birth and death records. According to Megasthenes, a committee of 30 members managed the capital of the Mauryas, Pataliputra and other cities. This committee was divided into 6 boards consisting of 5 persons each. Every board was responsible for some specific function.

The Sources of Revenue Collection

The Mauryan Empire's main source of income was land revenue, which varied from $1/3^{rd}$–$1/6^{th}$ of the entire produce that could be paid either in cash or in kind. The land tax was slightly more in case of irrigated lands. According to the Ashokan Edict, there were two kinds of taxes called *Bhaga* and *Bali*. Bhaga was charged at the rate of $1/6^{th}$ of the produce on the production of agricultural goods and cattle. Bali, on the other hand, was a tax paid on religious grounds. Taxes were also levied on manufactured goods of different kinds, license - fees, fines, gambling houses and liquor shops. Mines and forests also came under the ambit of tax collection. The state provided facilities like irrigation, roads, hospitals and other expenditures like maintaining a huge army and paying salaries to the various officials were done from these taxes.

The System of Spies

This was an excellent aspect of Mauryan administration, where the Emperor employed spies to get regular information about the workings of his state. Megasthenes named these spies "Overseers", while Kautilya named them *Gudhapurushas*, which means the Secret Agents. Since the King had to be aware of all matters concerning the bureaucracy, these spies collected valuable information for the king about his state, his army and the conduct of his officers.

Military Administration

The King was the supreme Commander of the armed forces and he personally lead his army both in peace and war. Historical records boast of a large army possessed by the Mauryas that consisted of 9000 war-elephants, 30,000 cavalry, 6,00,000 infantry and 1000 chariots besides the fleet of ships. The main arms used by this army were shields, bows, arrows, spears and swords. A military committee of 30 members controlled the entire army of the Mauryas which was further divided into six boards of five members each. These boards were as follows:

- Board of Infantry
- Board of Cavalry
- Board of War Chariots
- Board of War Elephants
- Board for Navy
- Board for managing Transport

The Mauryas also followed a well-laid policy of recruitment and paid the soldiers their salary in cash. For ensuring safety and security of the entire kingdom, the Mauryan kings had constructed various forts throughout the empire. Besides this, there were several factories for the production of the arms of different kinds.

Judicial Administration

The most remarkable and effective law of the Mauryas had been confirmed by Megasthenes to be related to criminal offence. Death penalty was the ultimate punishment for serious offenders of law and those who were involved in lighter crimes were chastised by shaving of the head of the guilty to humiliate him or cutting his nose off. Avoiding paying of taxes was considered to be a serious offence. During the Mauryan period, criminal laws were very strict and the punishments meted out were equally ruthless.

CHARACTER OF THE MAURYAN EMPIRE

The driving out of the foreign powers from India marked the Maurya's rise to power. With the passage of time, the Mauryas brought nearly all parts of India under their control, gradually taking the shape of an all Pan-India Character.

After defeating Seleucus, Chandragupta annexed the four provinces of Kabul, Herat, Baluchistan and Kandahar. Till the end of the reign of Ashoka, these four states remained with the Mauryan Empire. During the rule of Bindusara, certain parts of South India came under his control as well. With the passage of time, the Mauryas came to occupy most of the subcontinent, giving it an all-India character. The all India character of this empire could also be understood from the fact that Chandragupta breathed his last at Karnataka's Shravanabelagola.

The advantages of this Pan–Indian character of the Mauryan empire are :

- It heralded the end of single small states.
- It aided in establishing links with foreign nations on the grounds of trading.
- India became a strong country and assisted Mauryan kings to confront aggression from foreign invaders.
- With the Kalinga war, there came a change in the policy of the state, which marked the end of wars and conquests in India. This allowed the kings of the Mauryan Empire to concentrate on the economic as well social life of the ordinary people. Thus, this ensured an all-round development and economic prosperity.

DOWNFALL OF THE MAURYAN EMPIRE

Several factors led to the downfall of the Mauryan Empire. There is a discrepancy between two opinions, one of which suggests that it was Ashoka's pro-Buddhist policies that led to the development of counter-revolution from the Brahmanical order. On the other hand, the other group suggests that it was Ashoka's peaceful policies that were the root cause of the decline of the empire because it gave a chance to Pushyamitra Sunga to revolt and end the dynasty. However, the reasons for the decline of Mauryan Empire are as follows :

- According to the historians, the primary cause behind the decline of the Mauryan Empire was the accession of weak successors to the throne after the demise of Ashoka.

- The vastness of the Mauryan Empire demanded a strong hand to keep it from falling apart.
- However, the successors of Ashoka such as Dashratha, Sampati and Brihadratha failed to hold the reins of such a vast empire since they were weak rulers.
- After the Kalinga war, Ashoka adopted the policy of non-violence and stopped waging battles. This weakened the strength of his military power and encouraged foreign invasion.
- Moreover, the successors of Ashoka observed the policy of non-violence and dhamma vijaya, espoused by the Emperor Ashoka during his lifetime. They could not imagine of implementing aggressive policies, initiated by Chandragupta, At the other end of the spectrum, none of Ashoka's successors except Dhasaratha could comprehend the policy of Dhammavijaya, inaugurated by Ashoka. This led to the subsequent emasculation of the empire.
- There was a revolt from the chiefs of the Southern Province and Kalinga who had successfully freed themselves from the grasp of the Mauryan administration.
- The key to the efficient administration is money. But Ashoka emptied his treasury to spread Buddhism and works of public welfare. Consequently, it resulted in financial crisis and ruin which affected the efficiency of administration.
- The payment of the army involved massive expenditure on the part of the state. This great financial burden was met by the collection of taxes. The later kings of the Mauryas failed to collect taxes on time, thus maintaining such a huge army became a burden.
- Ashoka's patronage of Buddhism and his anti-sacrificial attitude affected the income of the Brahmins. So they developed antipathy against the Mauryas and their empire. Therefore, immediately after the death of Ashoka they began to work for the destruction of the Mauryan Empire and succeeded eventually in overthrowing it.
- The successors of Ashoka were unable to safeguard the North-western frontier against the Greek invaders. This particularly contributed to the fall of Mauryan Empire.

Under these tumultuous circumstances, Pushya-mitra Sunga, the Mauryan General killed the last Mauryan king, Brihadrath a around 187 BC. This marked the end of the Mauryan Empire.

In Retrospect

- ♦ *Rise of the Mauryan Empire :* The north-western part of India was under the rule of the Greeks. To free India from Greek control and topple the Nanda dynasty in Magadha, Chanakya trained Chandragupta Maurya. Chanakya was previously insulted by the last Nanda King.
- ♦ *Sources that Aid in Reconstructing the Mauryan Age :*
  - *Literary Sources :* Megasthenes' Indika, Vishakhadatta's Mudrarakshasa, Arthashastra by Kautilya.
  - *Archaeological Sources :* Pillars and Rock Edicts of Ashoka. Rules like truthfulness, non-violence, respecting teachers and being obedient to parents are etched on the Rock Edict XII to be followed by people.
- ♦ *Chandragupta Maurya :* Mauryan Dynasty's first ruler defeated Seleucus in 305 BC, conquered Punjab and North West and Magadha—maintained friendly relations with Seleucus, brought the regions of Kabul, Kandahar and Herat into the Mauryan Empire, Chandragupta remained in power for 25 years and was guided by Kautilya.
- ♦ *Bindusara :* Chandragupta Maurya's successor who reigned from 300–273 BC, followed the footsteps of his father in expanding his kingdom and conquering new lands, carried on good relations with the Greeks.
- ♦ *Ashoka :* Most significant period in the Indian History, Kalinga War of 261–60 BC, transformed Ashoka and converted him into a Buddhist from 259–58 BC, 3rd Buddhist Council that held in 250 BC, dispatched Buddhist delegation to several parts of Sri Lanka and India.

- *Ashoka's Dhamma* : Dhamma is a code of conduct, guidelines towards virtuous and moral living, issued in inscriptions or Stone Edicts and pillar edicts. The guiding principles of Dhamma are: Tolerance, True ceremonies, Domestic Life's purity and Life's Sanctity–Dhamma Mahamatras.
- *Administration of Mauryan Empire* : Centralization of the government with the King as the administrative, legislative and judiciary head–Council of Ministers comprising of governors, viceroys, heads of departments, ministers and subordinate officers, network of spies, Provincial Administration, Sources of Income, District Administration, Judicial Administration, City Administration.
- *Character of the Mauryan Empire* : Society was divided into various classes yet happiness and peace existed in the kingdom, Economic situations thrived on trade and agriculture, Art and Architecture flourished, Pillars reflect the Mauryan Administration accurately.
- *Analysis of the Administration of the Mauryas* : Nature of the Mauryan Administration can be learned from Arthashastra–officials who administered a large empire.
- *Downfall of the Mauryan Dynasty* : Peace-making attitude of Ashoka, Counter–revolution of Brahmans, Weak successors of Ashoka, insurgencies of Chiefs of the Southern Provinces and specifically of Kalinga.

EXERCISES

Part-I (Short Questions)

1. What are the two foreign literary sources of information of the Mauryan period ?
2. Name the famous book written by Megasthenes.
3. Who was Chanakya and which famous book did he write ?
4. What were the two most important archaeological sources of the Ashoka's reign ?
5. State the importance of Ashoka's Edicts.
6. Which dynasty ruled Magadha before the advent of Chandragupta in the scene ?
7. Name the four provinces that were won by Chandragupta Maurya after defeating Seleucus.
8. Who succeeded Chandragupta Maurya ?
9. What were the two titles that were assumed by Ashoka after his coronation ?
10. When was the Kalinga War fought ?
11. What were the reasons that led Ashoka to conquer Kalinga ?
12. What was the importance of the Kalinga war and what change did it bring in Ashoka's life ?
13. What was the impact of the Kalinga war on Ashoka's life ?
14. What does the term 'Dhamma' stand for ?
15. Enumerate the fundamental principles of Dhamma.
16. Discuss the steps taken by Ashoka to spread Dhamma.
17. Who were Pulsias and Prativedaka ?
18. State the roles of *Pradesika, Rajuka* and *Yukta* in Mauryan administration.
19. What were *bali* and *bhaga* ?
20. What was the name given to spies by Megasthenes and Kautilya ?
21. State two factors that led to the decline of the Mauryan Empire.

Part-II (Structured Questions)

1. Discuss Indika and Arthashastra to recollent the literary sources of Mauryan dynasty.
2. With reference to the archaeological sources of Mauryan empire, explain the importance of

(a) Ashokan Edicts

(b) Sanchi *Stupa*

3. Depending on the sources, highlight the political history under the Mauryas during the age of:

   (a) Chandragupta Maurya

   (b) Bindusara

   (c) Ashoka

4. Discuss battle of Kalinga and its impact on Ashoka's life.

5. 'The war of Kalinga filled the heart of Ashoka with remorse and regret'. In this context, explain :

   (a) Importance of Ashoka's *Dhamma*

   (b) Its Principles

   (c) Its Spread

6. Write a note on the extent of the empire established by Emperor Ashoka.

7. Write short notes on Military Administration and Judicial Administration of the Mauryan Empire

8. Discuss the factors that led to the dawnfall of the Mauryan Empire.

CHAPTER 5

THE SANGAM AGE

- Sources : Tirukkural and Megaliths.
- A brief study of Society and Economy.

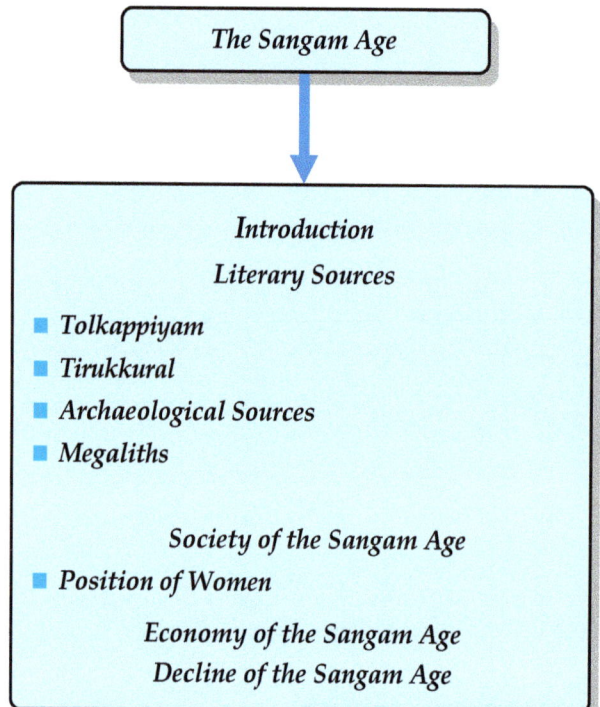

INTRODUCTION

The Sangam Age is considered to be 'the Golden Age of Tamil History'. This classical period of Southern India, extended from 600 BC to AD 300. The three major states that originated and flourished during this period were – the Pandyas, with their capital at Madurai; the Cholas, with their capital at Kaveripattanam and the Cheras with their capital at Vanji.

The word *'Sangam'* is a Sanskrit word which means assemblies or association. The Tamil Sangams therefore, refer to an assembly of Tamil poets or scholars, a literary academy which was established by the Pandya Kings. According to Tamil traditions, there existed three Sangams in ancient Tamil Nadu, popularly known as *Munchchangam*. They flourished under the royal patronage of the Pandyas. The first Sangam or *Talai Sangam* held at Madurai was attended by Gods and legendry sages but no literary work of this assembly is available. The middle or *Idai Sangam* was held at Kapadapuram, but all literary work except, *Tolkappiyam* has perished.

The third or *Kadai Sangam* held at the modern city of Madurai was attended by a large number of poets who produced voluminous literature. It is difficult to give an exact estimate of the period when the Sangams existed. However, the age of Sangam is the age to which Sangam literature belonged. Historically, the Sangam literature that we know today is accepted as having existed in the third Sangam age.

LITERARY SOURCES

The Sangam Literature acts as an important source of information about Sangam Age as it provides information about the ancient Tamil history. It is largely secular and dealt with everyday themes like love, war, trade, governance and bereavement. The literature contains a corpus of

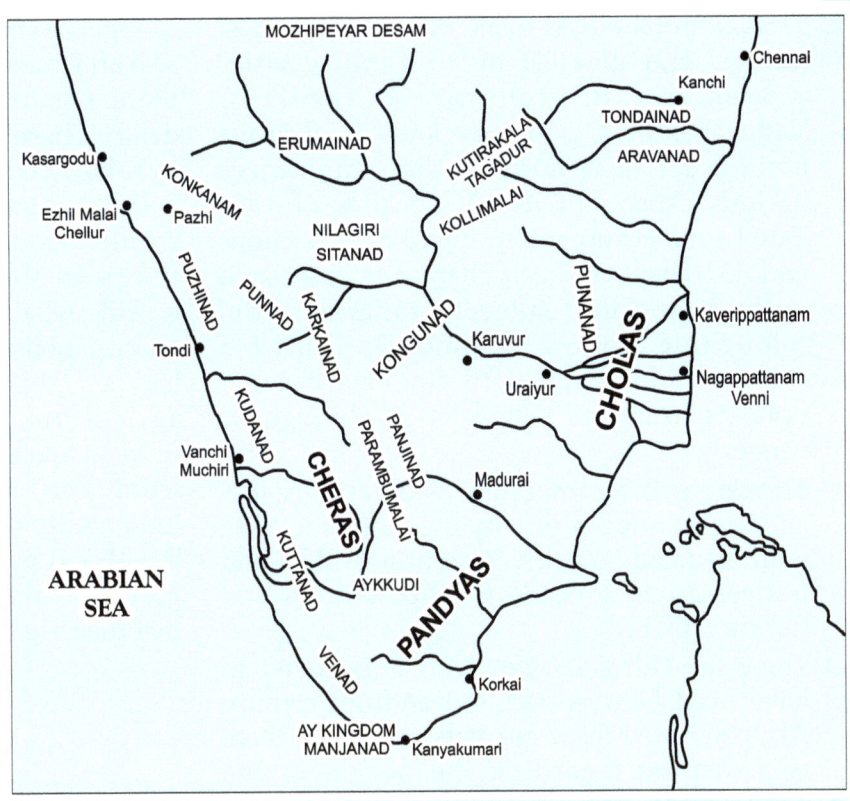

South India in the Sangam Period

poems composed by Dravidian Tamil poets that talk about the achievements of number of kings and princes. The verses from the text *Pathitripathu* act as an authentic source that reveals facts about the Chera Dynasty and helps in fixing the chronological position of the kings. Therefore, it is a significant source to reconstruct the history of the early Cholas, the Pandyas and the Cheras. The Corpus of Sangam Literature is divided into two texts which are narrative and didactic :

- ❏ The first text, *Melkannakku* or Eighteen Major Works is narrative.
- ❏ The second text, *Kilkanakku* or Eighteen Minor Works is didactic.
- ❏ **Composition of Sangam Literature :** Sangam literature comprises the most archaic Tamil works such as Tolkappiyam, Ettutogai (Eight Anthologies), the Pattuppattu (Ten Idylls), the Padinenkilkanakku (Eighteen major works) and the three epics (*Cilappatikaram, Manimegalai* and *Sivagi Sindamani*).

These texts indicate several stages of social evolution. Besides these texts, the literary sources include gems like :

- ❏ *Tolkappiyam* is the earliest literary work of Tamil literature written by Tolkappiyar. It is the most authoritative treatise on Tamil grammar, prosody and culture. It classifies the Tamil language into Sentamil, which is a classical Tamil language almost exclusively used in literary works and Koduntamil, the dialectical Tamil spoken by people in different regions of ancient Tamilagam. It is inclusive of three books, namely, *Solladikaram, Ezhuttadikaram* and *Poruladikaram.*

Every book is again dissected into nine chapters. The exact period of the work is precarious. It is dated between the third century BCE and the 10th century CE. Some modern scholars want to mark it as a layered creation and not an homogeneous entity.

Thiruvalluvar

- ***Tirukkural*** (abridged name '*Kural*') is the most famous and greatest of all Tamil classics written by Thiruvalluvar in Tamil (or Valluvar as he is popularly known). It is the earliest set of aphorisms that emphasizes various aspects of life. It consists of 1330 Tamil couplets organized into 3 main sections and 133 chapters. Each chapter is associated with a specific subject, ranging from 'ploughing a piece of land' to 'ruling a country' and contains 10 couplets each. It upholds truth and simplicity all through its verses.

  Tirukkural is an important widely translated and interpreted work in the universe. The work is dated between 5th centuries BCE and is deemed to precede Cilappatikaram (1st Century BCE).

- The poet Thiruvalluvar, who is believed to have lived between the 2nd and 6th century AD, composed these couplets. Although there is a dispute regarding the period of the composition of *Thirukkural*, many scholars hold that it was created in the late Tamil Sangam period.

- Ettutogai stands for Eight anthologies in the Sangam literature. The Purananuru is a Tamil work of poetry in the main text of Ettutogai (Eight anthologies). It reflects on the statecraft, kingship and governance.

ARCHAEOLOGICAL SOURCES

The early historiography looked at this civilization as representing the "classical" epoch of South Indian history, which rubbed shoulders with the Roman Empire. Historians assign a variety of archaeological sources to this period such as Megaliths, Herostones and inscriptions.

Megaliths

Before the Sangam age, the extreme south of India was inhabited by people called Megalith builders. These people are known as such from the pattern of their graves. Their graves are called *Megaliths* because they were encircled by huge pieces of stone which contained not only the skeletons of the people buried within but also pottery and iron objects such as arrow heads, spearheads, hoes and sickles.

Like the ancient Egyptians, the megalith builders also understood that there was life after death. These goods were buried with the belief that the dead would need these things in the next world. Also, tools and weapons meant for hunting, agriculture, and fishing excavated from the graves indicate that people of that period earned their livelihood by means of hunting and cultivation. Further, tridents have also been found indicating that they were worshippers of God *Shiva*.

Megalith site near Tiruvannamalai

SOCIETY OF SANGAM AGE

The Sangam Age as mentioned in literature witnessed prosperity in all spheres of life. The people of that period had a well-organized social life. The text *Tolkappiyam* refers to four caste systems prevalent in Sangam society-*Anthanar*, *Arasar*, *Vaislyar* and *Vellalar*. Like the Brahmanical society of the Vedic age, social inequalities also existed during this period. The ruling class was *Arasar*. *Anthanars* played a significant role in the Sangam polity and religion. The *Vellalar* was the agriculturist class whereas *Vaislyar* propagated trade and commerce. Hospitality was a special attribute of the Sangam Tamils. Chewing and offering of betel leaves was a common ritual.

Avvaiyar

Sangam literature also mentions that people of that period were religious minded and they worshipped their gods and goddesses with reverence. *Murugan* (son of Lord Shiva) was a very popular god among the people. Their exotic tribal dance was related to the worship of Murugan. Other gods worshiped during that period were *Mayon* (Vishnu), *Vendhan* (Indira), *Varunan* and the Mother Goddess *Kotrravai*. The text Manimegalai refers to the temple of Saraswati, which testifies to the Kapalikas (an austere class of Shaiva Ascetics). Religious occasions and festivals like Onam, Kaarthigai and Indra festival were organized to honour these deities. Besides, they also worshipped natural objects like sun, moon, earth, mountains and rivers. Neem trees were considered sacred by Sangam Tamils. 'Like every Indian society, there was a deep belief in incarnation, the effects of karma and the power of fate. People reposed faith in astrology and omens. A woman with dishevelled hair was considered a bad omen. To their belief, Banyan tree was the abode of gods.

Position of Women

The women of the Sangam Age enjoyed a respectable position in society. However, male chauvinism prevailed. Some women like *Kaakkai, Mudiyar* and *Avvaiyar* (the poets) were educated and contributed to Tamil literature and their courage was appreciated in many poems. Some of them had knowledge of politics and at times they even used to advise the kings. Chastity was the most important virtue of Tamil women. They were allowed to choose their life partners. However, the life of widows was miserable. They had to shave their head, abandon all ornaments and consume only the bland food. The tonsure of widows (tying of tali at the marriage ceremony) was supposed to be a pre-Aryan influence. Subsequently, this custom permeated the whole indigenous subcontinent. The practice of *Sati* system was also prevalent in the higher strata of society.

ECONOMY OF THE SANGAM AGE

Agriculture was the chief occupation of the people dwelling in the Sangam Age. Paddy was the common crop. Some other crops that were also cultivated included ragi, millets, cotton, sweet potato, pepper, ginger, sugar cane and jackfruit. Paddy was the chief crop in the Chola and Pandya dynasty while jackfruit and pepper were famous in the Chera dynasty. Ring wells and tanks were the artificial sources of supply of water during the dry season for irrigation. The food-habits of the people were based on financial status and included fish, meat and tinai rice. The evidences from Sangam literature reflect a very interesting aspect of Tamil economy, which is the existence of five physiographic divisions of the land. *Tolkappiyam* text also refers to the five-fold division of land namely, *Kurinji* (hilly tracks), *Mullai* (pastoral), *Marudam* (agricultural), *Neydal* (coastal) and *Palai* (desert). The life of the people in these divisions differed as they had their respective chief occupation as well as gods for worship which are as follows :

Land	Chief Deity	Chief Occupation
Kurinji	Murugan	Hunting and honey collection
Mullai	Mayon (Vishnu)	Cattle rearing and dealing with dairy products
Murudam	Indira	Agriculture
Neydal	Varunan	Fishing and Salt manufacturing
Palai	Korravai	Robbery

The handicrafts of the Sangam period were very popular. They included weaving, spinning, metal works and carpentry, ship building and making of ornaments using beads, stones and

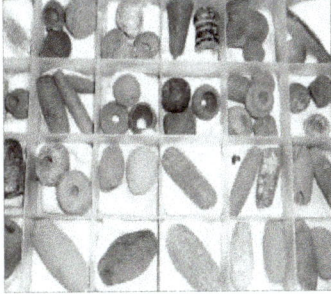
Various Beads of Sangam Age

ivory. There was a great demand for these products as the internal and external trade was at its peak during that period. Spinning and weaving of cotton and silk clothes attained a high quality. According to Periplus of the Erythrean Sea, Uraiyur was an important center for cotton trade. The poems from Sangam literature mention the cotton clothes as thin as a cloud of steam or a slough of a snake. There is a reference that cotton clothes woven at Uraiyar and Madurai were in great demand in the western world.

The Tamil literature mentioned about a hair pomade (togaram). It also referred to the building of rope charpoys by pulaiyans. The Pattinappalai alluded to the life and society of fishermen of Puhar, the paradavar that involved some of their vacating recreations.

Sangam literature and archaeological evidence throws light on the fact that people of that age used to trade in a variety of things. Both internal and foreign trade was well organized. Initially, barter system prevailed in internal trade. The wholesalers, retailers and hawkers exchanged their commodities with the neighbouring regions. For instance, people living in Kurinji region exchanged honey with the people residing in Neydal region for salt and fish. Mullai people exchanged milk products with people of Marudha, for obtaining rice from them in return. Gradually, with the usage of coins, local markets called *Angadis* came into existence and the scope of trading also expanded which resulted in the development of towns. This age also witnessed remarkable growth in foreign trade with Rome, Greece, Africa, Sri Lanka and South East Asia due to increasing demands for luxury goods. Saliyur in the Pandya country and Bandar in Chera are the two most significant ports mentioned in the Tamil poems.

Pandya Coins

Cheras Coins

The main exports were precious gemstones, ivory, sandalwood, pearls, cotton and silk textiles. Indian spices, cotton fabric and stones were the chief products exported to Greece and Rome. A number of inscriptions have been found which confirmed the existence of several trade guilds like those of metal workers, potters, blacksmiths, carpenters, silversmiths, goldsmiths, ivory workers, hydraulic engineers and corn-dealers. The important guilds used to act as financiers and bankers as well.

Decline of Sangam Age

The Sangam age witnessed its decline towards the end of the 3rd century AD. The Kalabhras occupied Tamil country. Jainism and Buddhism became prominent during this period. The Pallavas in northern Tamil Nadu and Pandya in southern Tamil Nadu drove the Kalabhras out of the Tamil country and established their own rule.

In Retrospect

- ♦ *Sangam Age* : Extended roughly from BC 600 to AD 300. According to historians, there were three Sangams held during this age in three different cities out of which the two early cities were washed out by the sea. There is no historical evidence of the early Sangams but the last Sangam was held in Madurai during 5th century BC.
- ♦ *Literary Sources* : The main literary sources are Thirukkural, Tolkappiyam.
- ♦ *Archaeological Sources* : The main archaeological sources are megaliths.
- ♦ *Society* : The society was divided into four categories-Anthanar, Arasar, Vaislyar and Vallalar, women were respected, many gods were worshipped, and hospitality was their special attribute.
- ♦ *Economy* : Agriculture was the chief occupation. Based on physiographical attributes, land was divided into Kurinji, Mullai, Murudam, Neydal and Palai. The Chola, Pandya and Chera were the three prime kingdoms in the Sangam Age. International trade flourished due to the increasing demands for luxury goods like valuable stones, spices, silks and cotton textile.
- ♦ *Purananuru* : The Purananuru is a Tamil poetic work in the Ettuthokai, one of the eighteen melkanakku noolgal. It is a treatise on Kingship : What a king should be, how he should act, how he should treat his subjects and how he should show his generiosity.

EXERCISES

Part-I (Short Questions)

1. Which period of Indian history is called the Sangam Age ?
2. Name the three states that flourished during the Sangam Age.
3. How many Sangams were held during the Sangam Age ? Which one was the most important ?
4. Name two groups into which the Sangam literature is divided.
5. Who composed *Tolkappiyam* and *Thirukkural* ?
6. How many chapters are there in *Thirukkural* ?
7. What is *Purananooru* ?
8. What are megaliths ? What is their striking feature ?
9. What were the four divisions of the Sangam Society ?
10. Name the deities worshipped by the Tamil people.
11. Who were *Kaakkai, Mudiyar* and *Avvaiyar* ?
12. What was the chief occupation of that period ?
13. Name the crops cultivated by Pandya, Chola and Chera dynasty.
14. What are the five divisions of land that decide the duty and occupation of the residents living in a particular region ?
15. Name three items that were exported during that Age ?

Part-II (Structured Questions)

1. Write a brief note on *Thirukkural* and its significance in understanding the Sangam Age ?
2. With reference to archaeological sources of the Sangam Age, write a short note on Megaliths.
3. Write in detail about :
    (a) The society during Sangam Age
    (b) The economy during Sangam Age

CHAPTER 6

THE AGE OF GUPTAS

- Sources: Account of Fa Hien, Allahabad Pillar Inscription.
- Political History and Administration (Samudragupta and Chandragupta Vikramaditya); Contribution to the fields of Education (Nalanda University), Science (Aryabhatta) and Culture (works of Kalidasa, Deogarh Temple)

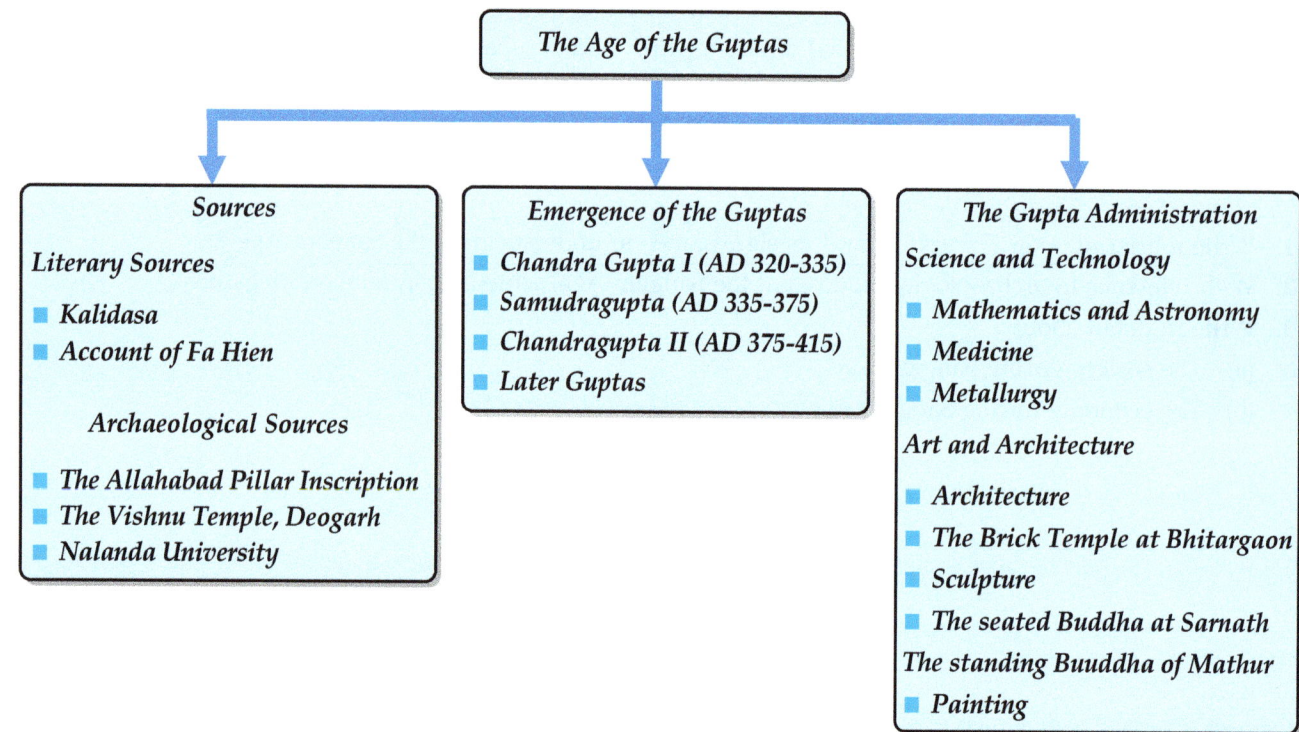

After the decline of Mauryan Empire in BC 187, India torn apart into separate kingdoms. For about 500 years, these smaller kingdoms fought against one another for land and power. India witnessed massive changes in the economic, political, religious and social life of the people with the downfall of the Mauryas. Invasion of the north-west frontier by foreign powers occurred repeatedly. Sunga dynasty and Kanva dynasty came to power and ruled for around 160 years. In the beginning of around AD 320, a second great empire arose in India : The Gupta Empire.

The empire began under a ruler named Chandragupta I, who was the first great ruler of this dynasty. At the height of their power, the Guptas ruled most of the Northern India and their empire was the largest that India had known since the days of the Mauryas. They also strengthened the power of their kingdom through matrimonial alliances with several other kingdoms. India experienced a Golden Era in the Gupta Period, that lasted until about AD 540, which was so called due to the high standards of culture and civilization that existed during this period. This period not only saw the revival of Hinduism but also the unrestrained flow of powerful creativity in the sectors of arts, literature, architecture, education and science. It was at this time, India also ventured into expanding its influence beyond its own borders.

SOURCES

Literary Sources

The history of the Guptas can be reconstructed from the works of Kalidasa and literary accounts of various foreign travellers like Fa Hien and Hieun Tsang. From all these literary accounts, information on the political, social, economic and religious environment of the country during the time of Guptas can be acquired.

Kalidasa

The greatest of all Indian poets ever, Kalidasa lived in the court of Chandragupta II in the 5th century AD. His amazing poetic and dramatic works are a major source for reconstructing the history of the Gupta age. His plays and poetries were exclusively based on Indian Puranas. The four major poetic works of Kalidasa are *Raghuvamsa*, *Ritusamhara*, *Kumarasambhava*, and *Meghaduta*. The three dramatic works for which he is renowned are *Vikramor vashiyam*, *Abhijna nashakuntalam* and *Malavikagnimitram*. *Abhijnanashakuntalam* has immortalised Kalidasa, as it narrates the love story of Shakuntala and King Dushyanta. It is noted that Kalidasa created the hero of *Malavikagnimitram* in the image of Chandragupta Vikramaditya. Another potent lyrical work by him is the *Meghaduta* or 'The Cloud Messenger'. The literature in the Gupta period was written in Sanskrit. However, the entire collection of his works has been translated into several major languages of the world.

Kalidasa

Account of Fa Hien

Fa Hien was the first Chinese Buddhist pilgrim who visited India in AD 399 during the reign of Chandragupta II. He has left behind the *Smritis* and some interesting accounts which are the chief sources of knowledge about the life of people during Gupta Dynasty. He observed that India under Guptas was peaceful and flourishing. There was a degree of balance and harmony among the social life of people. He characterizes the Gupta administration as mild and benevolent. There was no capital punishment and offences of any kind were ordinarily punished by charging fines and death sentence was completely unknown to people. Crimes were negligible and in cases of repeated attempts, the offender's right hand was cut off. The People of that time were law-abiding, honest and free from pointless restrictions. On the whole, the administration was more liberal than that of the Mauryas.

In his book, *Fo-kwo-ki*, (means 'The Travels of Fa Hien') he described Pataliputra to be a thriving city that had many charitable institutions exemplified by a hospital funded by caring and wealthy citizens. He praised the people as well as the King (himself a *Vaishnava*) of the city since a multitude of religions like *Vaishnavism*, *Shaktism*, *Shaivism*, *Jainism* and *Buddhism* all co-existed harmoniously in the society which was quite affable.

According to Fa Hien, trade and commerce flourished during the Gupta Period. Large groups of people were agriculturists while others followed professions such as carpentry, spinning, weaving, pot-making, gold smithery and animal husbandry. There was no poll-tax or land-tax but agriculturists had to pay a part of their produce as tax to the ruler. The roads were kept safe for travelers.

Archaeological Sources

The Allahabad Pillar Inscription

Evidences of the Majestic Guptas can be found in this epigraph. The Allahabad Pillar inscription is deemed to be the most significant historical record of the classical Gupta Age. It is composed in refined Sanskrit language in Gupta script (eventually known as Brahmi script). Harisena, the Court poet of Samudragupta, composed the contents that are inscribed on this Pillar at Allahabad. The writings on this stone pillar give an exhaustive account of the political career of Samudragupta and the kingdoms conquered by him. It was written in Sanskrit and consists of a single sentence of 33 lines, of which only some lines are readable now. This inscription is extremely important due to India's political geography as it also gives glimpses of the social conditions of the ages to which Guptas belonged. The names of various kings and people who populated the country at around the 1st half of the 4th century AD are part of this inscription.

The Vishnu Temple (Dashavatara Temple)

The Vishnu temple also called Gupta temple at Deogarh is an important archaeological source to reconstruct the Gupta age. This temple was constructed in the 6th century AD and was built of stone on a raised platform that measured 1.5 m in height. Tales from the *Ramayana* adorn the outer walls of this temple, while the pillars and the main entrance are decorated with innumerable carvings and paintings. There is an additional outer wall that stands surrounding the entire temple. The temple is presided over by Lord *Vishnu*, the God responsible for preservation of this world, which is depicted to be sleeping on a giant serpent that is coiled underneath Lord Vishnu. This giant serpent is known as *Sheshnaga*.

The Vishnu Temple also called as the Dashavatara Temple at Deogarh

Nalanda University

The Guptas were patrons of education. They built many colleges and universities throughout their empire. Of these, the Nalanda university at Nalanda in Bihar's Rajgriha was the most popular and respected educational institution of ancient India. Kumaragupta I established this university in the 5th century AD. The university had 10 temples, many classrooms, meditation centers and a big library. Initially this was a Buddhist monastery but later became a university. Subjects like Hinduism, grammar, logic and astronomy were taught at Nalanda. Many Buddhists taught at Nalanda and students were instructed in Buddhist and Hindu Philosophy. This university flourished under the rule of the Guptas and was later patro-nized by Harshavardhana of the Pushyabuti dynasty.

Ruins of Nalanda University

Nalanda University acted as a guiding light for the people up to the 12th century AD. Subsequently it faced destruction at the hands of Muhammad-bin- Bakhtiyar Khalji, who was a general of Muhammad Ghori. Of this grand structure, only the relics now exist.

EMERGENCE OF THE GUPTAS

Chandragupta I (AD 320–335)

The founder of the Gupta dynasty was Sri Gupta. He was the successor and son of Ghatotkacha who ruled from AD 320–335. He was the first to assume the title *Maharajadhiraja*, which meant the great King of Kings. He strengthened the power and prestige of his dynasty by a matrimonial alliance with

Maharajadhiraja, Chandragupta I

the Lichchavi clan. His marriage with Kumaradevi, a Lich-chhavi princess helped him in amassing great political gains by adding the Lichchhavi principality to Magadha and thereby extending his domi-nion over Awadh as well as along the Ganges and as far as Prayaga or Allahabad. Thus, Chandra gupta's empire included a part of Bengal, Bihar and eastern Uttar Pradesh. Chandragupta I is generally considered to be the herald of the Gupta era that commenced on 26th February, AD 320. This era commemorated the epoch of his accession to the throne.

Samudragupta (AD 335–375)

After Chandragupta I, his son Samudragupta succeeded him to the throne. He was one of the greatest rulers of the Gupta dynasty who ruled till around AD 375. The Allahabad Pillar Inscription provides a detailed account of his conquests and boundaries of the Gupta Empire as mentioned earlier in the chapter. Harisena, the Court Poet of Samudragupta composed this inscription in Sanskrit.

As per the inscription, he defeated nine kings of Northern India and wrested control of the western parts of Uttar Pradesh and present day Delhi. Next, he conquered the eastern part of India by defeating the Kingdoms of Nepal, Assam and Bengal and made them to pay him tribute. Then, he advanced towards the Southern kingdoms and defeated 12 rulers among which the regions of Andhra, Orissa and Tamil Nadu were included. Although he conquered these lands, he didn't take possession of these kingdoms because he felt that it would be difficult to control them from the North. He allowed the rulers to rule as branches of the Gupta Empire, under his suzerainty. He had close contacts with the kingdom of Ceylon, Indo-China, East Indies and Malay peninsula and South East Asian colonies. In the inscription, he has been described as the hero of a 100 battles. Moreover, impressed by Samudragupta's conquests and generosity, the Sakas and Kushana principalities on the west and north-west of India surrendered to him and decided to pay tribute to the Gupta emperor. They attended his court, concluded matrimonial alliances with the Guptas and used imperial coins as their currency. Due to his extensive military achievements, Samudragupta was called the 'Napoleon of India' by a famous historian, Vincent Smith.

After these military victories, Samudragupta performed the horse sacrifice or *Ashva medha Yajna*. He issued gold and silver coins of eight different varieties with the legend 'restorer of the 'ashvamedha'. He was a follower of Brahmanism and believed in sacrifices of the Vedic religion. In spite of this belief in Brahmanism, he had respect towards all other religious faiths. This can be testified by the fact that he allowed the king of Ceylon to build a Buddhist monastery at Bodhgaya.

Gold coins by Samudragupta to commemorate the Ashvamedha ritual

Coin of Samudragupta playing the veena

Kaviraja (King of Poets) is a term used by Harisena for Samudragupta, which described him as a patron of poetic arts, musician, scholar and poet himself. One of his coins even depicted him playing a flute or Veena. His court was full of literary figures and great scholars from various places. Thus, Samudragupta was not just a very powerful ruler but also a patron of arts.

Chandragupta II (AD 375–415)

Chandragupta II, also called Vikramaditya-I, succeeded his father Samudragupta in AD 375 and it was under his rule that the Gupta Empire attained glorious peaks. Some historians believed that the immediate successor of Samudragupta was his son Ramagupta, the elder brother of Chandragupta-II. A drama by Vishakadatta, Devichandraguptam explicates that Ramagupta agreed to surrender his queen, Dhruvadevi to the

Saka chief, Basana. At this critical juncture, Chandragupta-II saved the honor of the queen by killing the Saka chief. Subsequently, he usurped the throne and married the widow of Ramagupta. He extended the Gupta Empire by a judicious combination of the policies of diplomacy and warfare. Through matrimonial alliances with the powerful Vakatakas he strengthened his political power. The political importance of this alliance lies in the fact that the Vakatakas occupied a geographically strategic position in the Deccan which served a useful purpose when he undertook his campaign in western India against the Sakas.

The greatest military achievement of Chandragupta II was the defeat of the last ruler of the Saka satraps of western India. As a result of this conquest, his territories in western Malwa and the Kathiawar Peninsula were annexed into the Gupta Empire. After this victory he performed the horse sacrifice and assumed the title *Sakari*, meaning, 'destroyer of Sakas. Thus, Chandra-gupta II gained control over the Arabian Sea gaining access to Broach, Sopara, Cambay and other sea ports under his reign. This enabled the Gupta Empire to control trade with the western countries. The western traders poured Roman gold into India in return for Indian products. The great wealth of the Gupta Empire was manifest in the variety of gold, silver and copper coins issued by Chandragupta II.

Gold coin of Gupta king Chandragupta II

Chandragupta II is also known for his personal wisdom, humane administration and his patronage of literature, arts and architecture. The nine gems or *Navratnas* adorned his court, which included famous poet Kalidasa and Amarasimha.

Later Guptas

Chandragupta II was succeeded by his son Kumaragupta I in AD 415. He took the control of the empire and had a successful rule for 40 long years. During his reign; art, literature, music and foreign trade prospered.

Kumaragupta I was succeeded by his son Skandagupta. During Skandagupta's reign, he faced the invasion of the nomadic tribe Hunas in AD 458 from the Central India. However, the invasion of the Hunas was completely crushed by Skandagupta, which made the Hunas never to dare again to enter India. After Skandagupta, Purugupta ruled for a short period that remained uneventful. After his death in AD 477, the process of disintegration began for the Gupta Empire. However, the line of the Imperial Guptas, is supposed to have ended with the last known king Vishnugupta, who had probably died in that year.

THE GUPTA ADMINISTRATION

The Gupta kings assumed titles like *Maharajadhi-raja, Parambhattarika, Vikramaditya, Samrat* and *Chakravartin*. The king was assisted in his civil administration by a *Mantri* or *Sachiva* while the *Senapati* was commander-in-chief of the army. The king maintained a close liaison with the provincial administration through a class of officials called *kumaramatyas* and *ayuktas*. Numerous inscriptions mention *dutaka* or *duta* who communicated royal commands to officers and the people concerned. Another important official mentioned in the Gupta inscriptions was the minister for foreign affairs called *Sandhibigrahika*.

The empire was divided into several provinces called *Bhuktis* or *Desas*. The provincial governors who usually belonged to the royal family were called *Uparika, Maharaja* or *Pradeshikas*. They were mostly chosen from among the princes. A *Bhukti* was divided into districts called *Vishayas*, which were ruled by *Vishwapatis*. Other important district level officials were *Prathamkayashtha* who wrote letters, *Pushtapal*, the record keeper and *Nagarshreshti*, the chief Banker. Each village was under a village headman or *Gramika*. A village council in the maintenance of law and order assisted him. The *Gramika* and his council presided over all important social and economic activities.

Science and Technology

India, during the rule of Guptas, saw great advancement in the fields of sciences like medicine, astronomy, mathematics and metallurgy.

Mathematics and Astronomy

Aryabhata and Varahamihira were the major astronomers and mathematicians of that period.

Aryabhata (late fifth and early sixth century AD) was the first to point out that earth is a sphere which rotates on its own axis and that eclipses were caused by the moon coming within the earth's shadow or between the earth and the sun. His contribution in mathematics is equally valuable. He was the first to discover the number 'zero' and the decimal system of notation. The Arabs learnt the numerical system from the Indians and later these numericals came to be known as Arabic numerals when they were taken to Europe. In his famous book, *Aryabhatiyam*, he has dealt with different branches of mathematics including arithmetic, algebra and geometry. Trigonometry also developed during this time and Aryabhata was the first to give the exact value of pi (π) as 3.1416 and the formula for calculating the area of a triangle.

Aryabhata

Varahamihira (Sixth Century AD) was another great astrologer and mathematician of that period. He authored two renowned books, *Brihat-Samhita* and *Panch-Siddhantika*. His book, *Panch-Siddhantika* is a treatise on mathematical astronomy and it summarizes five earlier astronomical treatises, namely the *Surya-Siddhanta*, *Romaka Siddhanta*, *Paulisa Siddhanta*, *Vasishtha Siddhanta* and *Paitamaha Siddhanta*, while *Brihat-Samhita* is an encyclopedia of science which dealt with astrology, planetary movements, eclipses, rainfall, clouds, architecture, growth of crops, manufacture of perfume, matrimony, domestic relations, gems, pearls and rituals. He even studied planetary movements under the influence of the Greeks and gave proofs for his claim that the moon rotates around the earth, which in turn rotates round the sun.

Brahmagupta (late Sixth and early Seventh Century AD) was a great astronomer and mathematician of his age. He is known to provide the description of the gravitational law in his book *Brahmasphuta Siddhanta* and *Khanda Khadyoka*.

Medicine

Sushruta, Dhanvantari and Charaka were the most distinguished physicians of this period. *Charaka Samhita* and *Sushruta Samhita* were important works on Ayurveda. Their conclusions are presented in *Ashtanga Sangraha* by Vaghbhatta. There was usage of mercury and iron in medicine during that period which indicates that the people of that era had knowledge of chemistry and they even practiced it. Substantial development took place in the field of medicine for curing digestion and eye diseases. A book named *Navanitaka* deals with different kinds of powders, oils, elixirs and children's diseases. Veterinary science also developed during the Gupta period. Hastyayurveda or the veterinary science was composed by Palakapya during this period. A book called *Asvasistra* lists the symptoms and treatment of various animal diseases.

Metallurgy

The scientific study of metals is called metallurgy, which reached great heights under the rule of the Guptas. The famous Iron Pillar at Mehrauli, near the Qutab Minar stands as a silent witness to assert the high standards of metallur-gical skills and metal casting of the artists of the Gupta

Iron Pillar at Mehrauli and detail showing the inscription of Chandragupta II

Period. Despite being exposed to sun and rain for the last 1500 years this pillar has not rusted or corroded. The copper statue of Buddha at Nalanda and Gupta gold coins are the best specimens of artistic excellence in the field of metal casting. Nagarjuna is mentioned as a great chemist. However, no books dealing with chemistry and metallurgy of the Gupta age have been found.

Art and Architecture

During the Gupta Period, with the revival of Hinduism, changes were seen in the sculpture, art and architecture and painting done by the artists of that era.

Architecture

The artists of the Gupta period constructed the structure of the temples with intricate details. They initiated use of permanent materials like brick and stone instead of perishable materials like bamboo, wood, etc. Instead of cave temples, structural temples were built for the convenience of idol worship. The interiors of these temples were plain and the most holy place *Sanctum* or *Sanctorum* was provided with a flat roof to worshippers. The Vishnu temple of Deogarh that has already been described and the Brick Temple at Bhitargaon are the two finest examples of Gupta temple construction.

The Brick Temple at Bhitargaon was constructed in the 5th century AD. The structure of the temple has a pyramid for its roof and the exterior walls have been adorned with various figures and statues. Inside the *Garbagriha* of the temple, a *Shiva Linga* has been placed. The main architectural feature of this temple is an arch, which is a curved structure laying support to the weight of the roof. This curved structure or arch developed during the reign of the Guptas became a new trend for the time and thereafter.

The Brick Temple at Bhitargaon

Other than these two remarkable structures, the temple at Sanchi with its flat roof and various *Chaityas*, *Stupas* and *Viharas* were built under the rule of the Guptas. One feature of the columns of the Sanchi Temple placed in the portico had bell capital on top of them. On the other hand, the Stupas, Chaityas and Viharas of the Ajanta and Ellora caves were rock-cut temples that were carved out of the cave rocks.

Sculpture : The Gupta Period saw the art of sculpture reaching the highest peak of perfection. Sculptors created statues out of stone, wood, bronze and terracotta clay. Many of these sculptures portrayed Buddha or Hindu deities and some showed scenes from the lives of important people. The two finest specimens of Gupta sculpture are discussed below:

Seated Buddha

The Seated Buddha at Sarnath : The figure of seated Buddha at Sarnath near Varanasi dating back to the 5th century is shown sitting in a Yogic position and preaching his first sermon to disciples.

The Standing Buddha of Mathura : This 217 cm high Buddha sculpture made of red sandstone dates back to the 5th century. Here Buddha wears a robe, which is held in his left hand and the robe folds and drapes all around him.

Standing Buddha

The distinctive features of sculptures from the era of the Guptas are :

❑ The style evolved out of two different schools of art– the Sarnath School and the Mathura School. Later on another school came into existence that was based on Pataliputra.

❑ Buddha is depicted here with curly hair, quite unlike the clean-shaven head of the images of

Buddha as portrayed by the artists of Gandhara School of Art.

- In the previous art schools, the circle of light or halo surrounding the head of the God was plain, without any sort of decoration. This changed in the Gupta period, where the artists made elegant designs in the halo itself.
- These sculptures had truly Indian touches, without any kind of influence from foreign schools of art.
- The *mudras* or poses of Buddha are very different than those seen in the art forms of other schools.
- The background of the sculptures of the Gupta Period was always based on spirituality.
- In these sculptures, attention has been paid to details like drapery in both forms, being folded or kept plain.

Painting

The art of painting gained a secular character under the rule of the Guptas. The cave paintings of Ajanta murals in Maharashtra and Bagh near Gwalior were the best representation of Gupta paintings. These paintings mostly illustrate episodes from the life of Buddha as depicted in the Jataka stories. Some of the Ajanta murals reflect Buddhist values such as love and understanding. Many of the scenes include graceful images of kings, queens, musicians, dancers and forests decorated with flowers, trees and complex patterns. The arts of Ajanta and Bagh bear testimony to the 'Madhyadesi School' of painting.

Jataka stories depicted on the walls of Ajanta Caves

Thus, Gupta artists were skilled painters and their paintings have been praised for their range of designs, richness, bright colour and dynamic finish even today.

In Retrospect

- **Sources to Reconstruct the Age of Guptas :** Literary sources: Accounts given by Fa Hien, works of Kalidasa; archaeological sources: Allahabad Pillar Inscription, Nalanda university and Deogarh's Vishnu Temple.
- **Chandragupta I :** Founder of the Gupta Dynasty, ruled from AD 320 to AD 335, through a matrimonial alliance with the Lichchhavi clan strengthened the Gupta power.
- **Samudragupta :** Fondly called Napoleon of India, extended the Gupta Empire and brought rulers of North and South under his control by annexing the kingdoms, acknowledged by all powerful leaders, Allahabad Pillar Inscription lays down all his achievements, Worshipper of Lord Vishnu, scholar as well as patron of music and art.
- **Chandragupta II :** Grandest of all Gupta rulers under whose rule Gupta Empire reached new, heights of glory led operations against Saka Satraps, made Ujjian his Capital by dint of annexations and marital alliances, he extended the Empire Navratnas or Nine Jewels of his court, Patron of literature and arts, the Iron Pillar close to Qutab Minar gives details about his conquests.
- **Later Guptas :** During Kumaragupta's reign, peace and prosperity prevailed, succeeded by Skandagupta who defeated Hunas.
- **Scientific Advancements :** Authors like Varahamihira, Aryabhata and Brahmagupta brought new scientific and technical treatises, metallurgy flourished Mehrauli's Iron pillar is an example, Medicine also developed during the Gupta period, use of mercury and iron in medicine indicated their knowledge of chemistry.
- **Architecture :** Special highlights of the architectural skills of the Gupta Period is Temple of Vishnu at Deogarh, Bhitargaon's brick temple close to Sanchi Dasavatara Temple; Sculpture : exquisite Buddha statues in standing posture at Mathura and sitting position at Sarnath suggest a superior sense of sensibility of art and thought; Painting : Themes of paintings are inspired from the Jataka tales, Paintings at Bagh and Ajanta Caves is one of the finest examples.

EXERCISES

Part-I (Short Questions)

1. Which period is regarded as the Golden Age of Indian culture and why ?

2. Who was Kalidasa ?
3. Name the four major poetic works of Kalidasa.
4. Who was Fa Hien? State any two observations made by him of India during Gupta dynasty.
5. Who wrote the writings inscribed on Allahabad Pillar Inscription ?
6. State two characteristic features of the Vishnu Temple at Deogarh.
7. Name the university that flourished during this period and the subjects that were taught at this university.
8. Name the founder of Gupta dynasty How he strengthened the power and prestige of his dynasty ?
9. Name the greatest ruler of Gupta dynasty.
10. Why is Samudragupta called the 'Napoleon of India' ?
11. Name the inscription which tells us about the nature and military accomplishments of Samudragupta.
12. Under whose rule did the Gupta Empire reach its glorious peak ?
13. What was the greatest military achievement of Chandragupta II ?
14. After whose death did the Gupta Empire gradually decline ?
15. What was the role of dutaka or duta ?
16. Who is Sandhibigrahika ?
17. Who wrote *Aryabhatiyam* ?
18. State any two major contributions of Aryabhata.
19. Name two books composed by Varahamihira.
20. What does the use mercury and iron in medicine indicate ?
21. Name the finest example of metallurgical skills that developed during Gupta period.
22. State two distinctive features of the Sculpture of that period.
23. What was the subject matter of Gupta paintings ?
24. Point out any two important features of the Ajanta paintings.

Part-II (Structured Questions)

1. With reference to the intellectual progress seen in the Gupta period, write notes on:
   (a) Works of Kalidasa in enriching Sanskrit Literature.
   (b) Works of Aryabhata and Varahamihira
2. With reference to the architectural sources of the Gupta period, write short notes on:
   (a) The Allahabad Pillar inscription
   (b) The Vishnu Temple
3. With reference to Nalanda university, answer the following questions :
   (a) Who established Nalanda University ?
   (b) Where was it situated ?
   (d) Give three of its special features.
4. Give a detailed account of the Chinese pilgrim Fa Hien.
5. 'Samudragupta had a strong reputation of being the greatest vanquisher and king'. Give a detailed explanation of his conquests and personal achievements.
6. During Guptas reign, India saw great advancement in the fields of sciences. In this context discuss:
   (a) Mathematics and Astronomy
   (b) Medicine
   (c) Metallurgy
7. What are the distinctive features of a sculpture of the Gupta era ?
8. Write a note on the Cave architecture and temples of the Gupta period.

CHAPTER 7

THE CHOLAS

- Sources : Inscriptions; Brihadishwara Temple.
- Political History and Administration (Rajaraja I, Rajendra I)

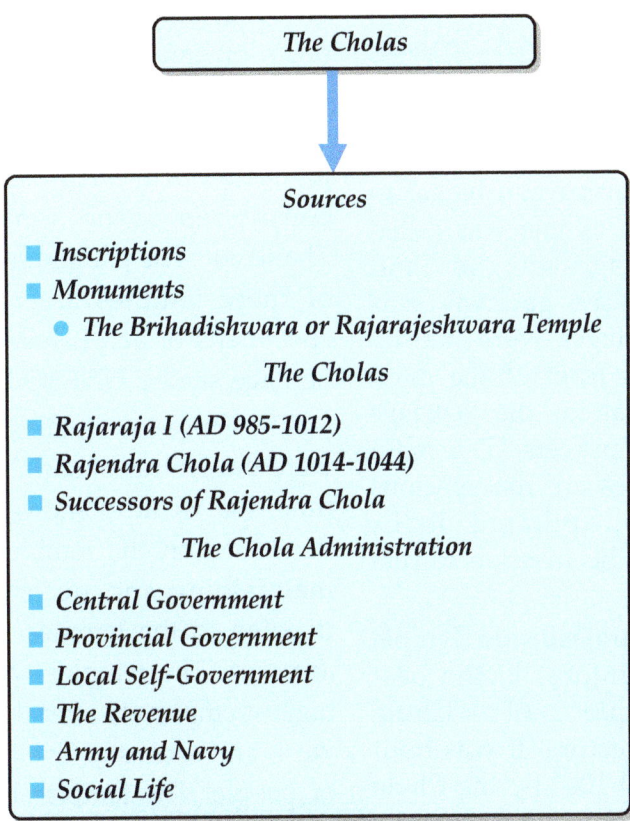

Southern India geographically refers to an area south of the Vindhyas around the region of River Krishna and River Narmada. The Dravidians inhabited the southern part of the Indian Peninsula and it was the home to three powerful kingdoms the Cheras, the Pandyas and the Cholas. From contemporary sources like the Sangam literature and royal inscriptions, we learn that the Cholas were the most powerful of these kingdoms and dominated the political scene in South India for over two centuries.

INSCRIPTIONS

The history of this period can be constructed fairly accurately from the numerous copper plate inscriptions that have been found by archaeologists. Records of grants of land, villages, plots of farmland or other privileges given by kings to private individuals or institutions such as a temple are inscribed on copper plates or on pillars. Most of them are written in Tamil but some are bilingual and are written in Sanskrit as well. They tell us about the kings who ruled as well as the social conditions and artistic inclinations of the people of the time. The Tiruvalangadu grants of Rajendra Chola I and the Kancheepuram inscription of Raja Raja Chola tell us the history of these two Chola Kings.

Monuments

The Chola rulers were considered to be the great lovers of art and architecture. They built many beautiful temples, roads, canals, palaces and cities. Majority of the Chola temples were built in the Dravidian style. The Chola temples in the early period were simple structures but later, the temples became grander and bigger in size. The main shrine of the temple was called *garbhagriha*, where the images of gods and goddesses were kept and the gateway was known as *gopuram*. The images were mainly built of bronze or stone. In front of the main shrine was the audience hall or the *mandapa* where people gathered for prayers. The main features of the Chola temples are the spacious courtyards, interconnected pillared halls, magnificent sculptures and the massive towers or *vimanas*.

The **Brihadiswara** or **Rajarajeshwara** Temple at Thanjavur (formerly Tanjore) is the best example of Chola architecture. It was built in AD 1000 by the Chola king, Rajaraja I and was. It was completed in 1035 AD and dedicated to Lord Shiva. The bronze image of Lord Shiva as 'Nataraja' or Lord of Dance displays grace and vigour and has been considered the 'cultural epitome' of the Chola period. The entire temple structure is made of granite. It consists of an inter-connected *Nandi mandapa*, a pillared portico and an assembly hall. The 57 metres high tower or *vimana* comprises thirteen storeys and its top is crowned with an 8.6 metres high single block of stone that weighs almost 80 tonnes. In this temple, a carving of a man's head with a European hat is located (in a subsidiary structure), who is interpreted as Marco Polo (13th century) Venetian traveler. The temple's interior walls are decorated with magnificent sculptures and elaborate paintings. Another fine example of Chola architecture is the temple built by the King Rajendra Chola in his capital, Gangaikon-da cholapuram and the temple of Gangaikonda Cholapuram (also attributed to Lord Shiva or Brihadesvara), the masterpiece of Rajendra Chola. It overshadowed the architectural capabilities of his predecessors in every possible way. The temple is considered to be similar to the temple at Thanjavur. The paintings and designs on the walls of these temples are considered to be good specimens of art. It has been declared a world heritage site by UNESCO.

The Chola inscriptions inform that the temples were the centres of social activity. During festival time, the wealthy showered large offerings and donations on the temples which were used for maintaining and decorating them. The lands donated to the temples were called *devadana* or *devadaya*. The temples were also considered the biggest employers after the State as they provided work and means of livelihood to a huge number of people. The temples looked after the welfare of its workers by providing food, housing facilities and clothing to them. They established hospitals for taking care of the disabled and sick employees. Since there were no separate schools, the priests of the temple were the local teachers and the schools were held in the courtyards of temples. The students were taught in both Tamil and Sanskrit. Since texts like Vedas had to be studied, the religious teachings were in Sanskrit while Tamil

Brihadiswar Temple at Thanjavur

THE CHOLAS

was taught to the students as it was the widely spoken language in the Chola kingdom.

THE CHOLAS (AD 846–1279)

The Cholas were based in the Kaveri delta and their empire extended along the Coromandel Coast. Around 3rd to 4th century AD, the Cholas endured harsh defeats at the hands of the Pandyas, Pallavas and the Cheras.

In Tamil land, the Chola rule was re-established by the Chola ruler, Vijayalya (C.848) during the middle of the 9th century. He started his career as a subordinate commander or *vassal* of the Pallava king and soon captured Thanjavur or Tanjore from the Muttaraiyar chiefs making it the capital of his kingdom. His son, Aditya I (AD 871–907) succeeded him and inflicted a crushing defeat on the Pallavas.

Aditya I was succeeded by his son, Parantaka I who ruled for 48 years from AD 907 to AD 955. He defeated the ruler of Pandaya and extended his empire by capturing Madurai, the Pandyan capital. He also invaded Ceylon. However, towards the end of his reign he suffered defeat at the hands of the Rashtrakutas in the famous battle of Takkolam. After a gap of thirty years, the Chola power rose to imperial greatness with the accession of the Rajaraja I.

Map showing the extent of Chola Empire

Rajaraja I (AD 985–1012)

Rajaraja I was originally regarded as Arumolivarman, the son of Parantaka II. He was also known as Rajaraja Chola, was a brilliant commander. It was under his reign that the Cholas rose to a position of supremacy in southern India. He began his career by the conquest of the Chera and the Pandya kingdoms. To celebrate his victory over the Cheras and the Pandyas, he assumed the title of *Mummudi Chola*. He also conquered the Eastern Chalukya kingdom of Vengi and put his own nominee on the throne. He extended his dominion by conquering parts of Karnataka, Travancore, Mysore, Kalinga and Coorg.

Later, Rajaraja I decided to prove his strength along the South Indian coast as he was aware of the importance of controlling the sea. He carried out raids into the territories of Western Chalukyas. Though he took out a naval expedition and attacked both the Maldives Islands and Sri Lanka, he was unsuccessful in controlling them. Later, he invaded Sri Lanka and annexed its northern part and towards the end of his rule, he conquered Maldives. The money that came

Rajaraja Chola I

from overseas trade made the coasts of Ceylon, Kerala and the Maldives Islands quite rich. Spices, textiles and precious stones were sent to West Asian countries by India. The Arab merchants from Western Asia traded in these goods in exchange of money.

Rajaraja mural, found in Brihadishwara temple, Thanjavur

Besides being a great conqueror, Rajaraja I was a capable administrator, a patron of arts and literature and a great builder. His achievements are inscribed on the walls of Brihadishwara temple built by him in Thanjavur. Though he was a staunch follower of Lord Shiva, he ensured religious tolerance and patronized all religions Vaishnavism, Saktam, Jainism and Buddhism alike. This is evident from the fact that he granted a village at Nagapatam in the Malay Peninsula to the Buddhist *Vihara*. The vihara came to be known as 'Chudamani Vihara' after the name of the father of Sri Mara. According to historians, Rajaraja I initiated the process of prefacing the inscriptions of the reign with a set account of events.

Under the rule of Rajaraja I, the Cholas became the paramount power in Southern India. He made himself the overlord of almost the entire region of the present State of Tamil Nadu, parts of State of Karnataka and its adjoining regions, Sri Lanka and other islands. Owing to these conquests, he was considered to be one of "the foremost warriors and empire builders of ancient India.'

Rajendra Chola (AD 1014–1044)

The Chola power rose to its zenith during the reign of Rajaraja's I son, Rajendra Chola. He was an able successor who continued the policies of his father. He sent a fleet across the Bay of Bengal and conquered Pegu (in Burma) as well as Andaman and Nicobar islands. His campaigns also advanced up to the banks of river Ganges, where he defeated Mahipala, the Pala king of Bengal. To commemorate his victory in the Gangetic plains, he adopted the title of *Gangaikonda* and built a new capital called *Gangaikonda Cholapuram* which is now identified as Modern *Gangaikonda puram*.

The most daring campaign of Rajendra was in South-East Asia. For centuries, Indian merchants had been trading with several parts of South-East Asia and southern China through the Straits of Molucca, which was held by the kingdom of Srivijaya. The Indian merchants from the Chola Kingdom appealed to Rajendra Chola for help as the merchants of Srivijaya were creating problems for them. Rajendra Chola sent out a huge navy and defeated the Srivijaya king. Thus, Indian trade with southern China and South-East Asia continued, thereby enriching the Chola kingdom to a great extent. In AD 1025, he sent out a naval expedition for the conquest of King Shailendra's territories of Sumatra and Java. Rajendra Chola I sent two diplomatic missions to China mainly for political and administrative purposes.

According to RC Majumdar, "*King Rajendra I had the proud satisfaction of seeing his banner floating from the banks of the Ganga to the Island of Ceylon and across the Bay of Bengal over Java, Sumatra and the Malaya Peninsula*".

Successors of Rajendra Chola

Rajendra Chola was succeeded by his son, Rajadhiraja I. Rajadhiraja subdued the rebellions in Pandya, Kerala and Ceylon kingdoms. He started a mission to reinstate Chola power in Vengi. He defeated the enemy forces of Western Chalukyas. At Yadgir, he installed a pillar of victory with the 'tiger' emblem embossed in it. After conquering Kalyani, he performed the Virabhisheka (coronation of victory) ceremony and adopted the title of 'Vijayarajendra'. In AD 1052, Rajadhiraja I lost his life in the Battle of Koppam. After his death, Rajendra II (AD 1052-1063) and his younger brother, Virarajendra (AD 1063-1070) succeeded the throne. Both of them were brave rulers and fought fiercely against Chalukyas but they could not check the decline of Chola power. Kulottunga was the last Chola ruler who ruled between AD 1070 and AD 1120. The Chola power declined during the thirteenth century. The successors of Kulothunga had very little energy and strength and as a result, Kerala, Sri Lanka and the Pandyas proclaimed their Independence. With the rise of the Hoysalas, the Chola Empire became completely fragmented.

THE CHOLAS

THE CHOLA ADMINISTRATION

In the words of Nilkanta Sastri, the Chola administration combined 'vigorous central-control with a very large measure of local autonomy'. The Chola administration provided a pattern for kingship that was followed by other rulers of South India. The system was highly efficient and organized, with the King as the pivot of administration and all authority resting in his hands.

Central Government

The huge resources of the kingdom, vast palace establishment and splendour of the Court enhanced the power and glory of the King. The King discharged his responsibilities and duties with the advice and help of his Council of Ministers. In order to keep a check on the administration, the King often went on tours. A large number of officials operated the administrative system. Officers of higher rank were known as *Perundanams* and the others holding a lower rank were known as *Sirudanams*. The officers were encouraged and rewarded with titles and paid by giving them assignments in revenue bearing lands. In fact, many of the offices had become hereditary. The princes were actively employed in war and peace and were associated with the ruling sovereigns. The Central Government looked after matters like internal peace and order, external defence, cultural progress and promotion of general prosperity of the empire.

Provincial Government

The Chola kingdom was divided into several provinces known as *Mandalams*. Each province was placed under the charge of a Viceroy, usually one belonging to the landed nobility or a prince of the royal family. Apart from that, there were territories of those rulers who paid tributes, in terms of money or goods to the Chola kings, in return for protection.

The provinces were further subdivided into divisions or *Kottams*. The other units of administration were districts or *Nadus*, groups of villages or *Kurrams* and the village or *Gramam*. All of these territorial divisions had their respective assemblies comprising notable persons and those representing vocational and economic groupings. For instance, such an assembly of a whole *mandalam* was consulted, in connection with the exemption of land revenue because of severe drought in the province.

Local Self-Government

The exceptional efficiency of the village institutions was the most remarkable feature of the Chola administration. In many villages, the villagers themselves carried out the administration. The villages had three types of village assemblies, namely, the *Ur*, the *sabha* and the *nagaram*. The *Ur* was the common type of assembly of normal villages, where the land was held by people of all classes, who were, therefore, members of this local assembly. The *sabha* was an exclusively Brahmin assembly of the *brahmadeya* villages, where all the land belonged to the Brahmins. The *nagaram* was an assembly of merchants and belonged to localities where traders and merchants were in dominant position. In these councils, the life and work of the village was discussed. Since it united the people in the village, it was considered a source of popular strength.

In the management of local affairs, these assemblies enjoyed full power. Villagers who owned land were chosen for the council by vote. The method of election included the name slips of all candidates thrown and mixed up in a pot and a small boy pulling out the slips one by one. The village priest announced the results. Within the village, the village assemblies administered justice, except in cases involving serious crimes. They gathered taxes, regulated water supply and administered all charitable institutions like schools and temples. They could even donate or sell land for religious purposes. The accounts were maintained with meticulous care and if somebody stole money, he was severely dealt with. The village assembly carried on its affairs with the help of smaller committees, each of which looked after specific matters like settlement of disputes, gardens, tanks, justice, temples and general management.

The Revenue

An efficient department of land revenue, regarded as the Puravuvaritinaik-kalam was in vogue. The revenue of the Chola kingdom came from the produce of the land and taxes on land. The land revenue was fixed at one-third of the gross produce for wet land and one-sixth for dry land. The officials collected the taxes on land from the village councils. The other important sources of income were the taxes on trade, handlooms, mines, water courses and the customs (meaning duties on imported goods). While a fraction of the revenue was setaside for the king, the rest was used on public works like building of tanks and roads, paying for the navy and army, on salaries of officials and on building of towns and temples. The Cholas splurged huge amount of money on irrigation projects like tanks, wells, canals and dams. Rajendra I, near his new capital, *Gangaikonda Cholapuram*, dug an artificial lake. Also, the roads that were constructed by the Cholas were a boost to the economy of the land in terms of commerce, trade and communications.

Army and Navy

The Chola rulers maintained an effective naval force and a large well trained army. The soldiers of the Cholas kingdom comprised two types: the Kaikkolar who formed royal troops and received regular pay from the treasury. The second one, Nattuppadai formed the militia men recruited for local defence. The army included archers, horsemen, foot soldiers and war elephants. The soldiers lived in *Kadagams* or cantonments that were situated in various parts of the empire.

Social Life

The caste system greatly prevailed in southern India. Society was divided into different castes. Apart from the prosperous Brahmins, the merchants and traders also emerged as a powerful class by virtue of their wealth. The poor and unprivileged people lived in slums. The practice of untouchability prevailed and social status of the lower castes was pitiable as they were not allowed to enter temples nor were they allowed to draw water from the common wells. Greater social freedom prevailed among the upper classes. Professionals like carpenters, weavers, blacksmiths, masons, goldsmiths also existed.

Women were given high status and freedom in the Chola society. They were appointed as officers in the Chola Government. Chastity and modesty were considered important. There were child marriages among the higher castes. Women who were talented in music and dance performed during festivals. The women of the upper classes enjoyed the right to property. Some queens were associated with the administration of the kingdom and were patrons of temples. Queens such as Kundavai and Mahadevi gave liberal donations to temples. However, Sati System was commonly practiced among the women of the royal family. Writings of Morcopolo and some inscriptions speak about the position of women during the Chola period.

In Retrospect

- **Background :** The southern part of the Indian Peninsula was home to three powerful kingdoms– the Cheras, the Pandyas and the Cholas. The Cholas were the most powerful of these kingdoms and dominated the political scene in South India for over two centuries.

- **Sources :** The history of this period can be constructed from inscriptions that have been found by archaeologists. Monuments: The main features of the Chola temples are the spacious courtyards, interconnected pillared halls, magnificent sculptures and the massive vimanas (towers), Brihadeshwara Temple at Thanjavur constructed by Rajaraja I was dedicated to Lord shiva.

- **The Cholas :** They were based in the Kaveri delta and their empire extended along the Coromandel Coast. Aditya I (871–907 AD) succeeded and inflicted a crushing defeat on the Pallavas. The Chola power rose to imperial greatness with the accession of the son of Sundara Chola. Rajaraja I : He was a brilliant commander and under his reign the Cholas rose to a position of supremacy in southern India. He carried out raids into the territories of Western Chalukyas. He also invaded Sri Lanka and annexed its northern part and towards the end of his rule, he conquered Maldives, Ceylon and several other islands, built Brihadishwara temple. Rajendra Chola : He defeated Pala king of Bengal and adopted the title of Gangaikonda, in order to commemorate the victory. He built a new capital known as Gangaikonda

Cholapuram, defeated the king Sri Vijaya, trade with south-east Asia brought prosperity to the Chola Empire. The successor of Cholas had very little energy and strength and as a result, with the rise of the Hoysalas, the Chola Empire became completely disintegrated.

- ◆ *The Chola Administration :* The system was highly efficient and organized with the King as the pivot of administration, the village at grassroot level, local self-administration was the most remarkable feature of the Chola administration, Assembles like Ur, sabha and the nagaram performed important functions, huge amount of money was allocated for irrigation projects like tanks, wells, canals and dams, land revenue was the main source of revenue which was fixed one-third of the gross produce for wet land and one-sixth for dry land. The army included archers, horsemen, foot soldiers and war elephants. The soldiers lived in Kadagams or cantonments that were situated in various parts of the empire.

- ◆ *Social Life of Cholas :* Caste system prevailed, merchants emerged as a powerful class, society was divided into different castes, poor and unprivileged lived in slums, social status of the lower castes was pitiable as they were not allowed to enter temples nor were they allowed to draw water from the common wells. Women were given high status and freedom, enjoyed the right to property, chastity and modesty were considered important and were appointed as officers in the Chola Government.

EXERCISES

Part-I (Short Questions)

1. Name the three major ruling kingdoms of South India.
2. Which ruler established the rule of the Cholas ?
3. State any two architectural features of the temples built by the Cholas in the Dravidian style.
4. Which temple is considered to be the best example of Chola temples ?
5. Which king built the Brihadishwara Temple ? Which God is mainly invoked in the temple ?
6. Mention any two features of the Brihadishwara Temple.
7. What is *gopuram* ?
8. State the two languages that were promoted by the Cholas.
9. State any two purposes for which the temples were put into use during the Chola period ?
10. Name any two great rulers of the Chola dynasty.
11. For what purpose did Rajaraja I undertake a naval expedition against Maldives and Ceylon ?
12. State any two victories won by the Cholas, under Rajaraja I.
13. What is the name of the new capital that was built by Rajendra Chola ?
14. State any two achievements of Rajendra Chola.
15. What made the Chola administration effective and strong ?
16. Mention the names that were given to the territorial divisions of the Chola kingdom, namely, the Province and the District.
17. What was the method of electing members of the village assembly during the Chola rule ?
18. Mention any two duties assigned to a village assembly under the Cholas.

Part-II (Structured Questions)

1. With reference to the South Indian temples, explain :
   (a) The typical features of Chola temples.
   (b) The role of the temple as an employer and centre of learning

2. The most glorious epoch of the Cholas began with the accession of Rajaraja I (AD 985-1014) and Rajendra Chola (AD 1014-1044). In this context, explain :
   (a) The growth of kingdom during their reign
   (b) The extent of the empire
   (c) Their activities as a Ruler and Great Builder
3. The Chola Empire was raised to the pinnacle of glory by King Rajendra I (AD 1014-1044). In this context, briefly explain :
   (a) The position of the Chola Monarch
   (b) The functioning of the local self-government or autonomous rural institutions
4. With reference to the Chola administration, explain :
   (a) The three types of village assemblies
   (b) Taxes imposed by the Cholas

CHAPTER 8

THE DELHI SULTANATE

- Sources : Inscriptions, Qutub Minar.
- Political History and Administration (Qutub ud-din Aibak, Alauddin Khilji and Muhammad Bin Tughluq).

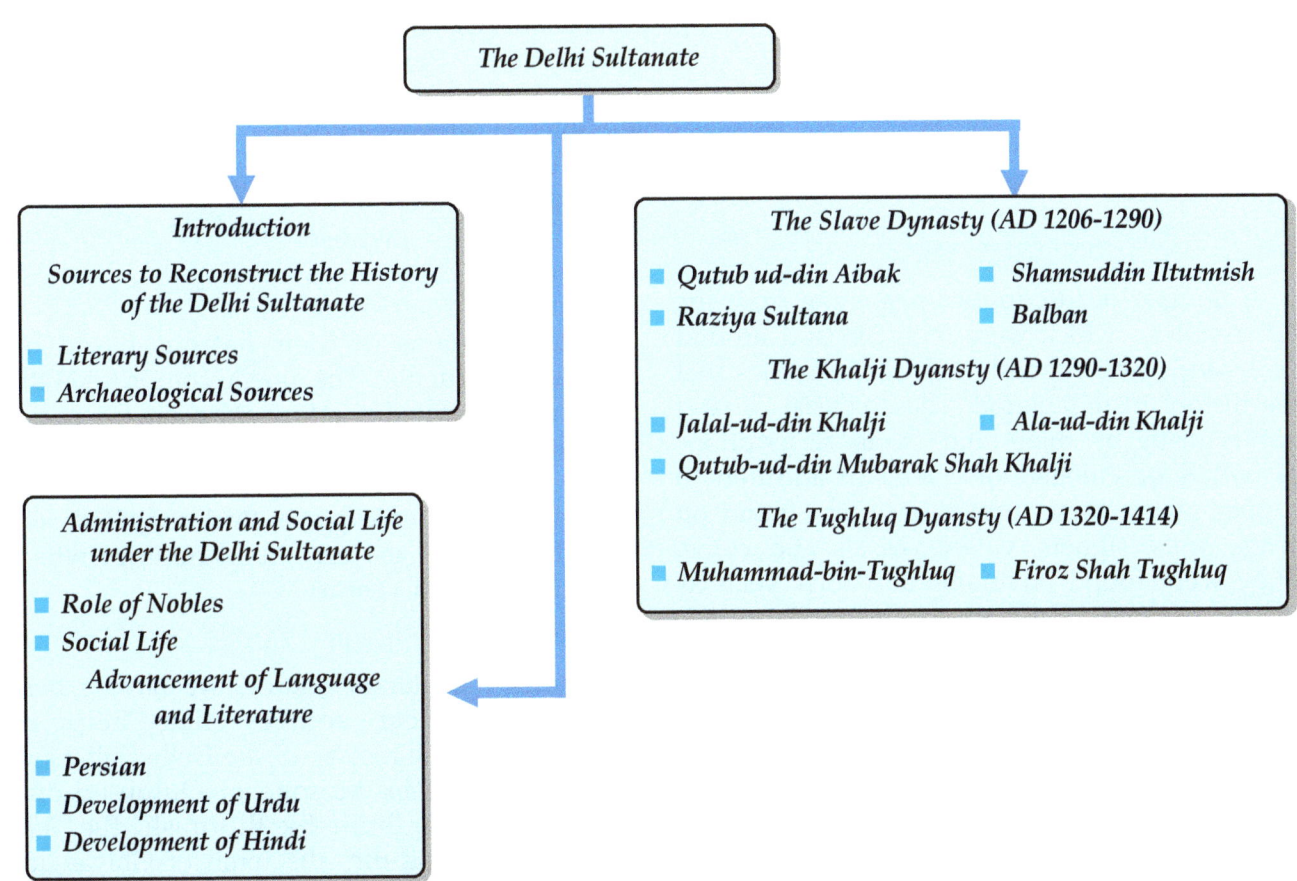

INTRODUCTION

The conquests of Muhammad Ghori became the nucleus of a new political entity in India– The Delhi Sultnate. He conquered Ghazni and established his Ghori dynasty at Ghor in Afghanistan in the twelfth century. Unlike Mahmud of Ghazni (ruler of Ghazni before Muhammad Ghori), who came to India only to plunder and acquire wealth, Muhammad Ghori was looking to settle down and establish an empire in India. Muhammad Ghori invaded

India and occupied Punjab and Sindh by AD 1190. This led to two battles fought between him and Prithviraj Chauhan, who was the Rajput ruler of Ajmer and Delhi. The defeat of Prithviraj Chauhan in the second battle of Tarain in AD 1192 by Muhammad Ghori heralded an era of Muslim rule in India. The sudden death of Muhammad Ghori in AD 1206 and his failure to lay down proper succession procedures pitted his three slaves, Taj-ud-din Yalduz, Nasir-ud-din Qubacha and Qutub-ud-din Aibak against each other. Of these, Qutub-ud-din Aibak began to rule independently.

The period between AD 1206 and AD 1526 in Indian history is known as the *'Period of the Sultan Rulers'*. This period can be divided into 5 distinct dynasties, viz.

- The Slave dynasty (AD 1206-1290)
- The Khalji Dynasty (AD 1290-1320)
- The Tughluq Dynasty (AD 1320-1414)
- The Sayyid Dynasty (AD 1414-1451)
- The Lodhi Dynasty (AD 1451-1526)

INSCRIPTIONS

A number of inscriptions beginning from the 12th century, which were found in and around Delhi and Uttar Pradesh, help us to reconstruct the history of this period. These consist of land grants made by rulers and chiefs, descriptions of battles or eulogies of rulers. In addition to copper plates, these inscriptions were found on arms, seals, signets, vases, vessels and coins. They were found on tombs and forts such as the inscription in Hauz Khas, which tells us that it was a tank to supply water to the people of Siri. They were written in Sanskrit, Arabic, Persian and Urdu. They were sometimes bilingual, Arabic with regional languages like Gujrati or Bengali.

Literary Sources

The Delhi Sultanate witnessed some of the most illustrious Persian Chronicles of the Medieval World that throw a great deal of light on the polity, society and economy of the times. Noteworthy among these are *'Tarikh-i-Firuz Shahi'* by Zia Barani and *'Prithviraj Raso'* by Chand Bardai.

Ziauddin Barani's (1285 - 1357AD) *Tarikh-i-Firuz Shahi,* is a major historical source of information of the Tughluq dynasty. It gives detailed accounts of the reign of Ghiyas-ud-din-Tughlaq, Muhammad-bin-Tughluq and Firuz Shah Tughluq. It also provides a useful account of the reigns of the previous Delhi Sultans (from Balban's rule) till the accession of the Tughluqs, describing their systems of revenue administration elaborately. Barani also wrote the *Fatwa-i-Jahandari*, a complementary volume to the *Tarikh-i-Firuz Shahi,* in the 14th century. This text provides a detailed narrative of the Socio-Politico-Religious and economic conditions of the Sultanate during this period.

Chand Bardai (1149 - 1200 AD), the court poet of the King Prithviraj Chauhan III, composed the poem ***Prithviraj Raso***. He accompanied the king in all his battles and belonged to the community known as 'Charans', whose traditional occupation is to compose poems and ballads in praise of their patrons based on historical incidents.

Chand Bardai

The poem comprises 1400 stanzas and provides information on the social and clan structure of the *Kshatriya* communities of northern India. In the literary tradition, Chand Bardai's epic poem Prithviraj Raso (or Chand Raisa), is the earliest manuscript which dates to the 12th century.

Archaeological Sources

Besides the literary sources we have a host of archaeological sources that help in reconstructing the history of the Delhi Sultanate. The *Quwat-ul-Islam* Mosque of Qutub-ud-din, the *Qutub Minar* built by Iltutmish, the *Alai Darwaja* of Ala-ud-din, the tomb of Ghiyas-ud-din Tughluq and the numerous mosques, gardens, public baths, rest houses built by Firoz Tughlaq stand as evidence of the greatness and grandeur of the Delhi Sultans.

One of the most magnificent archaeological sources constructed by Turks (founded by Qutub ud-din Aibak in AD 1199 and completed by

THE DELHI SULTANATE

Iltutmish in AD 1230) in the 13th century was the Qutab Minar at Mehrauli in South Delhi. Many historians debated regarding the origin of the name of the minar. According to some it was named in honour of Qutub-ud-din Aibak, the first Muslim ruler of India while others contend that it received its name from Khwaja Qutub-ud-din Bakhtiar Kaki, a Muslim saint of Uch, who was highly venerated by Iltutmish. The purpose behind the construction of the *Minar* was to help *Mu'azzin* (crier) to give calls for prayer.

Qutub Minar in Delhi

Its main features are :

- The circular tower of the *minar* that rises to a height of 72.5 metres was dedicated to the Sufi saint Qutub ud-din Bakhtiar Kaki.
- It originally consisted of four storeys. The last storey was damaged by lightning and it was reconstructed into two storeys by Firoz Shah Tughluq. It was obviously not constructed for the Muazzim to give the call for prayer as his voice would not be heard from such a height. The purpose seems to be symbolic, to mark the axis of the earth.
- Each storey is separated from the other by balconies, which encircle the tower.
- The entrance to the tower is through the doorway on the northern side. Inside the tower, there are 379 stairs, which lead to top.
- The Minar is divided by several decorative bands of Quranic verses and balconies supported by characteristic Islamic decorations.
- The Minar contains numerous inscriptions in Arabic and Nagari characters, which narrate its history.
- Red sandstone, marble and grey quartz have been used to construct the tower. It is the tallest stone tower in India.

THE SLAVE DYNASTY (AD 1206–1290)

After victory at the Battle of Tarain in AD 1192, Muhammad Ghori appointed a number of his slaves as officers and made his slave general, Qutub-ud-din Aibak, viceroy for the conquered and annexed lands in India. On Muhammad Ghori's death in AD 1206, Qutub-ud-din Aibak assumed sovereign powers and independently founded a new dynasty, called the Slave dynasty. Under this new dynasty, Aibak founded the Delhi Sultanate. The early rulers of the slave dynasty were known as the '*Mamluks*' or sultans, since these sultans were earlier either the slaves or sons of the slaves of the Turks.

Qutub-ud-din Aibak (AD 1206–1210)

Qutub-ud-din Aibak

Qutub-ud-din Aibak was the founder of the Delhi Sultanate, with Lahore as is capital. He was well known for his generosity and for this reason he earned the title of *Lakh-baksh* or giver of lakhs. He built two mosques, one at Ajmer and the other at Delhi - the *Quwat-ul-Islam* Mosque which is called as the first mosque in Delhi. He also laid the foundation of the Qutub Minar in Delhi to honour the famous Sufi saint, Qutub-ud-din Bakhtiyar Kaki. This monument remained incomplete as Qutub-ud-din Aibak died of a sudden fall from a horse, while playing *chaugan* or polo at Lahore in AD 1210. Later, Iltutmish finally completed the Qutub Minar.

Shams-ud-din Iltutmish (AD 1211–1236)

Shams-ud-din Iltutmish was a slave of Qutub-ud-din Aibak and occupied the throne of Delhi in AD 1211 after deposing Aram Bakhsh. Aram Baksh (1210-11), son of Qutub-ud-din Aibak, had a brief stint with the Delhi Sultanate and was eventually succeeded by Iltutmish. He was a very capable ruler and is regarded as the 'real founder of the Delhi Sultanate'. He made Delhi his capital in the place of Lahore. He also saved Delhi Sultanate from the wrath of Chengiz Khan, the Mongol leader, by refusing to give shelter to Khwarizm Shah, whom Chengiz was chasing. Thus, the Mongol policy of Iltutmish saved India from the wrath of Chengiz Khan. Iltutmish proved to be an able conquerer in a brief period. In 1228, Multan and Sindh were annexed to the sultanate. At the same time, he wielded control over Bengal and Bihar. With the assistance of Rajput chiefs, he became successful in suppressing the conquests. The conquest of Ujjain was detrimental to the existence of many ancient Hindu temples in the region. Subsequently, the ancient Mahal temple was decimated by the sultan. His military expeditions in the Hindu regions of Benaras, Badaun and Kannauj had truly overshadowed the might of the Hindu rulers.

In AD 1229, Iltutmish received a deed from the Abassid Caliph of Baghdad, which formally recognised his independent position as a Sultan. There after a new governing class or nobility was formed by Iltutmish, which was the ruling elite of the period and was known as *Turkan-i-Chahalgani* or *Chalisa* (a group of forty). He divided his kingdom into several small and big *iqtas*, as assignment of land instead of *salar*. In the medieval Indian currency system, the reign of Iltutmish stands out to be a milestone as he was the first Turkish ruler to introduce a purely Arabic coinage. He introduced the two basic coins of the Sultanate period, the copper coin (*jital*) and the silver coin (*tanka*). He also completed the construction of Qutub Minar, which was started by Aibak.

Silver Tanka of Iltutmish

Raziya Sultana (AD 1236–1240)

Since Iltutmish did not consider any of his sons to be capable of becoming a Sultan, he nominated his daughter, Raziya, as his successor. But the Turkish nobles opposed this move since

Raziya Sultana

they considered it below their dignity to be ruled by a woman and instead placed Rukn-ud-din Firoj on the throne. However, within seven months, Rukn-ud-din was removed from the throne and Raziya became the first and last woman among the Muslim rulers of Delhi Sultanate in AD 1236.

Raziya was a brave and able ruler and had all the qualities to rule Delhi Sultanate; the only weakness was that she was a woman. Besides dressing like a man, she led the armies in the battlefield. She held open court, gave up *purdah*, listened to the problems of her subjects and exercised general supervision over each department's work. As a result, some provincial governors and her own brother became hostile and rose against her. She tried to crush their revolt but was unsuccessful. She was defeated and imprisoned and her Abyssinian slave, Yakut was also killed. Though the leader of the rebels Altuniya defeated Raziya, she later married him. With his help, she tried to recover Delhi but in AD 1240, she became the victim of a conspiracy and was assassinated near Kaithal (Haryana).

After Raziya, Nasir-ud-din Mahmud the youngest son of Iltutmish ascended the throne after about six years of internal strife in AD 1246. He was a weak and pleasure loving king and left the administration to Ghiyas-ud-din Balban, the leader of the forty nobles, called the *Chalisa*.

Balban (AD 1266–1287)

Ghiyas-ud-din Balban ascended the throne in AD 1266 after killing Mahmud. He adopted a policy of severity and sternness in the sultanate. He was fully aware of the graveness of the situation. He understood that the Chahagani posed a real threat to the existence of the monarchy. As a matter of fact, he introduced rigid court discipline and practices, such as sijda (prostration before the sultan) and paibos (kissing the sultan's feet). At the same time, he initiated the Persian festival of Nauroz to convince the nobles and other subjects. According to Balban, monarch was the vice-regent of the almighty and was pure in principle. As a sultan, he considered himself to be the shadow of God on earth and the receiver of divine sanctions.

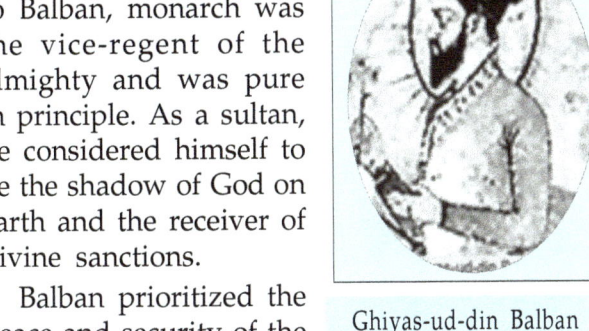
Ghiyas-ud-din Balban

Balban prioritized the peace and security of the state. Therefore, he established a centralized military department (dewan-i-arz) and reorganized the army. Earlier, the roads of Uttar Pradesh and Delhi were highly unsafe and infested with thugs, Balban installed military depots to check the corruption and internal crises. He also countered the Mongols who posed a serious threat to the Delhi Sultanate.

After Balban's death in AD 1286, one of his grandsons Kaiqubad was made the Sultan of Delhi. But after four years of his incompetent rule, the Slave Dynasty came to an end.

THE KHALJI DYNASTY (AD 1290–1320)

The history of Khalji Dynasty is marked by brutal wars and internal conflicts among the rulers.

Jalal-ud-din Khalji (AD 1290–1296)

The Khalji Dynasty started with the crowning of Jalal-ud-din Khalji by the nobles in the year AD 1290. He won the hearts of the people by his generosity, justice and affection. Since he came to the throne after killing Kaiqubad, he lavishly rewarded those people who helped him ascend the throne. He gave high titles and posts to his sons, relatives, friends and helpers and permitted the officers of the old regime to continue. He even tried to win over his enemies by love. In AD 1296, Ala-ud-din Khalji, his nephew, who proclaimed himself as the Sultan, treacherously murdered him.

Ala-ud-din Khalji (AD 1296–1316)

Ala-ud-din Khalji, whose real name was Juna Khan, was the most powerful ruler of this dynasty. On his accession to the throne, Ala-ud-din Khalji had to face the rebellion of Mongols who had earlier settled near Delhi. When he heard of the rebellion, he got some 20,000 to 30,000 Mongols killed in a single day. Afterwards, he brought the Rajput kingdoms of Malwa, Mewar, Marwar and Ranthambhor under his control. There is a legend associated with the Ala-ud-din Khalji, where the Queen Padmini had to commit Jauhar and die to save herself from Ala-ud-din Khalji. He tried to capture Chittor, the capital of Mewar by killing Rana Ratan Singh, her husband. After this, Ala-ud-din occupied several portions of Northern India by AD 1305.

Ala-ud-din Khalji

It was his policies of market regulations that made Ala-ud-din a popular historical character. He created three kinds of markets in Delhi and set the price of every commodity ranging from food grains to goods. The three markets were specified for food items and food grains, expensive cloth and thirdly for horses, slaves and cattle. *Shahna* or the controller of the market was in charge of the market that meted out severe punishments for under weighing goods and cheating of various kinds. In addition, there were other staffs, such as barids (intelligence officers), and the munhias (secret agents). They submitted their independent market-survey reports to the Sultan. Every merchant was registered with the commerce ministry. They signed a bond that guaranteed the regular supply of goods in which they traded. Ala-ud-din was the first Sultan who sent a Deccan expedition under the military commander Malik Kafur. All the kingdoms of the Deccan, namely, Warangal's Kakatiyas, Devagiri's Yadavas, Madurai's Pandyas and Dwara samudra's Hoysalas were occupied by Ala-ud-din by AD 1313, but were not conquered. These kingdoms had to accept Ala-ud-din's lordship and pay him tribute annually to protect their kingdoms and maintain peace.

Steps taken against Nobility : Owing to the rebellions caused by nobles, Ala-ud-din Khalji took some steps in handling the nobility. These steps were:

- The nobles had to seek permission of the Sultans to carry out any parties or festivities and form marriage alliances.
- Gambling, use of intoxicants and wine were forbidden and the gamblers were punished strictly.
- To keep a check on the actions of the nobles, Ala-ud-din set up an efficient system of spies, who along with the soldiers were paid in cash and not in land.

Military Reforms : Ala-ud-din Khalji was the first ruler of Delhi who laid the foundation of a permanent standing army. Besides importing quality horses, he started the system of branding horses, *dagh* so that the soldiers cannot replace them with horses of substandard quality. Also, he introduced the system of *chehra* that involved giving a kind of identity card to every soldier. He himself approved all recruitments to the army and paid cash salaries to the soldiers from the royal treasury.

Revenue Reforms : In order to get maximum revenue, Ala-ud-din Khalji introduced a number of important measures. He brought all the land of his kingdom into his direct control and introduced the practice of measuring the land and fixing the state share accordingly. He revoked all land grants made as gifts to Muslim clerics or Muslim landlords. He increased the land revenue, from one-third to one-half. He demanded the revenue to be paid in cash and not kind and appointed special officers for the purpose of collecting land revenue. Also, typically harsh treatment was meted out by him to Hindu landlords known as *Chaudharis* or *Muqaddams*.

In short, Ala-ud-din "once more revived the power and prestige, if not the dignity of the Court of Balban." He believed in the *"majesty of the Monarch and in his being God's representative on earth"*.

Qutub ud-din Mubarak Shah Khalji (AD 1316–1320)

Muhammad-bin Tughluq

After the death of Ala-ud-din in AD 1316, his son, Qutub-ud-din Mubarak Shah, succeeded him to the throne and became the third and last ruler of the Khalji dynasty in India. He was the weakest amongst all rulers of this dynasty and during his reign all taxes and penalties were abolished. He liberalised the strict administrative policies of Ala-ud-din and released all prisoners of war who were captured after waging gruesome battles. He was ultimately murdered by Khusrau Khan in AD 1320 thereby bringing the Khalji dynasty to an end in India.

THE TUGHLUQ DYNASTY (AD 1320–1414)

In AD 1320, Ghazi Malik succeeded the throne and assumed the title of Ghiyas-ud-din Tughlaq. He was the founder of the Tughluq dynasty.

Muhammadbin Tughluq (AD 1325–1351)

In AD 1325, Jauna Khan, the son of Ghiyas-ud-din ascended the throne and took the title of Muhammadbin Tughluq. He was one of the most significant rulers of his age who laid stress on efficiency. He had complete command over astronomy, mathematics, medicine and had great interest in philosophy and religion. Besides, he was a great lover of Persian literature, fine arts, music and calligraphy. However, historians have different views about the character of Muhammadbin Tughluq. According to them, he was known for his cruel and brutal punishments even for minor mistakes.

His five ambitious projects led him to ruin. Though his projects were well conceived, but they failed as he did not take the right steps to make them work. For this reason, some historians call him 'a mixture of opposites,' 'wisest fool,' 'a visionary,' 'mad man' and 'an idealist'.

Taxation in the Doab : The Sultan made an ill-advised financial project in the Doab in AD 1326 between the Ganges and Jamuna. He not only increased the rate of taxation but also revived and created some additional *Abwabs* (or land tax) in the fertile region of Ganga-Yamuna Doab, in order to get more revenue. But a severe famine broke out in the area at that time and people refused to pay the extra taxes and rose in rebellion. But the Sultan's tax collectors showed no compassion and took strict measures to collect the taxes. This behaviour made a number of the peasants desert their lands and escape to the jungles.

However, efficient steps were taken by Muhammadbin Tughluq to fight the famine and save the situation. He advanced loans to the peasants, ordered free distribution of grains and improved irrigation facilities but these measures came too late and agriculture suffered a heavy setback. In fact, numerous people had already starved to death by then.

Transfer of Capital : His second project was the spread of his kingdom to the south. In AD 1327, he shifted his capital to Devagiri, near modern Aurangabad and renamed it Daulatabad. There were many reasons for shifting the capital from Delhi. Firstly, Daulatabad was centrally located from where he could control the Deccan territories, in much better fashion. Secondly, Delhi was constantly threatened by the Mongol invasions. Lastly, Delhi was in the grip of severe famine. Therefore, he ordered the people of Delhi, including religious heads to shift to Daulatabad. However, after a couple of years, he decided to abandon Daulatabad largely because he soon found that just as he could not control south India from Delhi, he could not the North from Daulatabad. Thus, the decision of shifting the capital and coming back caused a lot of hardship for the people.

Introduction of Token Currency : The introduction of the 'token currency' was another controversial project taken by Muhammad-bin Tughluq in AD 1329. He introduced bronze *tanka* instead of silver *tankas*, as there was shortage of silver. This experiment failed, owing to the circulation of fake or forged coins on a very large scale that caused chaos in commerce and trade. According to Barani, the court historian of Muhammad-bin-Tughlaq and Firoz Shah Tughluq, the heaps of bronze coins rose like mountains near Tughlaqabad. Soon the new coins began to be greatly devalued in markets and consequently, the token currency was withdrawn by Muhammad-bin Tughluq.

Bronze Coin of Muhammad-bin Tughluq

Proposed Khurasan Expedition : The Sultan had a vision of universal conquest. For this purpose, he organised a huge army and paid the salary of one full year in advance to his soldiers. He decided to conquer Persia (Iran), Khurasan and Iraq. But the project was abandoned and the army was disbanded by Muhammad-bin Tughluq. He also sent an expedition to the Kumaon hills in the Himalayas. In this expedition, only 10 people out of an army of 10,000 returned and the rest perished. The royal treasury was depleted by these expeditions.

Qarachi Expedition : This expedition was launched in AD 1330 to counter Chinese incursions. It also appears that the expedition was directed against some refractory tribes in Kumaon-Garhwal region with the object of bringing them under Delhi Sultanate. The first attack was a success but when the rainy season set in, the invaders suffered terribly.

Since the experiments of Muhammad-bin Tughluq failed, his popularity also fell. He began losing the support of his people and many of his nobles and *ulema* (scholars of Islamic learning). Since revolts broke out in various parts of his empire, he had to move from one part of the country to another to suppress the rebellions. This not only wore out his armies but also exhausted his treasury. He died in AD 1351, while suppressing a revolt in Sindh.

Firoz Shah Tughluq (AD 1351–1388)

Since Muhammad-bin Tughluq had no male heir, his cousin Firoz Shah Tughluq ascended the throne. The long regime of Firoz Shah Tughluq (37 years) witnessed the resurgence of Sharia laws that were epitaphed by the Sultan on an octagonal tower near Firozabad Jami Mosque. Wazir Khan-i-Jahan Maqbul, a converted Muslim, preserved the legacy and prestige of the Sultan during that period. Though he was a distinguished military leader, he faced a difficult situation as the empire had already started breaking upduring the regime of Mohammad-bin Tughluq. Through land grants, he won the support of nobles and the *Ulema*. He established four new towns, Firozabad, Fatehabad, Jaunpur and Hissar. He introduced several reforms in the field of irrigation and also constructed roads, gardens, mosques and manufacturing centres called *karkhanas* (factories). Trade and agriculture flourished during his period and there was an increase in the general prosperity of the people. He built many schools and was a patron of scholars such as *Shams-i-Siraf Arif* and *Zia-ud-din Barani*. He also set up a department of charity known as *Diwan-i-Khairat* and gave financial help to the needy and the poor. A separate department was also set up by him to look after the slaves. However, the two major mistakes of his reign were, firstly to impose the *Jaziya* tax on Hindu pilgrims, which turned his Hindu subjects against him and secondly, he neglected the defence of the North-West Frontier.

The Tughluq dynasty would not survive much after Firoz Shah's death in AD 1388. The Sultanate grew very weak and shrunk in size as Malwa, Gujarat and Sharqi (Jaunpur) kingdoms broke away. Everywhere, the provincial governors and other ambitious chiefs hoisted the flag of revolt.

The final blow to the Tughluq dynasty was the invasion of Timur in AD 1398. He was a Mongol chieftain who invaded India during the reign of Nasir-ud-din Mahmud, the last Sultan of the dynasty. Timur easily defeated the army that was sent to resist him. During his stay of fifteen days, his army mercilessly sacked and plundered the people of Delhi. On his way back to Central Asia, he also looted places like Hardwar, Meerut, Jammu and Nagarkot. Timur returned to Central Asia, leaving a nominee Khizr Khan as his deputy in India who established the Sayyid dynasty in AD 1414.

After the Tughluq dynasty disintegrated, the Sayyid dynasty rose to power. The dynasty had four rulers who claimed to be the descendants of Prophet Mohammed.

After the death of Muhammad Shah, his son took over the throne under the title of Alam Shah. A quarrel between him and his *Wazir*, Hamid Khan, made it possible for Bahlul Lodhi to seize Delhi in AD 1451. He ruled Baduan till he died in the year AD 1478. With his death the Sayyid dynasty came to end.

The Lodhis were Afghans by race as it was established by the Ghizlai tribe of the Afghans. They formed the last phase of the Delhi Sultanate. There were three main rulers in the history of the Lodhi dynasty, viz., Bahlul Khan Lodhi, Sikandar Lodhi and Ibrahim Lodhi.

ADMINISTRATION AND SOCIAL LIFE UNDER THE DELHI SULTANATE

The Sultan was the supreme executive, judicial, legislative and military authority. A council of ministers advised him, including the '*wazir*' who acted as the Prime Minister and supervised the work of other officials. Though the Sultan depended greatly on the advice and efficiency of the wazir, the Sultan always took the final decisions. The Sultan also appointed people to sensitive posts and kept an eye on the expenditure and revenue. The chief judge was the '*Qazi*' who advised the Sultan on religious and civil matters.

During the Sultanate period, the kingdom was divided into '*Iqtas*' or provinces. Each province was placed under officials known as '*muqtis.*' The provinces were further divided into '*shiqs*' and '*parganas*' or districts in order to facilitate local administration. The lowest administrative unit was the village. The officials who worked at the village level were the '*muqaddam*' or the village headman, '*mushrif*' or village accountant and '*patwari*' or record-keeper. In order to settle local disputes, each village included a panchayat of wise men who were capable of resolving such matters.

Role of Nobles

The nobles held positions of military commanders and provincial governors and therefore, formed an extremely powerful group. They lived in great luxury and were given generous grants.

During this period, the practice of giving revenue grants from a territory was known as the 'iqta system' and the grantees were known as the 'iqtadars.' The iqtadars not only had to maintain themselves and their families out of this grant but also some soldiers used by the Sultan during the times of war. In fact, several of these 'iqtadars' functioned as independent rulers of the territories under their command when the central authority became weak.

Social Life

The Muslim nobility consisted of Turks, Persians, Mongols, Arabs, Afghans and the Indian Muslims. The Indian Muslims were looked down upon by the other races but the émigré Muslims also had differences among themselves. The Social Hierarchy was divided among Amirs, Maliks and Khans while the Ulema were also among the elites. Among the subject, the Hindus, the Chaudhuris or Landlords and the Merchants made up the higher castes and classes while the ordinary peasants were oppressed by both the Sultan and his Hindu intermediaries.

Persian Literature

The Delhi Sultans showed their inclination towards the advancement of Persian literature. In the aftermath of Islamic conquest of India, many Central Asia scholars flocked to the capital city, Delhi. Al-Beruni, accomplice of Mahmud Ghazni, was a remarkable Persian scholar and demonstrated his flair in writing Persian literary pieces. He gave a vivid account of India's plight during the 11th century in his notable work.

The Sultans of Delhi highly patronized the Persian scholars and they adorned their court with their presence. This led to the development of Persian literature in India. Khwaja Abu Nasr, poetically surnamed Nasiri, Abu Bakar Bin Muhammad Ruhani, Taj-ud-din Dabir and Nur-ud-din Muhammad Awfi were the phenomenal gems at the court of Sultan Iltutmish. *Nur-ud-din* wrote *Lubab-ul-Albab* and Amir Khusrav used Hindi dialects in the poetic verses and couplets.

Hindi Literature

The era of Delhi Sultanate saw the glimmering beginning of regional literature. There was a cascade of Hindi literature that mostly developed in Western Uttar Pradesh. The growth of Khari-boli and Braj-Bhasa culminated in the development of Hindi literature. For instance, *Prithviraj Raso* of *Chand Bardai*, the court-poet of Prithviraj Chauhan, the *Hammir Raso and the Hammir Kavya* by *Sarangdhar* and the *Alha-Khanda* produced by *Jagnayaka*. The prolific writer, *Vidyapati Thakur* who wrote in Sanskrit, Hindi and Maithili languages gave an impetus to the development of Maithili literature towards the start of the 15th century.

Urdu Literature

Initially, Urdu language was known as Hindavi. Both Hindi and Urdu shared common Indo-Aryan lineage and legacy. However, Urdu is closely linked with the Nastaliq script style of the Persian calligraphy and the script reads from right-to-left. The earliest sprinklings of Urdu literature started from the Muslim conquest of Sind in 711. Urdu language and literature developed decisively during the Sultanate and Mughal periods. Prominent works of Urdu are selected Poetry by *Muntakhib Kulliyat-I Zafar* or commonly known as *Bahadur Shah Zafar*, the drama of Akbar by *Muhammad Husain Azad* and Pushto-Urdu dictionary of *Khairullah*.

In Retrospect

- **Delhi Sultanate**: Five dynasties make the period of Delhi Sultanate namely, the Slaves from the period of, AD 1206 to AD 1290, the Khaljis from the period of AD 1290 to AD 1320, the Tughlaqs from the period of AD 1320 to AD 1413, the Sayyids from the period of AD 1414 to AD 1451, the Lodis from the period of AD 1451-1526.

- **Sources**: Tarikh-i-Firuz Shahi by Zia Barani and Prithviraj Raso by Chand Bardai are major literary historical sources that throws light on the history of sultanate. Archaeological sources- Qutub Minar in Delhi is major archaeological source of Delhi sultanate, it was founded by Qutub-ud-din Aibak in AD 1199 and completed by Iltutmish in AD 1230.

- **The Slave or Ilbari Dynasty**: Qutub-ud-din Aibak: Founder of the Slave Dynasty chose Lahore to be his capital and later shifted to Delhi, mainly devoted his attention to setting up law and order, initiated the construction of Qutub Minar, Iltutmish: He was a very capable ruler and is regarded as the real founder of the Delhi Sultanate, used diplomatic skills to maintain peace with Mongols, divided his kingdom into iqtas, introduced the two basic coins, the copper coin (jital) and the silver coin (tanka), Raziya Sultan: Medieval India's first Muslim woman ruler, dressed in men's attire and abolished the purdah system, nobles opposed her, Altunia rebelled and defeated, Altunia married her later she faced defeat and murder at the hands of Bahram Shah in AD 1240, Balban ruled between the years AD 1266–1287, broke the power of Chalisa, established the military department Diwani-i-Arz, exalted the position of kingship. His successors were weak and failed to keep the empire intact.

- **The Khalji Dynasty**: Jalal-ud-din Firoz Khalji was this first ruler of this Dynasty, known for his generosity, justice and affection, Ala-ud-din Khalji ascended the throne in AD 1296 and initiated the grandest phase of the Sultanate, conquered Gujrat, which was his first major conquest, he overpowered the Rajput rulers of Chittor, Ranthambhor and various parts of South India, introduced many reforms, handled the Mongols, the kingdoms of Warangal, Devagiri, Madurai and Dwarasamudra were defeated by Malik Kafur, his commander, and brought under the empire, Steps taken by Ala-ud-din regarding administration and revenue helped in regulation of good's prices, Qutub-ud-din Mubarak Shah Khalji turned the severe policies of Ala-ud-din into liberal policies, Khusrau Khan killed him.

- **The Tughluq Dynasty**: Ghiyas-ud-din Tughluq was the founder of Tughluq dynasty, founded the city Tughlaqabad; Muhammad-bin–Tughluq: A mix between eccentricity and scholarly personality, criticised for five of his projects which were, transferred his capital from Delhi to Devagiri, introduced token currency, raised the taxation rate in the Doab region, sent expedition for conquering Iraq and Khurasan, occupation of Qarachi, all of these policies failed, Firoz Shah Tughluq: took over populist tactic in administration that won over the Muslim clerics and made the Hindu subjects turn against him, encouraged agriculture and was an expert builder, was the founder of numerous cities, his successors were all weak that led to the attack of Timur which resulted in the final blow of Tughluq dyansty.

- **Administration and Social Life**: Theocracy prevailed, Islam became the State religion in the name of God, Sultans ruled, despotism of the Sultan, Islamic law was followed, wazir was the highest ranking officer, Chief Judge of the state was the Qazi, Naib Sultans or the provincial governors were in charge of provinces, Paraganas, Shiqs the smallest unit of the administration was the Village.

EXERCISES

Part-I (Short Questions)

1. Who was the founder of the Delhi Sultanate in India?
2. Name the five dynasties that formed the Delhi Sultanate.
3. Who laid the foundation of Qutub Minar?
4. Who was the founder of Slave Dynasty in India?

THE DELHI SULTANATE

5. What do you mean by the term *'Mamluks'*?
6. How did Iltutmish save India from Chengiz Khan.
7. Who was the only woman to sit on the throne of Delhi? She belonged to which dynasty?
8. What measures were taken by Balban to crush the Turkish nobles?
9. Who considered himself as God's shadow on earth?
10. What was *paibos*?
11. Which ruler established the Khalji dynasty?
12. Who established Tughluq Dynasty and when?
13. Describe how Ala-ud-din Khalji expanded his empire.
14. What measures did Ala-ud-din Khalji take for regulating prices and augmenting his resources?
15. Why Muhammad-bin Tughluq was referred as 'wisest fool' by some historians?
16. Name any two schemes of Muhammad-bin Tughluq that failed and led to his unpopularity.
17. Who was the successor to Muhammad-bin Tughluq? What were the various reforms introduced by him?
18. Who was Timur? What did he set out to procure from India?
19. Name the person who invited Babur to invade India.
20. Which battle marked the advent of the Mughal Empire?

Part-II (Structured Questions)

1. With reference to the sources, briefly discuss the important features of Qutub Minar
2. With reference to the Slave dynasty, write in detail about the main achievements of the following rulers:
   (a) Iltutmish
   (b) Balban
3. Who was Ala-ud-din Khalji and what reforms did he introduce?
4. Discuss in detail the failures of Muhammad-bin Tughluq in reference to:
   (a) Issuing of Currency
   (b) Transfer of Capital
   (c) Raising Taxes in Doab
5. Discuss the administration and social life under the Delhi Sultanate.

CHAPTER 9

THE MUGHAL EMPIRE

- Sources : Ain-i-Akbari, Taj Mahal, Jama Masjid and Red Fort.
- Political History and Administration (Babur, Akbar and Aurangzeb).

The Mughal Empire

Introduction
Sources for reconstructing the History of Mughal Empire

Literature
- Ain-i-Akbari
- Akbarnamah

Monuments
- Red Fort
- Taj Mahal
- Jama Masjid

The Mughal Emperors
- *Babur (AD 1526-1530)*
- *Humayun and The Suri Dynasty (AD 1530-1556)*
- *Sher Shah (AD 1540-1545)*
- *Akbar (AD 1556-1605)*
- *Jahangir (AD 1605-1627)*
- *Shah Jahan (AD 1628-1658)*
- *Aurangzeb Alamgir (AD 1658-1707)*

Administrative and Social Developments
- *Rajput Policy of Akbar*
- *Administrative System of Akbar*
  - *Mansabdari System*
  - *Land Revenue System*
  - *Religious Policies of Akbar*
- *Policies of his Succesors*

Decline of the Mughals

INTRODUCTION

Before Babur's invasion of India in AD 1526, various independent kingdoms that arose on the ruins of the Delhi Sultanate ruled India without any potent central authority. The independent states of Mewar, Bengal, Gujarat, Jaunpur and Malwa were continuously combating against one another. These mutual rivalries helped Babur to establish the supremacy of the Mughals in the Indian subcontinent.

SOURCES FOR RECONSTRUCTING THE HISTORY OF MUGHAL EMPIRE

Mughal History can be reconstructed from the various historical evidences like monuments, chronicles, coins, account of foreign travellers, historical letters, royal *firmans*, inscriptions, religious literature and many more that were produced during the Mughal period. However, the most important sources of information come from the period of Akbar. These are :

Literature

Abul Fazl's Ain-i-Akbari and Akbarnamah

Abul Fazal, a minister and one of the famous Nine Jewels of the court of Akbar, authored these chronicles. These are immensely valuable sources for gathering knowledge about the culture and nature of administration during the rule of Akbar. His best known historical works are *Ain-i-Akbari* and the *Akbarnamah*. Written in elegant Persian, *Ain-i-Akbari* comprises five books, the first of which describes the royal household. The second book gives details about the civil and military services and the servants of the Emperor. The third book gives details about the administration of the empire that consists of the set of laws for the executive and judicial departments and discusses how the empire was divided. The fourth book provides information about science, literature, social customs and Hindu philosophy at that time. The fifth and the final book recounts the wise sayings of Akbar. The *Akbarnamah* is a primary source that informs us about Akbar's life, the royal household and the royal court. Some other important sources for the Mughal period are 'Tabaqat-i-Akbari' by Nizam-ud-Din Ahmed, 'Tuzuk–i-Jahangiri' by emperor Jahangir himself or the memoirs of Jahangir, Inayat Khan's 'Shahjahannama' and Muhammad Kazim's 'Alamgirnama'.

Monuments

Red Fort, Delhi

Shah Jahan built Red Fort or *Lal Qila* when he decided to transfer his capital to Delhi. Its construction began in AD 1639 and completed in AD 1648.

Architectural Features

- It is a huge structure made of red sandstone and marble.
- The fort is in the shape of a parallelogram with massive walls around it.
- It has two main Gateways of which the Lahori Gate was used for ceremonial purposes and other Gateway for private use.

Red Fort, Delhi

Some of the prominent buildings in this fort are the *Diwan–i-Aam*, the *Diwan-i-Khas* and the *Rang Mahal*. These buildings are decorated with pure white marble and inlaid with precious stones. The famous Peacock Throne studded with precious stones including the *Kohinoor* was historically kept in the *Diwan-i-Khas*.

Jama Masjid, Delhi

Jama or Jami Masjid is the biggest mosque in India and is situated near the Red Fort in the ancient town of old Delhi. Mughal Emperor, Shah Jahan built it during the AD 1650-1656.

Jama Masjid, Delhi

Architectural Features

- The mosque is built on a high platform with three onion-shaped domes of white marble decorated with strips of black colour.
- Its courtyard is 37 meters wide and can accommodate as many as 10,000 people at a time.
- It has four minarets in the four corners and a flight of 31 majestic steps leading to the imposing gateways on three sides of the courtyard.
- The face of the massive prayer hall consists of eleven arches. This is the most spectacular feature of this magnificent construction.

Taj Mahal, Agra

Taj Mahal is one of the supreme accomplishments of the Mughal Empire. Shah Jahan built this grand mausoleum in the memory of his beloved wife Mumtaz Mahal on the banks of the river Yamuna. Its construction began in AD 1634 and continued for almost 22 years. Ustad Isa was the architect who designed the monument.

Architectural Features

- It is made of pure white marble.
- It stands on a raised platform and is surmounted by *cupolas* at each corner.

Taj Mahal, Agra

- The bulbous dome in the centre has the appearance of an inverted lotus. There are four smaller domes at the four corners of the building.
- The Four *minarets* at each corner of the terrace are decorated with beautiful cupolas and pinnacles.
- The outer walls and the interior walls of tomb are richly decorated with flawless sculptures and inlaid design of flowers and calligraphy. The design is typical Persian import, regarded as 'Pietra Dura'. It is highly remarkable in the field of architectural work and designing monuments.

It has been rightly described as *'treasure in beauty'* and *'dream in marble'*. Because of its exceptional qualities, the Taj Mahal is considered to be one of the wonders of the world.

THE MUGHAL EMPERORS (CHRONOLOGICAL BACKGROUND)

Babur (AD 1526–1530)

Zahir-ud-din Muhammad Babur was the founder of Mughal Empire in India. He was the son of Umar Sheikh Mirza, the ruler of Farghana, a small principality of Central Asia. He was a direct descendent of Timur through his father and also a descendent of Chengiz Khan through his mother. Babur called his dynasty *'Timurids'* because of their connections with Timur but it is better known as the Mughal Dynasty.

At a tender age of 11 years, Babur succeeded to the throne of Farghana. Babur always wanted to occupy Samarkand, the capital of Timur, which he captured twice but was unable to keep. Giving up his dream of capturing Samarkand for long, Babur established himself in Kabul in 1504. He then directed his attention towards India and carried out five invasions. The first one was in 1519 when he captured Bhera and the last being in April 1526, where in the First Battle of Panipat, Babur defeated Ibrahim Lodi. With this victory, Babur secured his ownership of Agra and Delhi.

Babur

However, Babur's conquest of Hindustan was incomplete till he defeated Rana Sanga who was the leading Rajput prince of Mewar of that period. Consequently, in 1527, Babur defeated Rana Sanga in the Battle of Khanua, 60

THE MUGHAL EMPIRE

kilometres west of Agra. In 1528, Babur occupied Chanderi from a Rajput chief, Medini Rai and in 1529 he took on territories close to the confluence of Ganges and Ghagra River in the Battle of Ghagra, when he defeated the combined force of Afghan chiefs headed by Mahmud Lodi and the army of Nusrat Shah of Bengal. All these conquests consolidated Babur's hold on Hindustan. However, he could not enjoy his position for long as he died in Agra on 26 December 1530. His autobiography, *Tuzuk-i-Babari* or *Baburnamah* gives a detailed record about his entire career.

Humayun (AD 1530-1556)

Humayun, the eldest son of Babur, ascended the throne after his death. He divided the entire empire inherited from his father among his three brothers as Babur died before consolidating his empire. He had to face lot of trouble as imperial treasury was almost bankrupt. Political forces of Bengal, Malwa and Gujarat were against the Mughals. However, his greatest foe was Sher Shah Suri, the Afghan Chief who attacked and defeated Humayun at Kannauj and Chausa in 1540. Following this defeat, Humayun fled to Persia where he remained for 15 years (AD 1540–1555) in exile. Meanwhile, Humayun's wife Hamida Begum gave birth to Jalal-ud-din Muhammad in Sindh, in 1542. However, Humayun came back to India and regained his empire in 1555 after defeating the successors of Sher Shah with the help of the ruler of Persia.

Emperor Humayun

Humayun remained the emperor for a very short period after this and died after falling from the stairs of his library (now called Purana Qila) on 24 January 1556.

Sher Shah Suri (1540-1545)

Sher Shah Suri was the emperor of Islamic Sur-Afghan dynasty of 1540-57. He established a long standing bureaucracy, which was responsible to the ruler. At the same time, he created a stable and functional revenue system. After defeating the Bengal army, he reigned in Bihar. In early 1539, he attacked and annexed Bengal. On June 26, 1539, he betrayed the Mughal Emperor, Humayun at the Battle of Chausa and took up the regal title of Farid-al-Din Sher Shah. In May 1540, he betrayed Humayun again, and had driven his enemies away from Bengal, Bihar and other parts of India. He also subdued the Baluch chiefs on the North Western frontier. He had an intention of extending the horizons of the Delhi Sultanate. As a matter of fact, he besieged Gwalior and Malwa. However, he died during the capture of Kalinjar.

Sher Shah Suri

One of the important rulers of India, Sher Shah Suri rose to the height of greatness from the depth of obscurity. He was a great administrator of army and financial revenues. He embarked on the project of building roads, rest houses and wells for the mass at large. He adopted an 'impartial attitude' towards all religions. His tomb at Sasaram in the Bihar district of India sets a brilliant example of art and craftsmanship.

Akbar (AD 1556-1605)

Jalal-ud-din Muhammad, popularly known as Akbar, was the greatest of all Mughal rulers in India. He ascended the throne when he was 13 years old under the guardianship of Bairam Khan. After Humayun's death, Bairam Khan crowned Akbar at Kalanaur in Punjab. In 1556, the Second Battle of Panipat was fought under the leadership of Bairam Khan, who marched into Delhi and defeated Hemu taking Agra back as the capital of Mughal Empire. In 1560 Akbar asserted his position sending off Bairam Khan to Mecca. The year 1561 marked the beginning of Akbar's

Akbar

policy of conquest and building a vast empire by occupying Malwa and Gondwana. In 1561, he also earned the control of Chunar fort and in 1576 he seized Bengal. In 1578, Gujarat came under Akbar's control and subsequently in 1586 and 1587 Kashmir and Kabul fell to Akbar.

Akbar was the sole Mughal ruler who earned the alliance of the Rajputs and extended his reach towards the Deccan. By 1601, the areas of Khandesh, Ahmadnagar and Berar came under the control of the Mughals. He fulfilled his ambition of gaining control over the entire Indian subcontinent to reduce the increasing influence of the Portuguese in the South and the prosperous economy of the south. However, he had to retire to North India, where his son Salim revolted against him. Akbar spent his last years facing rebellion from his son and finally died in 1605, after he declared Salim as the heir to the throne.

Jahangir (AD 1605-1627)

Jahangir

Salim, who adopted the name of Jahangir, succeeded to the throne on 3 November 1605. Jahangir built on his father's foundations of excellent administration and his reign was characterized by political stability, a strong economy and impressive cultural achievements. Jahangir was reluctant to decide on religious matters. But it does not mean that he was atheist or agnostic. He highly prioritized the administration of his empire. His son, Shah Jahan, followed the religious policy of Akbar. At the other end of the spectrum, Jahangir embraced his father's foreign policy and far-sightedness both in Southern and Northern India. Akbar initiated the Rajput policy, which was moulded by Jahangir. He finished the annexation of Mewar, which was started by Akbar. As far as foreign relations were concerned, Jahangir received Sir Thomas Roe in his court in 1615. At his behest, the English merchants could freely conduct their trade in Gujarat. They secured the rights of establishing factories at Ahmedabad and Agra.

Shah Jahan (AD 1628-1658)

Shah Jahan

Before his accession to the throne, Shah Jahan countenanced a host of problems. Nur Jahan, mother of Shahryar, backed his son to ascend the throne of the Mughal Empire. After a brief span of power struggle with his half-brother, Shahryar, Shah Jahan ascended the throne in 1628. Eventually, Shahryar was blinded and arrested.

The epoch of Shah Jahan is characterized as the 'Golden Age' of Indian culture and architecture. This period witnessed cultural efflorescence that reached its zenith. At the same time, he is known to have pioneered the construction of several beautiful monuments that permeated the northern landscape ('Taj Mahal' of Agra and 'Red Fort' of Delhi are discussed earlier in the chapter). Shah Jahan also founded the modern city of Delhi. During that time, the city came to be known as Shahjahanabad.

After his advent in the political scene, Shah Jahan renewed the Deccan policy of the Mughals. Incidents of principal aggressions of the reign of Shah Jahan were the demolition of the Ahmadnagar Kingdom (1638), loss of Kandahar to the Persians (1653) and a notable Second war against the Deccani princes (1655). After the death of Shah Jahan in 1666, Aurangzeb ascended the Mughal throne.

Aurangzeb Alamgir (AD 1658-1707)

On 21 July 1658, Aurangzeb crowned himself as the emperor of Delhi taking up the title of *Alamgir* after a long and fierce power struggle. But his formal coronation took place on 5 June 1659 after the battles of Khanwa and Deorai. On being officially crowned in 1569, he abolished octroi tax (*pandari*) and the inland transit duties (*rahdari*). Many oppressive land revenues and taxes were also eradicated. Throughout the 50 years of his rule, Aurangzeb extended the reach of the Mughal Empire to its peak, ranging from Western Kabul to Eastern Chittagong and Northern Kashmir to the Southern River Kaveri. In spite of this success he had to face many rebellions and strife throughout his rule. For putting Quranic law into effect properly, censors of public morals (*muhtasibs*) were appointed in huge cities and rituals like *Jharokha darshan* and weighing the emperor on his birthday were stopped. He also discontinued the practice of inscribing the *kalmia* on the coins and the celebrations of the New Year's Day (*nauraz*). In the sphere of art and architecture, his reign was not highly remarkable. Aurangzeb constructed Moti Masjid (Pearl Mosque) in the Red Fort Complex in Delhi and also supervised the construction of Badshahi Mosque in Lahore. He constructed the largest mosque in Srinagar. In Aurangabad, the structure of Bibi Ka Maqbara was developed in memory of his wife Rabia-ud-Daurani. Moreover, Aurangzeb was noted for his brilliant calligraphy, which was inscribed in many inscriptions of the historic monuments.

Aurangzeb Alamgir

On the political and administrative front, the Deccan expeditions of Aurangzeb were divided into two parts– the first was invasion of Bijapur and Golconda and the other was the long-standing war with Marathas that continued for four generations. Besides his lack of wisdom in handling the Rajputs and the Deccan, he ordered the arrest and execution of the ninth Sikh guru Teg Bahadur that led to the creation of *Khalsa* and the growth of Sikh military under the last Sikh Guru Govind Singh. Aurangzeb died in 1707, leaving behind a crumbling empire.

ADMINISTRATIVE AND SOCIAL DEVELOPMENTS

Though Babur founded the Mughal Empire in India and Humayun reconquered it from the descendants of Sher Shah, yet it is Akbar who is regarded as the true founder of the Mughal Empire in India. His administrative and social policies were central to the development of the empire that continued for another two centuries. Some of his successors followed his example while others developed their own policies. We discuss them in the following section.

Rajput Policy of Akbar

In 1562, Akbar married a Rajput princess, the daughter of Raja Bharmal of Amer, following which he entered into many such marital alliances. This laid the foundation for smooth relations between the Mughals and the Rajputs; Akbar not only ensured freedom for his Rajput wives to follow Hinduism but granted honourable status to their parents and relatives. By the end of 1570, every Rajput kingdom had followed suit, except Mewar. All these conquests were done without resorting to arms, which marks the success of Akbar's conciliatory policy. Since the Rajputs were given equal status in the Mughal government, the centuries–old rivalry between Mughals and Rajputs was put to an end.

Administrative Systems of Akbar

Akbar organized his Empire and divided it into 12 *Subahs* at the top. These were again sub-divided into *Sarkars*, followed by further subdivisions known as *Parganas* or Mahals. The Prime Minister called *Vakil* seconded the Emperor. All the income and expenses were managed by the head of the Revenue Department, who was known as the *Wazir* or *Diwan* or *Diwan-i-ala*. *Mir Bakshi* headed the military department while *Mir Saman* was incharge of royal household. *Qazi* was the head of the Judiciary and *Sadar* was in charge of helpful and religious matters.

Mansabdari System

This system was made up of a group of *Mansabdars*, who were the officials of the Mughal Empire. These officers were given specific rank or mansab either in the bureaucracy, military hierarchy or the nobility. The lowest rank was 10 while the highest was 5000 and these ranks had two divisions. First was *Zat*, which indicated the status of a person and how much he is to be paid, while the other,

Sawar stands for the designated amount of cavalrymen, he had to maintain. Like for every 10 cavalrymen, 20 horses were to be kept.

Land Revenue System

Akbar had set up a uniform system for measuring land tax to which various schemes were added by Todar Mal, to enhance the imperial treasury. The State provided loans to deprived farmers in sectors of agriculture, trade and industry to ensure growth and progress.

Religious Policies of Akbar

Akbar was specially known for his numerous liberal religious policies, which brought harmony, peace and religious tolerance among his subjects and helped in maintaining good relations with the Rajputs. He removed *Jizyah*, a tax paid only by non- Muslims. He also prohibited conversion of war prisoners to Islam without their consent and eradicated the pilgrim tax, which non-Muslims had to pay for bathing at Banaras, Prayag and other holy places. Akbar built a Hall of Worship called *Ibadat Khana* at Fatehpur Sikri in 1575, where he invited selected theologians and mystics to foster philosophical discussions.

By issuing a 'Declaration' or *mahzar*, Akbar became the supreme authority in religious matters. Studying and comparing different religions, Akbar came up with a new religion called *Din-i-Ilahi or Jaukind-i-Ilahi* in AD 1580. Through this religion he propagated notions of divine monotheism or oneness of God and stressed on courage, justice and loyalty to God and to the emperor as well. *Sulh- Kul* or universal harmony was the purpose of formulating this religion that guided Akbar in all his public policies.

Policies of his Successors

Jahangir tried to follow Akbar's liberal policy from the beginning of his rule but not with great success. In 1606, Jahangir's son Khusrau rebelled against his father at Lahore, who was blinded and killed in 1622. Arjun Dev, the 5th Sikh Guru who sheltered the rebel prince was killed as he refused to pay fine for his act. This strained the Mughal–Sikh relations forever. With regards to administration Jahangir did not make any changes.

Aurangzeb faced numerous problems throughout his reign. The most serious of these was the Maratha Insurgency, that began under their charismatic leader Shivaji. Moreover Aurangzeb also disrupted relations between Mughals and Sikhs by killing Guru Teg Bahadur. This resulted in the creation of the *Khalsa*, which is the military sect of the Sikhs. The greatest loss to the empire was the loss of the Rajputs as allies who parted ways after Aurangzeb tried to meddle in the succession disputes of Marwar. Faced with these difficulties he adopted a number of harsh measures that made matters worse. By 1667, the Muslim merchants were excluded from paying the taxes unlike the Hindu merchants and celebration of any Hindu festival became restricted by 1668. *Jizyah* was also reintroduced on Hindus. Under Aurangzeb the Mughal Empire lost many of its valuable non-Muslim supporters, especially the Rajput's.

Aurangzeb's Deccan Policy

Aurangzeb's aggressive Deccan policies presaged the downfall of the mighty Mughal Empire. Due to the implementation of this policy, the sultan remained absent from the seat of governance in Delhi. As a matter of fact, the capital became the hub of discontent and heated rebellions. The adversaries like the Jats, the Rajputs and the Sikhs challenged the authority of the Mughal Empire. The Marathas began to ravage the towns and massacre households treasures. Aurangzeb rose staunchly against the Shia Muslim dynasties in South India, mainly Bijapur and Golconda. In order to firmly establish his policies in Deccan, he lost control over the capital, which resulted in the steady decline of the Mughal Empire. His protracted Deccan policy decimated Mughal power and influence in the North. The treasury was also eclipsed by the Deccan policy of Aurangzeb.

The Mughal Empire which had reached its zenith, began to decline after the reign of Aurangzeb. There were many causes for the downfall of the Mughal Empire.

Coming of Europeans

The Europeans, especially the British, played a major role in putting an end to the Mughal Empire. They obtained a *firman* to trade with India. Gradually, they started interfering in Indian politics and established a British Empire in India which lasted for about 200 years.

Foreign Invasions

The invasions of Nader Shah and Ahmad Shah Abdali proved fatal to the Mughal Empire. As a result, India also became an easy prey for foreign rulers. In 1739, Nader Shah, the Afsharid Shah of Persia invaded and sacked the Mughal Empire. He emptied the coffers of the empire and looted several valuables, including Shah Jahan's famous Peacock throne and Kohinoor diamond.

Ahmad Shah Abdali conquered India seven times from 1748 to 1767. To the opinion of JaswantLal Mehta, Durrani (Abdali) stirred the Afghan's "religious enthusiasm" to fire and "sword into the lands of infidels India."

All these factors led to the steady dounfall of the Mughal Empire.

In Retrospect

- *Sources that aid in Reconstruction of the Age of the Mughals* : Literary sources like Akbarnama and Ain-i-Akbari by Abul Fazal, autobiography of Jahangir and Shah Jahannama by Inayat Khan, Archaeological sources like Fatehpur Sikri's, buildings and monuments like Humayun tomb, Agra Fort, Red fort, Jama Masjid and Taj Mahal.
- *Babur* : Family history relates to Chengiz Khan and Timur, founder of the Indian Mughal Empire after winning the First Battle of Panipat against Ibrahim Lodi in 1526, he was victorious at Khanua, overpowered the joint forces of Bihar and Bengal, in 1529 Mewar's Rana Sanga was defeated by him, occupied Chanderi and overpowered the Afghan Chiefs, passed away in 1530 in Agra, this man of great valour.
- *Humayun* : Successor of Babur, Sher Shah overpowered him at Kannauj and Chausa in 1540, spent 15 years of his life in exile, after regaining his empire for a short period he died in 1556.
- *Akbar* : Succeeded Humayun at the age of 13 under the supervision of Bairam Khan, defeated Hemu in 1556, initiated a series of conquests and occupied Chunar and Malwa, gained the support of the Rajputs by matrimonial alliances, brought Surat, Bengal, Mewar, Bihar and Orissa, his achievements in areas of architecture, art and literature are remarkable, started a new religion called Din-i-Ilahi.
- *Jahangir* : Brought Mewar and Mughal Empire together in AD 1615, extended Akbar's territory, lost Kandahar to Persia, patronized art, architecture, literature and painting, established trade relations between England and India.
- *Shah Jahan* : Ascended the throne of Agra in 1628, suppressed rebellions and drove out the Portuguese from Hughli in 1632, brought Ahmadnagar, Golconda and Bijapur and appointed Aurangzeb as Deccan's viceroy. In 1658, Aurangzeb carried out an assault on Agra and imprisoned Shah Jahan till his death. Mughal Architecture reached its golden period under the rule of Shah Jahan.
- *Aurangzeb* : In 1658, crowned himself as emperor of Delhi and assumed the title of Alamgir, took measures to lessen the economic woes of the people, his period of rule can be divided into two parts; one spent in Northern India for 25 years, while the other in the Deccan, ordered the arrest and execution of the ninth Sikh guru Teg Bahadur that led to the creation of Khalsa.

EXERCISES

Part-I (Short Questions)

1. Who founded Mughal rule in India ?
2. Why did the Mughals call themselves *Timurids* ?
3. Name the two important literary sources of the Mughal rulers.

4. State the name of Babur's Autobiography.
5. Name the supreme architectural monument of Shah Jahan's reign.
6. Where did Humayun live in exile for 15 years ?
7. Mention the three obligations that the Rajput states had towards Akbar.
8. What was the last victory of Akbar and why ?
9. State the consequences of Akbar's policy of religious tolerance.
10. What is significant about the mansabdari system of Akbar ?
11. What were 'Din-I-Ilahi' and 'Sulh-kul' ?
12. What were the principles of Akbar's *Din-i-Ilahi* ?
13. What made the alliance between the Sikhs and the Mughals got disrupted ?
14. Why did Nur Jahan back the cause of Shahryar to become the heir apparent to the throne ?
15. Give the name of two significant centres of trade from the Mughal period.
16. State the two stages of Aurangzeb's moves in the Deccan area.
17. What were the reforms introduced in Deccan by Aurangzeb, when he was the Viceroy ?
18. What was the role of *Diwan-i-ala* ?
19. What was the *Mansabdari* system ?
20. What was *Jizyah* ?
21. What was the name of the new religion propounded by Akbar ?

Part-II (Structure Questions)

1. With reference to the sources of Mughal Empire, write short notes on :
   (a) *Ain-i-Akbari* and *Akbarnamah*
   (b) Architectural features of monuments built during Mughal period.
2. Discuss the battles fought by Babur to strengthen his position in India.
3. Describe the measures taken by Akbar to consolidate the position of his Empire in India.
4. Akbar is regarded as the true founder of the Mughal Empire in India. In this context, discuss :
   (a) Administrative system,
   (b) Religious policy of Akbar.
5. Answer the following question with reference to Jahangir and Shahjahan :
   (a) Jahangir's contribution to the growth of the Mughal Empire.
   (b) Shahjahan's contribution to the growth of Mughal Empire.
   (c) Which event took place during the last year of Shah Jahan's reign ? What was its result ?
6. Elucidate the steps taken by Aurangzeb that affected the Mughal Empire destructively.
7. What were the causes that led to the decline of the Mughal Empire ?

CHAPTER 10

EMERGENCE OF COMPOSITE CULTURE

- Sources : Bijak, Guru Granth Sahib, Ajmer Sharif, St. Francis Assisi Church (Kochi).
- Significance of Bhakti Moments and Sufism (Mirabai, Sant Jnaneshwar and Hazrat Nizamuddin).

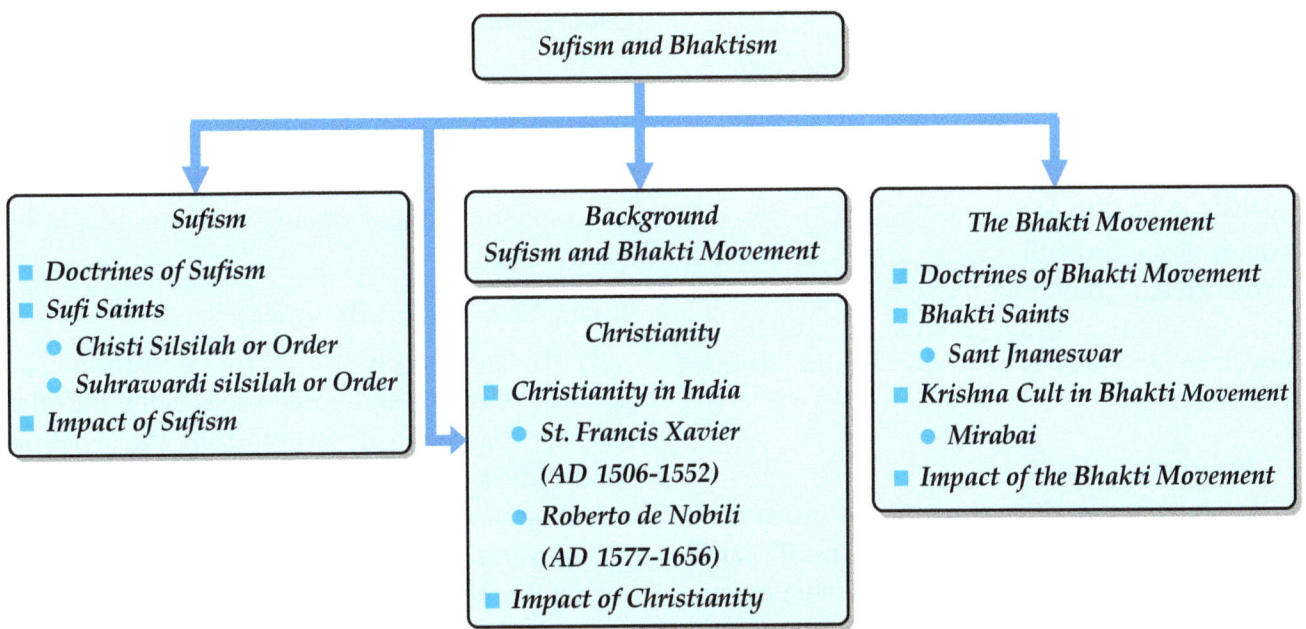

BACKGROUND

Culturally, the medieval period marks the beginning of a new stage in the growth of India's composite culture. The period saw the emergence of two great religious movements-The Bhakti Movement and the Sufi Movement. Both the movements condemned caste inequalities and laid stress on universal brotherhood. The mystics of the Bhakti movement composed hymns and sang *bhajans* to preach the message of love and universal brotherhood. The Sufis or the Muslim mystics also preached their message through music. Along with these movements, a new religion called Christianity also spread across India, which was preached by the Jesuit missionaries. They were members of the Society of Jesus, who preached the teachings of Jesus Christ through sermons and music. According to them, Christianity is based solely on faith in the salvation offered through Jesus Christ through the grace of God alone. It is not based on works, or particular acts of the worshipper. These movements played a leading role in combating religious exclusiveness and narrow-mindedness and in bringing the people of all communities together.

SOURCES

Bijak

Kabir was a 15th-century Indian mystic poet. He criticized both Hindus and Muslims for their meaningless ritualism, orthodoxy and dogmatic tradition. His teachings and philosophy are found in his book, Bijak. According to Carol E. Henderson, Kabir opined that the Hindus were misled by the orthodoxy of the Vedas. On the other hand, the Muslims were misguided by the rigor of Quran. He questioned the absurd religious customs like sacred thread and circumcision respectively. One of his poems states God is found not in temples, nor in mosques, nor in churches : not in crowds, nor in kirtans, nor in eating nothing but vegetables. When you really look for God, you will see him instantly, inside you. Another of his Dohas states; the river that runs through you also runs through me. Kabir was revered by Hindus, Muslims and Sikhs and many of his poems are found in the Adi Granth. Rabindranath Tagore also held Kabir in reverence and translated many of his poems. The Bijak is an important source of the Bhakti movement and tells us what the Bhakti movement was about.

Guru Granth Sahib

Another source of the Bhakti movement is the Holy Book of the Sikhs, the **Guru Granth Sahib,** which is considered to be the final, sovereign and everlasting Guru of the Sikhs. The Guru Granth Sahib is the spiritual revelation of not only the 10 Sikh Gurus but also the Bhakti saints like Kabir, Namdev, Jayadev, Surdas, Ramdas, Baba Farid, a sufi saint, among others. The Guru Granth Sahib teaches that there is only one God, that everyone is equal, that men and women are equal. One should live truthfully and according to God's will. One should practice humility, kindness, compassion and love. One should always keep an open mind and keep learning.

Ajmer Sharif

Ajmer Sharif or Ajmer Dargah is the shrine built over the grave of the Sufi Saint Hazrat Khwaza Muinuddin Chisti, which is located in Ajmer, Rajasthan. Khwaza Muinuddin Chisti was revered by people belonging to all religious groups because of his message of peace, selfless service, helping the poor and the needy and fellow feeling. Even today people flock to his Dargah specially during the Urs or his death anniversary because they believe that praying to him will take away all harmful things.

St. Francis Assissi Church (Kochi)

The Church of St. Francis of Assissi in Fort Kochi is another monument to build the composite culture of India. It was built by the Portuguese and once housed the remains of Vasco da Gama, which was later removed to Lisbon. The Portuguese were Roman Catholics. It was taken over by the Dutch who were Protestants and then taken over by the British and was an Anglican Church. Today it is under the Archaeological Survey of India and is a protected monument open to all the people of India.

Sufism and Bhakti Movement

With the advent of Islam, a number of cultural, religious and social ideas came into the country that were different from the existing Hindu ideas. The distinct cultural ideas of Islam including oneness of God, brotherhood of man and surrender of man to God's will, made an impact on the Indian reformers and thinkers. While the Indian thinkers were impressed by the Islamic open-door policy towards all men, irrespective of caste and non-ritualistic attitude towards religion, the liberal thinkers of Islam were impressed by the Hindu theory of *karma* - the belief that bad or good actions carry their punishments or rewards. This Indo-Islamic culture led to the development of two liberal religious reform movements in India, the Bhakti and Sufi movements. The essential unity of Hinduism and Islam was emphasized by a number of Bhakti and Sufi saints who laid stress on a belief based on devotion and love rather than on rituals. The Bhakti and Sufi movements played an important role in nurturing and fostering Indo-Islamic culture.

SUFISM

The word '*Sufi*', derived from the Arabic word '*Suf*' (wool), referred to the mystics who used to wear only a coarse woollen garment. Some scholars believe that the word 'Sufi' has come from the word '*safa*' that means purity.

Sufism was a liberal reform movement within Islam that started in Persia and Arabia as an endeavour to bridge the differences between the *Shia* and *Sunni* sects of Islam. Sheikh Ismail of Lahore was the first known Sufi who brought this movement to India in the eleventh century AD. According to Sufis, all religions were different paths for reaching the same God. They preached oneness of God, religious tolerance and brotherhood. The Sufi saints believed in simple living and personal devotion and love as a means of reaching out of God. The Sufi saints were respected by liberal Hindus and Muslims and their teachings were similar to the Vedantic philosophy.

Doctrines of Sufism

The main doctrines of Sufism were :
- Fundamental unity and respect for all religions.
- God is the supreme reality. He should be worshipped through love and personal devotion.
- The individual soul is the manifestation of the supreme God.
- Self-discipline and inner purity are basics for gaining knowledge of God.
- Meditation and chanting of God's name (*zikr*) are very important.
- Lead a simple life. Show charity towards the poor.
- Follow a *guru* or *pir* who would show the correct path.
- Brotherhood and equality of all human beings, irrespective of colour, caste, creed and religion.

The Sufi Saints

The Sufi saints of Central Asia and Persia were organized into 12 *silsilahs* or orders, each named after its founder. The literal meaning of the word 'silsilah' is chain and it signifies a continuous link between the disciple and the master. The leader or head of the order was known as the *pir* and the followers were known as the *murids*. The *pir* nominated a *wali* as his successor. Each Sufi order had a hermitage or *Khanqah*, which was the residence of the Sufi saints and their followers. The Sufi saints who settled in India belonged to the two very popular orders i.e., *Suhrawardi* and *Chisti* orders.

Chisti silsilah or Order : In AD 1161, Khwajah Muin-ud-din Chisti came to India with Mahmud of Ghazni and founded the Chisti Order. He advised his followers to live in peace and harmony with one another and to respect all religions. Till his death in AD 1236, he made Ajmer his headquarters. His *dargah* or tomb at Ajmer is considered an important pilgrimage centre and is visited by thousands of Muslim and Hindu devotees every year. An annual festival known as *Urs* is also held at this place.

Other popular sufi saints of the chishti silsilah were Sheikh Qutb-ud-din Bakhtiyar Kaki and his disciple Sheikh Farid *or* Baba Farid of Multan, Sheikh Salim Chisti of Sikri, Fari-ud-din Ganj-i-Shakar, Nasir-ud-din Chirag-i-Dilli and perhaps the greatest sufi saint ever, Hazrat Nizam-ud-din-Auliya, popularly referred to as '*Mehboob-i-llahi*' (Beloved of God) by his followers.

Nizamuddin Auliya : Nizamuddin Auliya was a saint of the Chishti order or silsila. He followed the footsteps of Baba Farid, Bakhtiyar Kaki and Muinuddin Chishti. He influenced the Muslims of Delhi to such an extent that Emperors, nobles and ordinary people changed their outlook and became more inclined towards doing good for others. Nizamuddin Auliya preached that love of God implied love of humanity. He believed in unity and equality and shunned differences based on religion, social or economic status. His Dargah is located in Delhi where his disciple Amir

Sheikh Farid

Khusro is also buried. His shrine is visited by people of all faiths throughout the year and specially during the Urs or death anniversary.

Suhrawardi silsilah or Order : The famous Sufi saint Sheikh Baha-ud-din Zakariya who was influenced by Sheikh Shihab-ud-din Suhrawardi founded this order. Unlike the Chisti order, the Suhrawardi saints did not believe in a life of poverty. The Muslim rulers employed members of this order. In India, the off-shoots of this order were the *Shattari* and *Firdausi* orders. They were active in Bihar and Bengal. Other famous Suhrawardi saints were Shah Alam Bukhari and Sheikh Shihab-ud-din Suhra wardi.

Impact of Sufism

- It promoted the feelings of universal brotherhood among Hindu and Muslims.
- It played an important role in promoting feelings of tolerance among the Muslim rulers.
- Irrespective of religion, people began to understand and appreciate the faith of other people.
- Sufism influenced the Persian and Hindi poets of the period such as Malik Muhammad Jayasi and Amir Khusrau, who composed poems in praise of the Sufi principles. They played a great role in promoting vernacular literature.
- A number of Sufi principles had similarity with those of the Bhakti cult. Hence, it led to the popularity of the Bhakti Movement.

THE BHAKTI MOVEMENT

The meaning of the word '*bhakti*' is 'devotion to God.' The movement originated as a reaction against ritualism and caste division in India. The Bhakti movement was started by the *Saivite* and *Vaishnava* saints of South India in the 8th century and became very popular in the 11th and 12th centuries. They were known as *Nayanars* and *Alvars* respectively and they preached 'personal devotion to God as a means to reach out to God.'

The simple democratic religion Islam did not believe in caste distinctions nor insisted on costly sacrifices and wasteful rituals. At the other end of the spectrum, many low-caste Hindus were attracted to this new religion. At the other end of the spectrum, the Bhakti cult was a reformist movement that aimed at reviving the Hindu religion. The Bhakti saints preached oneness of God, equality of all human beings without any discrimination on the basis of colour, caste, creed, religion and complete surrender of self to God. Between 11th and 15th centuries, these ideas began to spread to Northern India and soon they became quite popular. The basis of this cult has been traced to the *Upanishads*, the *Puranas* and the *Bhagawad Gita*. It also has its roots in the Shankaracharya's revival of the Hindu philosophy.

Doctrines of Bhakti Movement

The main principles of the Bhakti Cult were :

- God is one and he must be worshipped with love and devotion.
- All human beings are equal before God. The dignity of a man is not dependent on the privileges of birth but on his actions. Universal brotherhood of humanity is a reality that is to be accepted.
- The religious ceremonies, rituals and rites are devoid of substance. One can only reach God through absolute surrender to him.
- One can find salvation by following the path of true devotion or Bhakti. One should not follow empty ceremonies, blind faith and external rites.
- An enlightened teacher known as *Guru* is indispensable for realizing God or attaining salvation. Emphasis is laid on the *Krishnacult* and the *Ramacult* as both Krishna and Rama were regarded as incarnations of God on earth.
- One must avoid image worship, caste distinctions and class hatred.

The Bhakti Saints

Some of the notable saints of the medieval Bhakti cult were Madhavacharya, Mahatma Kabir, Guru Nanak Dev, Namdeo, Mira Bai, Ramanujacharya, Ramananda and Chaitanya

Mahaprabhu. These Bhakti saints believed in the Upanishadic philosophy of *Advaita* (non-duality of God).

Sant Jnaneswar or **Dnyaneshwar** was a 13th century Maratha saint, poet, philosopher and yogi. He was the first philosopher to write in the Marathi, language. Even though, he was a Brahmin, he had a bitter experience of the caste system and the dogmatism of scriptural learning. Therefore, he rejected caste system and identified with the common people. He chose to write and preach in Marathi and his ideas conveyed the message of the Bhakti movement. He wrote a commentary on the Gita called Dhyaneshwari and an independent philosophical work called Amrutanubhava. He popularlised Yoga and believed in Vithala or Lord Vishnu.

Sant Jnaneswar

Krishna Cult in Bhakti Movement

In North India, the Bhakti movement centered on the worship of Lord Krishna as an incarnation of Vishnu. The main theme of the *bhajans* or religious hymns of the saints were the childhood escapades of Krishna known as *Krishna Leela*. The cult of Krishna Vasuveda is an archaic form of worship in the domain of Vaishnavism. The tradition of Krishna cult melded with the later religious developments. The sources indicate that that the devotee associated with the cult of Krishna are called Vasudevaka.

The Harivamsa Purana explicates intimate relationships between Vasudeva, Praduyana, Aniruddha and Sankarsana. This relationship later culminated in the Vaishnava tradition.Some of the outstanding saints of the Krishna cult were Chaitanya of Bengal, Mirabai of Rajasthan, Narsi Mehta of Gujarat and Surdas of Sihi (now in Faridabad).

Mirabai (AD 1498–1547)

Mirabai was a Rajput princess who married into the ruling house of Mewar (Udaipur). A mystical singer and an ardent devotee, she discarded all worldly comforts and dedicated her life to the worship of Lord Krishna. She had been offering prayers to Lord Krishna in the form of poetic incantation since her childhood. She was one of the most significant figures of the Vaishnava bhakti movement, who believed that one could achieve salvation through complete devotion to Krishna. Some 1,200–1,300 prayerful songs or *bhajans* attributed to her are popular throughout India and sung even today. The characteristic of her poetry is complete submission to almighty or Lord Krishna. Her longing for union with Krishna is predominant in her poetry: she wants to be 'coloured with the colour of dusk' (the symbolic colour of Krishna).

Mirabai

Mirabai occupies a high place in the history of Indian religious thought. She wrote many books; among them *Raag Govind, Phutik Alpaada* and *Geet Govind Ki Teeka* manifest her single minded devotion. Mirabai composed as many as 1300 songs related to enthusiasm, adoration and complete submission to her beloved master, Lord Krishna. Mirabai epitomizes an 'emancipated figure' who had successfully debunked 'feminine stereotypes' and clichéd society.

Impact of Bhakti Movement

The Bhakti movement helped to establish a personalised approach to religion. Like Sufism, profound changes were brought about by the Bhakti Movement in terms of social and religious outlook of people.

❑ Universal brotherhood was preached by the Bhakti saints. They also emphasized on the equality of all men.

❑ The teachings of Ravidas, Guru Nanak and Kabir helped in reforming Indian society. By denouncing caste distinctions and following the

> **Similarities Between Sufi And Bhakti Saints**
> - Emphasized on salvation through love and devotion to the supreme God.
> - Criticized social barriers of caste, class, religion and challenged orthodoxy.
> - Condemned rituals and idol worship.
> - Emphasized on the importance of teacher to guide the devotee's life.
> - Composed devotional songs in local languages that were understood by people.

principle of equality, they tried to evolve a new social order. Also, they did away with the domination of priests by exposing the futility of empty rituals. Thus, this movement brought social changes in India.

❑ Since the Bhakti saints preached in the language of the people, languages like Bhojpuri, Oriya, Hindi, Bengali and Maithili became popular. Some of the important works of this period were *Gurumukhi* litera-ture of the Sikh Gurus, *Ramcharit Manas* by Tulsidas and the Vaishnava literature in Bengal.

CHRISTIANITY

Christianity developed out of Judaism in the 1st century CE. It is a religious faith founded on the life, teachings, death and resurrection of Jesus Christ. He was the son of Joseph and Mary and those who follow him are called Christians. The four canonical gospels written by Matthew, Mark, Luke and John are the main sources of the life and teachings of Jesus. Christianity has many different branches and forms with accompanying variety in beliefs and practices. The three major branches of Christianity are Roman Catholicism, Eastern Orthodoxy and Protestantism. The sacred text of Christianity is *The Bible*, including both the Hebrew scriptures (also known as the Old Testament and the New Testament).

Jesus Christ

Jesus's twelve companions were instrumental in spreading his teachings and the Christian religion after his death. Until the later part of the 20th century, most adherents of Christianity were in the West, though it has spread to every continent and is now the largest religion in the world. Christianity is also noted for its emphasis on faith in Christ as the primary component of religion.

Christianity in India

The thread of the Christian faith in India can be traced into the misty haze of the distant past to the early years of Christianity itself. According to the Indian tradition, St Thomas the Apostle, in AD 52, visited Kerala and preached along the Malabar Coast. The Malabar Christian community had close associations with the churches in Mesopotamia and Persia. In this context, the term 'Firangi' should be mentioned. Etymologically speaking, the term 'Firangi' is derived from the old French word 'Franc', which means a white person or British.

St. Thomas, the Apostle

They accepted a number of Hindu rites and rituals while keeping their own.

In AD 1498, Vasco da Gama, was surprised to see churches and crosses in Kerala but they did not see non-Catholics as true Christians. Further more, the Christianity that existed in Kerala probably looked more like a caste than a religion. In AD 1510, after the Portuguese commander, Albuquerque, took Goa, the first Catholic establishment took root there. In AD 1514, when the king of Portugal entered into an agreement with the Pope to share the administrative and religious authority over the areas under Portuguese control, Franciscans, Dominicans, Augustinians, Carmelites and Jesuits came to India to spread Catholicism.

St. Francis Xavier (AD 1506-1552)

Of all the missionaries Europe had sent out to India, St. Francis Xavier was undoubtedly the

ENERGENCE OF COMPOSITE CULTURE   161

St. Francis Xavier

greatest. He was one of the 12 apostles of Christ and had all the virtues necessary for a missionary namely, unabiding love of God, undying zeal for his glory, sympathy for the poor and needy and a strong will to labour for God and fellow men. He was a rare combination of the contemplative and the man of action. In AD 1542, he came to India with the Portuguese Viceroy of Goa and immediately undertook the task of influencing the Goan people. Much of his next three years were spent among the *Paravars*, *katesar/kadaiyar Pattamkattiyars* (head of fishery coast) and *mukkuvars* along the eastern coast of southern India. He went from street to street to spread the message of Jesus Christ, asking people to attend his meetings and listen to his sermons. Though he did not master the local language, he took the help of Goan scholars and translated the Creed, the Lord's Prayer, the Ten Commandments and the Ave Maria.

He built nearly 40 churches along the coast and from these St. Stephen's Church, at Kombuthurai find its mention in his letters, dated AD 1544. He intensively catechized paravars, children and baptized the inhabitants of 30 villages. He then focused on converting the king of Travancore to Christianity and also visited

Relics of St Francis Xavier encased in silver casket in the Basilica of Born Jesus Church at Goa.

Ceylon (present-day Sri Lanka). Dissatisfied with the results of his activity, he set his sights eastward in AD 1545 and planned a missionaryjourney to Makassar on the island of Celebes (today's Indonesia). Against the wishes of the Portuguese viceroy, he proceeded to China to spread Christianity. He died of fever on 2 December, AD 1552 in the Sancian Island, China. His relics are kept in a glass container encased in a silver casket in the Basilica of bon Jesus church at Goa.

Robert de Nobili (1577-1656)

Robert de Nobili (1577-1656), was a remarkable figure, who dispersed evangelical messages to the people of India. He was born in an Italian noble family. In the middle of his education, he became disillusioned and entered the Society of Jesus. Emboldened by the stories and folklores of the Jesuit Mission to Africa and Japan, de Nobili embarked on the new missions. He travelled to India and reached Goa in 1605.

In the initial stage, de Nobili lived within the orbit of Portuguese habitat, encompassed by varied aspects of European culture. Subsequently, he picked up Tamil, the local dialect of the region and mingled with the mass at large. He accepted the gauntlet from his superiors and endeavored to convert people living in the fringes of the society. In this way, he entered into the interiors of the country. De Nobili understood the nature of the Hindu society and got to know that the Portuguese formed the lowest rung of the society. As a matter of fact, he assumed the Brahmin lifestyle and stopped eating meat, and carried the water jug and walking stick used by Hindu monks. In order to read holy books of Hinduism, he learned Sanskrit language and translated Christian psalms into Tamil and Sanskrit languages.

De Nobili spent major parts of his life as an ascetic Hindu holy man. By employing this strategy, he could manage to proselytize hundreds of men hailing from the lower segments of the society and save them from the rigidity of Hinduism. He died in 1656 after adhering to his Catholic faith and the spiritualism he embraced in the Hindu milieu.

Impact of Christianity

Christianity in Delhi dates back to the Mughal Emperor Akbar's era. Emperor Akbar was known for his secular theology. In AD 1579 Akbar sent his ambassador to Goa with a letter asking for two learned priests to be sent to his court to provide him and his Muslim and Hindu courtiers knowledge about Christian doctrines. Father Antony Monserrate, Father Rodolfo Acquaviva and Brother Francis Henriques reached Fatehpur Sikri as his companions. Akbar received them with extra-ordinary warmth and involved them in the religious meetings held in the *Ibadat Khana* (Hall of worship) at Fatehpur Sikri.

Akbar, the Great at the Ibadat Khana. Left is Fr. Acquaviva with his companion Fr. Henriques at his side Illustraing to the Akbarnama.

The Jesuits made determined efforts to convert the Mughal emperor. However, their inability to stand up to the Muslim and Hindu theologians in debates resulted in the first attempt ending in total fiasco. The second wave of missionaries consisted of more intellectual and sophisticated Jesuits. Their efforts lasted over three years but once again met with little success. Akbar was very friendly with the missionaries but had no intentions of converting into Christianity; however, he did add a Christian wife to his substantial and diverse *harem*. He also commissioned Father Jerome Xavier to translate the Life of Christ into Persian as the *Dastan-i-Masih* which was completed in AD 1602.

Jahangir (AD 1605-1627) was even more supportive of Christianity than his father. However, he too was not interested in converting to Christianity. The next two Mughal emperors Shah Jahan and Aurangezeb, particularly the latter, were much less supportive of the Jesuits. In mid AD 18th century the Jesuits had five churches: one each in Marwar, Jaipur, Agra and two in Delhi.

Christianity also fascinated the Mughals in art and architecture. Jesuit priests who visited

Islamic nativity scene of Jesus' birth.

the courts often took religious images with them which intrigued the emperors. Akbar commissioned his artists to copy scenes from the Bible, particularly the Nativity. The painting depicts the child Jesus and his mother Mary sitting under a tree outside a wooden garden pavilion. Mother Mary is being attended by Mughal serving girls wearing saris and dupattas. The miniature illustrating this Nativity scene was one of a great number commissioned by the Mughal court under the emperors Akbar and Jahangir

Emperor Akbar was fond of the sayings of Jesus which can be depicted through his famous architectural monument Buland Darwaza in Fatehpur Sikri. The calligraphy that lined the inside of the arch of Buland Darwaza shows the Christian faith and it reads as follows– "*Jesus, Son of Mary (on whom be peace) said: The World is a Bridge, pass over it, but build no houses upon it. He who hopes for a day, may hope for eternity; but the World endures but an hour. Spend it in prayer, for the rest is unseen.*" This shows Akbar's tolerance and respect for other religions. His belief was "never for a moment forget God".

ENERGENCE OF COMPOSITE CULTURE

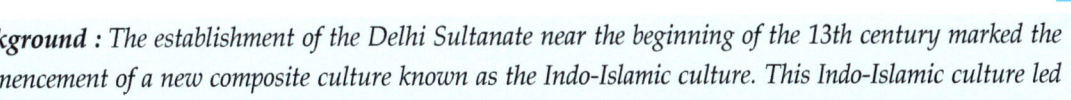

In Retrospect

- **Background :** The establishment of the Delhi Sultanate near the beginning of the 13th century marked the commencement of a new composite culture known as the Indo-Islamic culture. This Indo-Islamic culture led to the development of two liberal religious reform movements in India, the Bhakti and Sufi movements.
- **Sufism :** It preached oneness of God, religious tolerance and brotherhood. The Sufi saints believed in simple living and personal devotion and love as a means of reaching God. The Sufi saints of Central Asia and Persia were organized into 12 silsilahs or orders, each named after its founder. The Sufi saints who settled in India belonged to the two very popular orders i.e., Suhrawardi and Chisti orders. Khwajah Muin-ud-din Chisti and Hazrat Nizam-ud-din Auliya were the greatest of the Sufi saints in India.
- **Bhaktism :** The Bhakti cult was a reformist movement that aimed at reviving the Hindu religion. The Bhakti saints preached oneness of God, equality of all human beings without any discrimination on the basis of colour, caste, creed and religion and complete surrender of self to God. Some of the notable saints of the medieval Bhakti cult were Sant Jnaneshwar or Dnyaneshwar and Mira Bai.

- **Christianity :** The history of Christianity in India can be traced to the visit of the Apostle Thomas to the Malabar Coast in AD 52 Missionary activity started with the coming of the Portugese. St. Francis Xavier, one of the 12 apostles of the Christ came to India in AD 1542 and did considerable missionary work among the various low castes along the eastern coast of southern India.

EXERCISES

Part-I (Short Questions)

1. What do you mean by Sufism ?
2. Mention any two ways by which Sufism contributed to the religious unity of India.
3. State any two doctrines of Sufism.
4. Name the Sufi saints whose remains were buried in Delhi and at Ajmer.
5. Name two Sufi saints of the Chisti order
6. Name two Sufi saints of the Suhrawardi order
7. What do you mean by Bhakti cult ?
8. State any two doctrines of Bhakti cult.
9. Mention the names of the Bhakti saints who preached unity among the Hindus and the Muslims.
10. Mention two books of Mirabai.
11. Mention two similarities between the Bhakti and the Sufi saints.
12. What was the impact of Bhakti Movement on society and culture ?
13. Which apostle is said to have visited India in AD 52 ?
14. What does the term *Firangi* mean ?
15. Mention two local customs adopted by Roberto de Nobili.
16. Who was commissioned to translate the life of Jesus Christ in Persian ? Name the book.
17. Name the famous architectural monument which reflects Mughal's faith in christanity.

Part-II (Structured Questions)

1. With reference to Sufi movement, discuss :
   (a) Doctrines of Sufism
   (b) Works of any two Sufi Saints
   (c) Impact of Sufism on Indian society

2. With reference to the Bhakti Movement, discuss :
   (a) Doctrines of the Bhakti Movement,
   (b) About Sant Jnaneshwar
3. Discuss Krishna Cult in Bhakti movement.
4. With reference to Christianity, discuss :
   (a) Christian missionaries in India.
   (b) St. Francis Xavier and his work
   (c) Impact of Christianity on Mughal Art and Architecture

CHAPTER 11

THE RENAISSANCE

◆ Renaissance : Definition, Causes (Capture of Constantinople, Decline of Feudalism, New Trade Routes, Spirit of Enquiry and Invention of the Printing Press) and Impact on Art, Literature and Science (Leonardo Da Vinci, William Shakespeare and Copernicus).

```
                        The Renaissance
                              │
              ┌───────────────┴───────────────┐
              ▼                               ▼
```

Introduction

Causes for the Rise of Renaissance

- *Capture of Constantinople*
- *Collapse of Feudalism*
- *The Crusades*
- *Spirit of Enquiry*
- *The invention of the Printing Press*
- *New Geographical Explorations*
- *Art and Learning Flourished*
- *Progress in Science*

Impact of Renaissance

- *Art and Architecture*
- *Painting and Sculpture*
- *Literature*
- *Science*

Geographical Explorations and Discoveries

INTRODUCTION

The word 'Renaissance' is defined as a 'rebirth' or a 'reconstruction'. In French language, the word 'Renaissance' can be translated as 'Rinascita'. Historically speaking, 'Renaissance' indicates a phenomenal cultural and transitional movement, characterized by the resurgence of interest in the classical age of the Romans and the Greeks. Renaissance spanned roughly between the 14th to the 17th century, beginning in Italy in the Late Middle Ages and later spreading to the rest of Europe. Its influence affected literature, philosophy, art, politics, science, religion and other aspects of intellectual enquiry. Although the Renaissance saw revolutions in many intellectual pursuits as well as social and political upheaval, it is perhaps best known for its artistic developments and the contributions of

Leonardo-da-Vinci

Michelangelo

polymaths such as Leonardo-da-Vinci who inspired the term 'Renaissance Man'.

There is a belief that Renaissance began in Florence, in Italy, in the 14th century and then spread throughout the continent in course of time. Various theories have been proposed to account for its origins such as the social and civic peculiarities of Florence at the time, its political structure, the patronage of its dominant family, the Medici and the migration of Greek scholars and texts to Italy following the Fall of Constantinople.

While between the end of the Middle Age and the beginning of the Modern Age many parts of Europe underwent a period of renaissance, when viewed together these movements form an overall period of renaissance in Europe. The rebirths of different areas were, however, quite distinct from one another.

CAUSES FOR THE RISE OF RENAISSANCE

As Renaissance itself was not a single event, so were its causes which were embedded in European Politico-economic and cultural history over a great expanse of time and space. The main causes of Renaissance were :

Capture of Constantinople

Constantinople, the capital of Eastern Roman Empire and the cultural seat of Romans and Greeks for over 11 centuries was occupied by the Ottoman Turks in AD 1453. This marked the end of the Eastern Roman Empire called the Byzantine Empire. The fall of Constantinople compelled the Arab, Roman and Greek scholars to flee to Italy as its city states were then experiencing a flourishing age reminiscent of classical Greece. These scholars and learned men took their precious books and manuscripts with them to the Italian cities which then became the new seats of culture, thereby laying the foundations of Renaissance.

Collapse of Feudalism

Medieval European society and economy was feudal. In feudalism, the society functioned through the means of land tenure which bound everyone, right from the King to the smallest landowner through a series of defences and obligations. This feudal system declined in the 13th and 14th centuries mainly due to the revival of long distance trade. The growth of trade and markets stimulated a demand for luxury products. In order to procure them, the lords increased their exploitation of the serfs, who were virtually slaves. The slaves deserted cultivation and flocked to the newly developing towns. As a result, the feudal structure collapsed.

The Crusades

The Crusades or the wars fought between the Muslims and Christians between the 11th and the 13th century brought Europe in close contact with the economically and culturally rich Islamic world. The progressive ideas of Aristotle and Plato from the East migrated to the Western European nations that stimulated the imaginations of their people who started questioning blindfaith. These Crusades were also responsible for re-establishing trade and commerce between the East and West, which was highly conducive for the rise of Renaissance, as it helped in increasing the wealth and prosperity of the Italians. On the basis of their wealth, various renaissance scholars and artists were patronised.

Spirit of Enquiry

During the Middle Ages, religion played the most significant role in people's life. The church controlled education and knowledge made available by the church authorities had to be accepted without asking any questions. However, modern time scholars not only got endowed with scientific thinking but an enquiring spirit as well. This made them challenge the traditional beliefs of the church. The strong belief of thinkers such as Roger Bacon, Thomas Aquinas and Peter Aberald to attain excellence and happiness without any help from religion was one of the foremost causes of Renaissance.

The invention of the Printing Press

Invention of Printing Press with metal types acted as the most significant factor for ushering in Renaissance. Earlier, in the middle ages, books and manuscripts had to be copied manually and the cost of books was very high. But the invention of paper and a printing device brought about revolutionary changes in the growth of intellectual sphere. Books were made available in large numbers and on various subjects at very low prices. Therefore, knowledge did not remain the monopoly of a single class. With the spread of knowledge, the hold of superstitious and blind faith was loosened and people developed self-confidence which brought a new awakening in the European continent. Hence, it is evident that the paper and the printing devices were some of the most important causes influencing Renaissance.

Johannes Gutenberg launched the metal casting of individual letters of the alphabet around the middle of the 15th century. This led Gutenberg to establish his first printing press in AD 1455 in Germany and publish the first printed book in history, *The Gutenberg Bible*. These printing presses allowed large production of books and by AD 1500 books on a wide range of topics were printed.

The Gutenberg Printing Press

New Geographical Explorations

With the Turkish capture of Constantinople in AD 1453, the overland trade route from Europe to Asia via Asia Minor closed. So the European traders and Mariners started to look for an alternative route to Asia. Besides the growth of trade encouraged traders to find new sources and markets for their products. Many new sea routes were discovered. Bartholomew Diaz reached the Cape of Good Hope located at the southernmost tip of Africa. In 1492 Columbus reached the Caribbean. Vasco da Gama discovered India in 1498 and Magellan circumnavigated the earth. Due to these discoveries, contacts with the East developed and people become more adventurous.

Art and Learning Flourished

The breakdown of the church monopoly over learning in the latter half of the Middle Ages was responsible for the rapid dissemination of art and education throughout Europe. Various Cathedral schools along with several universities were established at Paris, Oxford, Padua, Cambridge, Montpellier, Naples, Bologna and Salamanca which took the responsibility of disseminating information and developing eagerness towards learning and thinking.

There were some families in Italy who supported traditions in fostering art and learning along with offering economic support to the painters, scholars, architects, sculptors, scientists, musicians etc. The most notable among them was Lorenzo de Medicis, who patronized men of letters and art like Michelangelo.

Progress in Science

Skills related to thinking and scientific understanding and a spirit of enquiry was fostered by the progress that was seen in Science during that time. New ideas came into existence with proof like the earth revolves around the sun was proven by Copernicus. Roger Bacon could plan the use of flying machines and horseless carriages while Galileo became famous for inventing the telescope. With these innovations in town, people could open up their mental outlook and bring an end to age-old traditions and beliefs.

Galileo : Inventor of Telescope

IMPACT OF RENAISSANCE

The most notable changes experienced during the Renaissance were in the fields of art and architecture, literature and science. It was in these disciplines that new trends and fresh styles emerged which was inspired by Europe's ancient history.

Art and Architecture

The greatest impact of renaissance was on art and its various forms such as painting, architecture and sculpture. The last quarter of the 15th century witnessed the glimmering inception of magnificent pieces in the sphere of art and architecture. The period from 1490-1520 marked the 'high noon of Renaissance', which saw the culmination of scientific forms of art and architecture. The roots of architecture in the Renaissance were majorly influenced by the medieval and ancient times. In the initial phase of 'Renaissance', the art of the

St. Peter's Basilica Dome

Archaicperiod was counterfeited remotely and was considered to be a source of aesthetic beauty and accuracy. In the later phase, art was scientifically and empirically evaluated. The new artistic notions were comprehended and embraced by the educated humanists of the city-states of Europe. In the later phase, varied disciplines like technique of art and scientific theory, anatomy, usage of geometric patterns and 'Universal man' of the humanists' philology were deployed. Most of the Renaissance architects were inspired by the building plans of the Roman Churches. This adoption of the schemes led to the development of architecture that had its basis in cross-like plan for the floor that was adorned with arches, decorative columns and dome. In the architectural works of Renaissance, harmony, proportion and balance in the buildings were highlighted. One of the most popular architectures of this period can be seen in St. Peter's Basilica in Rome. Michelangelo and Donato Bramante (AD 1444-1514) were the artists to design this grand structure.

Painting and Sculpture

There is a distinct shift in the themes of sculptures and paintings done by early and later Renaissance painters. In the middle Ages sculptures and paintings were used to promote religion. Unlike the artistic styles of the earlier Middle Ages which placed more importance on symbolism than reality, renaissance art was more lifelike and contained perspective. They began to depict the human form with increasing accuracy, which was enabled by a better understanding of human anatomy. This anatomical knowledge was gained from advances made in the field of medicine during the Renaissance period. They also adapted Greco-Roman style and developed other techniques such as studying light, shadow and human anatomy to find the mechanism underlying gestures and expressions.

The field of sculpture also saw presentation of saints and usage of religious themes in the medieval times, which changed with Renaissance. Previously, all the sculptures were made as a part of some building or some structural background. However, during Renaissance development of free standing sculptures earned the respect of separate artworks. The knowledge of the human anatomy and celebration of the beauty of mankind also inspired the sculptors to create works. During this phase, many renowned sculptors concocted new themes, motifs and techniques. Out of these, octagonal dome of Florentine Cathedrals, resurgence of classical columnar system and a spatial integrity in all public and private structures came into being.

In the sphere of painting, the golden epoch was divided into two phases: low and high phases. In the early phase, Masaccio, Pisanello and Umbrian genius Pierodella Francesca dominated the scene. They introduced fresco style paintings, linear-style painting and many other forms existed. In the high phase, more refined versions of paintings came into being.

Much of this new knowledge can be attributed to the pioneering Renaissance figures like Leonardo da Vinci, Raphael, Michelangelo, Donatello and Lorenzo Ghiberti. Other notable artists included Sandro Botticelli, Pon-tormo, Bronzino and Rosso Fiorentino, among others.

Leonardo da Vinci : Even though Leonardo da Vinci is known as a painter he infact personified the Renaissance and therefore is known as the Renaissance Man. Though he is famous for his painting of Monalisa, he had other interests too. He has been described as a man of 'unquenchable curiosity'. His interests ranged

THE RENAISSANCE

from invention, painting, sculpting, architecture, science, music, mathematics, engineering, literature, anatomy, geology, astronomy, botany, writing, history and cartography. His designs conceptualized the idea of parachutes, helicopters and a type of armoured fighting vehicles vehicles such as a tank, even concentracted solar power and adding machines.

PAINTING AND SCULPTURE

Name	Profession	Creation	Details
Leonardo da Vinci (AD 1452-1519)	Painter Sculptor Artist	• Virgin of the Rocks • The Last Supper • Monalisa	**Virgin of the Rocks:** This painting exhibits Vinci's zeal for science, technical skill and his belief that the Universe is a well-organized place. **Mona Lisa:** This is a painting of a woman that echoes the various frames of mind of the human soul. **The last Supper:** This painting highlights the psychological reactions of the people on the painting that range from horror, surprise to guilt.
Michelangelo (AD 1475-1564)	Painter Sculptor	• The Last Judgment • The Fall of Man • Pieta • David • Descent from the Cross	The Last judgment and The Fall of Man are among the most beautiful frescoes on the ceiling of the Sistine Chapel in Vatican. **David:** This sculpture is about 13 feet tall, depicting self-confident affirmation of the beauty of the human form. **Pieta:** This statue presents a sitting Mary carrying Jesus body. **Descent from the Cross:** This statue had been placed at the tomb of Michelangelo, which depicts Virgin Mary mourning over the dead body of Christ.
Rafael (AD 1483-1520)	Painter	• Sistine Madonna • Painted the Chigi Chapel	His works reflect the love of the divine mother. He is mostly celebrated for his paintings of the 'Sistine Madonna' and Jesus Christ's mother.
Donatello (AD 1386-1466)	Sculptor	• David	The first nude 13 feet tall statue made of bronze stands in a victorious position over the body of an assassinated Goliath. It is an important statue as it depicts the beauty of the human form.

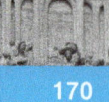

| Lorenzo Ghiberti (AD 1378–1455) | Italian artist | • Gates of Paradise Florence Baptistery | He belonged to the period of the early renaissance and was famous for sculpture and metal working. |

Literature

The Renaissance witnessed cultural efflorescence, revival of antiquity and cascade of renewed literary forms. Renaissance literature is also know as 'European literature', which was profoundly influenced by the influx of intellectual and cultural tendencies. The Renaissance literature came into existence in the 14th-century and persisted until the 16th century. Subsequently, it was spread across the continent and globe. The Renaissance literature was marked by the adoption of humanist philosophy and the revival of the classical antiquity. The writers of the period were inspired by the Graeco-Roman themes, revision of Platonic and Aristotle notions and rational inquiry. Simultaneously, new literary genres like essay (Montaigne) and Spenserian stanza were evolved. During the middle Ages, Latin was the popular language which significantly changed in the age of Renaissance. The impact was seen in the enrichment of languages like French, Italian, Portuguese, Spanish as well as Germanic dialects such as English, German, Dutch, Norwegian and Swedish. Writers and poets looked back to the poems and texts of Ancient Greece and Rome.

Renaissance literature dealt much more with human characteristics and behaviour, shifting away from religious and spiritual themes like heaven and hell of earlier Medieval books, poems and plays. With the invention of the printing press in the 1440s, information suddenly became much more accessible to the general public, which had a huge impact on the field of education.

The authors from the period of Renaissance also started concentrating on man and his problems. This emphasis on mankind led to the initiation of a movement called Humanism. This was possible only due to the contributions of various individual writers.

William Shakespeare : William Shakespeare was an English poet, playwright and actor. He is regarded as the greatest writer in the English language. If we read Shakespeare we get an idea what renaissance was all about. His stories are very complex compared to the simple stories written during the medieval period. They are full of human drama and has multiple, interweaving narratives. The idea of humanism and freedom of thought was also something new in Shakespeare's works. He is regarded as England's national poet and is known as the "Bard to Avon".

LITERATURE

Name	Profession	Creation	Details
Niccolo Machiavelli (AD 1469-1527)	Historian–known as Father of Modern philosophy	The Prince	His work outlines the political ideology of his age that prevailed in the Italian states during the close of the 15th and early 16th century. His ideas and suggestions was to separate political matters from religion.

THE RENAISSANCE

Dante Alighieri (AD 1265-1321)	Poet	The Divine Comedy	An epic poem that talks about the state of the soul and shows the social and religious life of the people of contemporary Italy.
Francesco Petrarch (AD 1304-1374)	Poet–known as the father of Humanism	Canzoniere, Triofoni, Secretum, De Otio Religiosorum, De Vita Solitaria, Sonnets to Laura.	Petrarch talked about the economic, social and political aspects of life. His lyrics and sonnets became very popular all through the European continent.
Giovanni Boccaccio (AD 1313-1375)	Prose Writer–Known as the Father of Italian Prose	Decameron, One Famous Women	In his collection of 100 novellas, morality and virtue were highlighted. His dialogue, prose and short stories surpass those of all of his contemporaries.
Geoffrey Chaucer (AD 1343-1400)	Poet–known as the Father of English literature	The Book of the Duchess, House of Fame, Legend of Good Women, Troilus, Criseyde, The Canterbury Tales.	He is widely considered the greatest English poet of the Middle Ages.
Thomas More (AD 1478-1525)	Author, English lawyer, Philosopher.	Utopia	'Utopia' was a name he gave to the ideal and imaginary island nation, where there is no exploitation and no class distinctions.

Name	Profession	Creation	Details
Roger Bacon (AD 1214-1294)	English philosopher– Known as Doctor Mirabilis (wonderful teacher)	Opus Majus Opus minus	He emphasized the study of nature through empirical methods.
William Shakespeare (AD 1564-1616)	Poet and Playwright	Julius Caesar, Antony and Cleopatra, Hamlet, A Merchant of Venice etc.	The greatest poet and dramatist of England enthralled readers globally. He elevated English literature to world status.
Martin Luther (AD 1483-1546)	Reformer	German translation of The Bible, the famous ninety five theses	Luther challenged blind faith, superstition and corruption through his works.

Science

Science and engineering were other fields that experienced major changes during the Renaissance. Many new and exciting discoveries were made, mainly in the areas of anatomy, astronomy and physics. Breakthroughs in engineering also paved the way for many of the world's most significant inventions, such as telescopes, clocks and spectacles. The willingness to question previously held truths and search for new answers resulted in a period of major scientific advancements that ultimately resulted in the Scientific Revolution. Pioneering Renaissance scientists and inventors included Galileo Galilei and Leonardo da Vinci.

Copernicus : Nicolaus Copernicus was a Polish astronomer and mathematician who fulfilled the Renaissance ideals. He lived in the fifteenth century and became a mathematician, an astronomer, a Church jurist with a doctorate in Law, a Physician, a translator, an artist, a Catholic cleric, a governor, a diplomat and an economist. As a student, Copernicus began to question what he was taught. He questioned the theories of Aristotle and Ptolemy. He disputed the theory that the Earth was the centre of the universe and said that it was the Sun which was the centre of the universe and that the Earth, the planets and the stars all revolved around the sun. This is called the Heliocentric idea of the universe.

SCIENTIFIC DISCOVERIES

Name	Profession	Discovery
Nicolaus Copernicus	Scientist	He was the first person to prove that the earth is round and it revolves around the sun that ideally stands in the middle of the planetary system. His theory is known as the Copernican theory, which revolutionized the field of astronomy.
Galileo Galilei (AD 1564-1642)	Physicist, mathematician, astronomer and philosopher	He disproved Aristotle's theory by proving the principle that the speed of a falling body depends on the distance it has to cover and not its weight. Some inventions of Galileo include the thermometer, hydrostatic balance and the improvisation of the telescope.
Johannes Kepler (AD 1571-1630)	Scientist, Mathematician, Astronomer and Astrologer	He proved Copernicus's theory of circular orbits wrong by proving that planets, including the earth, revolve round the sun along elliptical orbits and not along circular orbits.
Sir Issac Newton (AD 1642-1727)	Physicist, Mathematician, Astronomer, Philosopher and Theologian	Newton described universal gravitational law and the three laws of motion. He carried Kepler's work forward and presented proof of heavenly bodies moving as per the gravitational law. His monograph was the famous *Philosophiæ Naturalis Principia Mathematicia*.

Name	Profession	Discovery
Francis Bacon (AD 1561-1626)	Scientist and pioneer of the Scientific method	Bacon has been called the father of empiricism. He popularized inductive methodologies for scientific inquiry, often called the *Baconian method*.
Andreas Vesalius (AD 1514- 1564)	Flemish Anatomist and Physician	The author of one of the most influential books on human anatomy, *De humani corporis fabrica* (On the Structure of the Human Body) Vesalius is often referred to as the founder of modern human anatomy.
Edmond Halley (AD 1656-1742)	English Astronomer, Geophysicist, Mathematician, Meteorologist and Physicist	He was best known for computing the orbit of the eponymous Halley's Comet.
William Harvey (AD 1578-1657)	English Physician	He was the first person to describe completely and in detail the systemic circulation and properties of blood being pumped to the body by the heart.

GEOGRAPHICAL EXPLORATIONS

With the new spirit of enquiry of the Renaissance among the people, they liberated their minds from the collapsing notions of the medieval times and adopted a more adventurous and bold spirit. The outward demonstration of this spirit was reflected in form of various voyages undertaken to discover new worlds around the earth. The European countries

THE RENAISSANCE

became interested in the trade of spices which was extremely profitable. New routes to the East were discovered. The Renaissance men took up this challenge and the countries of Spain and Portugal led this quest. This was the beginning of the domination of the West and the rise of European colonial empires.

GEOGRAPHICAL DISCOVERIES

Name	Discovery
Bartholomeu Dias (Portuguese) (AD 1450–1500)	He reached the southernmost tip of Africa, called the Cape of Good Hope in AD 1488, which opened the way to reach various Eastern countries.
Vasco da Gama (Portuguese) (AD 1469–1524)	He discovered a new sea route to Calicut in India via the Cape of Good Hope in AD 1498. This discovery resulted in setting up of trade relations between Portugal, India, East Indies, Java, China, Japan, Sri Lanka and Sumatra.
Christopher Columbus (Spanish) (AD 1451–1506)	He sailed through the Atlantic and reached an island close to Cuban coast in AD 1492. Although, till the last moment of his life he was unaware of the fact that the country was not India, but a continent that was to be called America in the later years.
Amerigo Vespucci (Spanish) (AD 1454–1512)	He reached America following the footsteps of Columbus and after whom the country America is named. He was the one to provide confirmation of the fact that the 'New World' found by Columbus was very different from Asia.

Ferdinand Magellan (Spanish) (AD 1480-1521) 	He got the rare honour of being the first to circumnavigate around the world.
Walter Raleigh (English) (AD 1552-1618) 	He created a new colony called Virginia in America, which was named after the Virgin Queen.
Sir Francis Drake (English) (AD 1541-96) 	Made a voyage around the world.

In Retrospect

♦ *Renaissance :* A paradigm between the 14th century and the 17th century when a cultural movement based on classical sources, encompassing literature, science, art, religion and politics resurged.

♦ *Causes for the rise of Renaissance :* Downfall of Constantinople, Collapse of Feudalism, The Crusades, Black Death, Creation of Printing Press and New Geographical Explorations.

♦ *Impact of Renaissance :*
  ● *Architecture :* Harmony, proportion and balance in the buildings were extremely highlighted. St. Peter's Basilica in Rome is the popular example of architecture of that period.
  ● *Painting and Sculpture :* Renaissance art of painting and sculpture were more life-like and contained perspective. Leonardo-da-Vinci, Raphael and Michelangelo reflected the spirit of Renaissance most brilliantly.
  ● *Literature :* The new spirit of Humanism led authors to concentrate on man and his problems instead of spiritual themes like heaven and hell.
  ● *Science :* Science and engineering were other fields that experienced major changes; inventions such as telescopes, clocks and spectacles.

♦ *Geographical Explorations :* With the new spirit of enquiry of the Renaissance among the people, they liberated their minds from the collapsing notions of the medieval times and adopted a more adventurous and bold spirit. New routes to the East were discovered.

THE RENAISSANCE

EXERCISES

Part-I (Short Questions)

1. What do you understand by the term 'Renaissance' ?
2. Why did Italy become the centre of Renaissance ?
3. What role did the fall of Constantinople play in ushering Renaissance movement ?
4. In what ways was the feudal system opposed to advancement ?
5. How did the Crusades contributed in original thinking ?
6. Who provided encouragement to art and learning in Europe ?
7. Mention any two consequences of geographical discoveries.
8. What made the Renaissance artists pay great importance to the physicality of man's existence ?
9. Give the name of the two paintings that made Michelangelo famous.
10. Give the names of any two paintings of Leonardo da Vinci.
11. State any one renowned painting of Rafael.
12. What were the unique features of the sculptures from the time of the Renaissance ?
13. State the name of the writer of 'Canterbury Tales'.
14. Point out any two reasons behind the European nations taking upon geographical explorations.
15. Who ventured out in search for a new sea route to the Indies and reached America in 1492 ?

Part-II (Structured Questions)

1. With respect to the causes of Renaissance, write short notes on :
   (a) Capture of Constantinople
   (b) Geographical discoveries
   (c) Creation of Printing Press
2. Write short notes about the impact of Renaissance in fields like :
   (a) Paintings and Sculpture
   (b) Science
   (c) Literature
3. Write short notes about these thinkers, highlighting their contribution in the field of science :
   (a) Copernicus
   (b) Roger Bacon
   (c) Galileo
4. In reference to the geographical explorations, write notes about :
   (a) Background of the geographical exploration in the Renaissance
   (b) Adventures of the Portuguese explorers
   (c) Three effects of the geographical explorations.

CHAPTER 12

THE REFORMATION

- Reformation : Causes (Dissatisfaction with the practices of the Catholic Church and New Learning)
- Martin Luther's Contribution, Counter Reformation

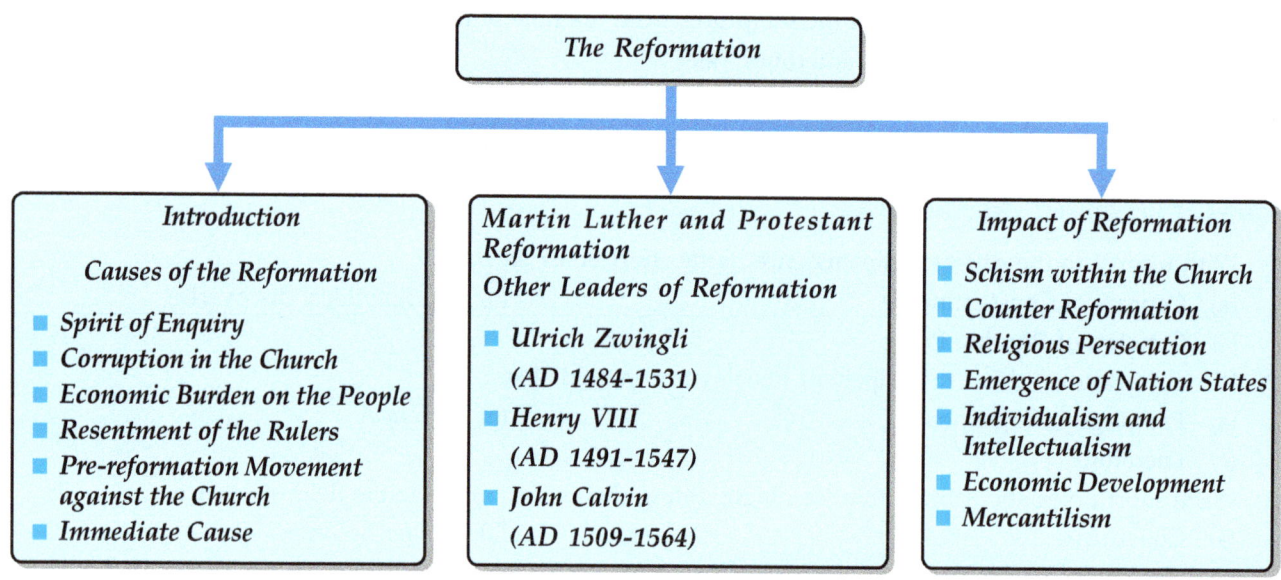

INTRODUCTION

Reformation is a general name that is given to a set of religious movements, encouraged by the Renaissance that broke out in the later Middle Ages. It developed a critical attitude and changed the mental outlook of people towards religion and traditional beliefs. People began to question the authority of the Pope, criticised the Church rituals and even the lifestyles of some clergymen. This change of attitude towards religious life led to a movement that aimed at reforming the Church. This movement called the **Reformation** or **Protestant Reformation** was initiated by a Christian priest named Martin Luther in Europe. By the 16th century, these religious movements came to a climax which had three dimensions :

❏ The church was split into two main divisions- the **Roman Catholics** and **Protestants.**

In the sphere of Protestantism, several radical and moderate folds came into vogue. These facets are Lutherans, Calvinists, Puritans, Anabaptists, Anglicans and Presbyterians.

❏ A large number of reforms within the Catholic Church were achieved by Counter-Reformation (in AD 1560), whereby a group of churchmen introspected and decided to purify the Roman Catholic Church of its abuses.

- Many European rulers resisted the church intervention in politics, which gave rise to Nation states.

CAUSES OF THE REFORMATION

Reformation was just not a mere religious movement. In the traditional sense, the Reformation indicates the split within the Roman Catholic Church, functioning under the Pope in Europe for centuries. It culminated in the development of a separate protestant Christianity. This schism of unity of Christendom was part of Reformation. The movement aimed to reform the Catholic Church from within and without. Reformation was not an over-night phenomenon. It was spurred by a series of political and cultural factors. Since it was a part of the political and social movement of that period, it did not take place impulsively. Various reasons were responsible for this movement, such as :

Spirit of Enquiry

The transition from the medieval to the modern period involved changes in every field in Europe. The Printing press came into existence and that made it possible to print the Bible in vernacular languages. This enabled people to start questioning the Church's superiority as they began to feel they could reach God without the intervention of a priest. Likewise, the original thinking of certain scholars led to a rise of a spirit of inquiry. People started feeling that the Church had numerous drawbacks owing to the factors like Renaissance movement, the revival of the secular and human spirit of ancient Greece and Rome, geographical discoveries, the Crusades, the contact with the east as well as the scientific inventions and discoveries. Thus, people began asking many questions to satisfy their endless spirit of enquiry.

Corruption in the Church

Reformation was mainly a revolt against the abuses and antagonisms of the Church. The clergy led an ideal life in the initial days that commanded respect in society, but with time a host of high-ranking religious officials and unworthy priests were appointed in the hierarchy of the Church through corrupt procedures. Some of these clergymen lacked necessary education, while others ignored their duties and lived luxuriously. Great scholars like Erasmus and Thomas Moore exposed the abuses rampant in the Church. There was a sale of Church offices and benefices, while church rituals and practices became a source of profits. Another corrupt practice was an unrestrained sale of relics such as objects supposed to have been used by Jesus Christ and the letters or *Indulgences* which was believed to reduce sin.

Economic burden on the People

The emergence of middle classes greatly contributed to the reformation. They protested against the dominance of the old church because it was largely controlled by the upper classes and administered largely for their benefit. Moreover the Church levied a variety of taxes like, *tithe* one-tenth of the income of each person), *Peter's Pence* etc. while nobles were exempted from taxation. This angered the common people as they were overburdened with tax and were hardly given anything in return for their money. In addition, the Roman Catholic Church pestered its members for varied services, such as confessions, burials, marriages and baptisms. Appeals procedures were very lengthy and tiresome. The economic burden of the Catholic Church was one of the significant factors that led to surmounting criticisms of the Papal authority. These pressing matters demanded Reformation in the Church.

Resentment of the Rulers

The monarchs of England, France, Spain and other nations supported the Reformation Movement as they hated the interference of the Pope in affairs related to politics. Over the issue of the ruler's right to tax on property of the Church, there was strife in the 13th century between the European rulers and their Popes, which ended with the defeat of the Papacy. Henry VIII, the English King didn't pay heed to the Pope and even passed an Act in AD 1536 to dissolve the monasteries.

Pre-reformation movements against the Church

Even before reformation, various anti-Church movements began to be organised in Europe.

These movements labelled the lives and certain practices of clergymen as scandalous and immoral. Several scholars raised their voices in opposition to certain Catholic teachings and practices.

Among them was John Wycliffe, an English priest and Oxford professor, who declared that the Pope was not Christ's representative on earth, but an anti-Christ. He also put emphasis on *The Bible* as the sole guide for salvation. His followers came to be known as the Lollards. He was condemned by the Pope and was expelled from the University for challenging the Church. Wye is regarded as the *"Morning star of the Reformation"*, since he challenged the church a hundred and fifty years before Martin Luther.

The dismal failure of Papal authority culminated in the development of purposeful religion and notions of apposite salvation. In Germany, developments in popular religion were apparent. A dearth of Papal authority led to the growth of doctrinal pluralism. On the eve of Reformation in Germany and many other countries of Europe, concept of 'popular piety' developed as people used to undertake religious pilgrimages abroad. Another facet of 'popular piety' was reflected in the famed mystical movement, 'the Modern Devotion' 'the Brothers and Sisters of Common life' instituted by Gerard Groote in Netherlands.

Immediate Cause

There had been some cases of protests against the power of the Pope, long before the open breach with Rome. The early reformers met with failure as these minor revolts were crushed with a heavy hand. Martin Luther, a German priest, accepted the challenge and raised a strong voice. A movement was launched by him against the authority of the Pope and the abuses of the Church. In fact, this proved to be the immediate cause of the Reformation.

MARTIN LUTHER AND PROTESTANT REFORMATION

Martin Luther (AD 1483–1546)- a German clergyman and professor of Theology at the Wittenberg University was the first to initiate the Protestant Movement in Germany. Martin Luther was called the 'morning star' of the Reformation. In AD 1514 Luther became priest at Wittenberg's Church. Meanwhile, he observed that the practice of granting 'indulgences' to provide absolution to sinners became increasingly corrupt. A friar named Johann Tetzel was selling indulgences in Germany to raise funds to renovate St. Peter's Basilica in Rome. He turned strongly against the Church and openly criticised the papacy for selling indulgences. He pointed out that no one on earth was capable of forgiving sins.

Martin Luther

Acting on this belief, he wrote *Ninety-Five Theses* that were statements highlighting the difference between the beliefs and the actual practices of the Church, which he later nailed on the door of the Wittenberg castle Church in AD 1517. In addition to the criticisms of indulgences, he emphasized the primacy of The *Bible* rather than Church officials as the ultimate religious authority in Ninety-five Theses, which later become the foundation of the Protestant Reformation. Pope Leo X condemned Luther's writings and ex communicated him from the Catholic Church.

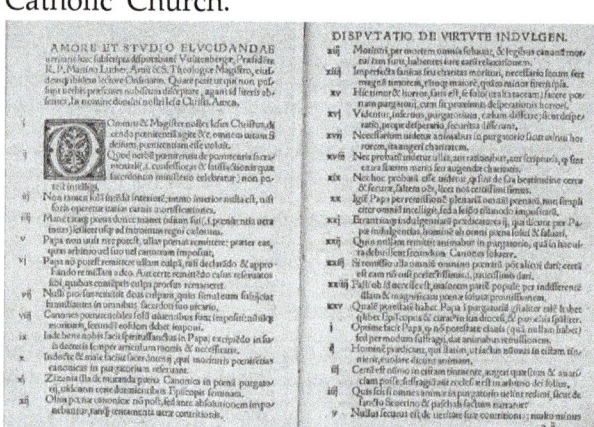

Martin Luther's Ninety-Five Theses

The **Diet of Worms**, which was a Council of high dignitaries and Princes of the Holy Roman Empire, ordered writings of Luther to be burned and banned in AD 1521 but he refused to recant. He concluded his testimony with the defiant statement: *"Here I stand. God help me. I can do no other."* His ideas, writings and speeches brought him the support of Frederick the Wise, Duke of Saxony. Gradually, a German Protestant Movement started as many German Princes raised the banner of revolt against the Church. Luther established an independent church and translated the Bible into German as he made German the language to be used in Church services. Since he didn't adhere to the hierarchy within the Catholic Church and Church's supremacy over state, he abolished most of the sacraments and Priest's special status, laying emphasis on faith only.

Luther's preaching of equality led to the rise of a new movement called **Anabaptism**, which promoted separation of Church and State. Luther enjoyed the support of the common people who asked for more freedom. This religious movement eventually took the shape of a political character, which led to Thirty Years War (AD 1618–1648) between the Catholic and Protestant princes that resolved with the Treaty of Westphalia. Luther died in AD 1555. By this time Lutheranism had spread to Denmark, Norway and Sweden and nine years later was also recognised as a legal form of Christianity. Lutheranism was followed in Northern Germany, while the south continued to follow Catholicism.

OTHER LEADERS OF REFORMATION

Ulrich Zwingli (AD 1484–1531)

Ulrich Zwingli Switzerland, which was then a confederacy of 13 states known as **cantons**. Under the leadership of Zwingli, the city-state of Zurich was the most powerful and important of all the cantons. He brought in the **Humanism of Erasmus** into the movement. The Bible was regarded by him as the sole guide to right living. He believed in simplicity and condemned idol worship and complicated ceremonies. The Swiss Reformation under Zwingli bore far-reaching repercussions in the social and cultural spheres. The Swiss Reformation emphasized the corporate character of the church, believing that clergy and laymen formed a 'holy community'. He was killed in AD 1531, in a religious war against the Pope.

Ulrich Zwingli

Henry VIII (AD 1491–1547)

In England, Reformation started more as a political propaganda than anything religious. In the academia, the English Reformation is hotly debated by the scholars. One view suggests that English Reformation emanated from above and the changes were enforced by the governmental actions with the advent of Henry VII's action (views of G.R Elton and Peter Clark). On the other hand, another view suggests that Reformation was deeply entrenched in religion and not in politics. They think that the early reformers like Lollards and other early protestants had created such milieu in English social and religious circuits. Henry VIII of England set up an indepen-dent Church known as the **Anglican Church**. He severed all relations with Rome, when the Pope refused to give him permission to divorce his wife, Catherine of Aragon. In AD 1534, he passed the **Act of Supremacy** through Parliament. By this Act, he became the clergy and the Supreme Head of the Church of England.

Henry VIII

John Calvin (AD 1509–1564)

Besides being a French scholar, John Calvin was a leading Protestant reformer in France. He had to flee to Switzerland as he was denounced as a heretic for his views on religion and bold criticism of the Catholic Church. In

John Calvin

fact, after the death of Zwingli, he popularised the Protestant movement in Switzerland and continued the work of his predecessor. Geneva became the centre of his religious activities. Calvin expressed his views on religion in the book known as *'Institutes of Christian Religion'*. Calvin was against all kinds of luxury, feasting, dancing, sports and games and wanted utter simplicity in the religion. This severe type of Protestantism was known as Calvinism. Religious sects with Calvinist beliefs were known as **Huguenots** in France, **Presbyterians** in Scotland and **Puritans** in America and England.

Erasmus

In Holland, the reformation was spearheaded by **Erasmus**. In his book *In Praise of Folly*, he denounced the evil practices of the Church and emphasized on a return to the Bible as a source of authority. He felt that reforms should be introduced in the field of religious practices. He was highly influential with the reformers and his thoughts influenced others in England, France and Germany.

IMPACT OF REFORMATION

Schism within the Church

The Western Schism or Papal Schism was a popular chasm within the Catholic Church, which spanned from 1378 to 1417. The political entanglements facilitated 'schism' within the Catholic Church, which was ended by the Council of Constance (1414-1418). These rival claims began to antagonize the Royal Papacy and subsequently, damaged the reputation of the office. This rival episode is sometimes referred to as the Great Schism. This split in the Western Roman Church occurred due to the 'resurgence of the papacy to Rome' under the aegis of Gregory XI on January 17, 1377. This led to the decline of Avignon Papacy and resulted in the estrangement of substantial parts of Western Christendom.

Counter Reformation

Counter Reformation was the movement launched by the Roman Catholic Church against the birth of Protestantism to reform the Church from within. Practises like selling Indulgences and violation of celibacy for the bishops and clergy were outlawed. Preaching in local languages was allowed, seminaries or centres of learning for the priests were introduced and the charging of fees for performing religious practices was forbidden.

Ignatius Loyola

The movement led to the revision of the service-books of the Church with an issue of a new edition of the Latin Bible, *Vulgate*, that became the Roman Catholic's official Bible. The Catholic Church was further strengthened by the Society of Jesus; whose members called the **Jesuits** dedicated themselves to the service of people. This society was founded by a Spanish noble, Ignatius Loyola in AD 1534. The efforts of the Jesuits were carried forward by St. Francis Xavier in Japan, China and India, which helped in restoration of the Roman Catholic Church.

Religious Persecution

An immediate and unfortunate effect of the reformation was intolerance, which expressed itself in cruel persecution and religious wars. Instead of generating the true spirit of Christ, the Reformation made thousands suffer on account of their religion. The subjects of the Spanish, Portuguese and Italian monarchs were forced to remain Catholic, or to suffer death or imprisonment at the hands of the Inquisition. King Philip II of Spain, and Mary, Queen of Scots persecuted the Protestants. Similarly, the Protestant princes of Germany punished their Catholic subjects.

Emergence of Nation States

The development of nation-states in Europe was a new phenomenon. Before the 1500s, the

THE REFORMATION

concept of 'Nation States' did not have any firm roots. During that time, people mostly lived in villages and identified themselves with their local lords. There was no uniformity in laws and regulations because it varied from one country to another. The ruler of the state assumed a titular position and the colossus power was exercised by the feudal lords or chieftains. Therefore, decentralized forces were very much in vogue during that time.

In the aftermath of the Reformation phase, the nation-states developed in full swing. In the early modern epoch, several monarchs began to wield power by enervating the feudal lords and liaising with rising commercial classes. For instance, France and Spain intervened in Italy at the behest of the Pope. However, some monarchs exercised control over their national churches leading to absolutism or absolute power. The concept of 'absolute states' assumed a new shape, which culminated in the development of national churches. In England, the spilt with the Catholic Church under the aegis of Henry VII led to the development of national church. The Papacy schism and subsequent development of nation states and church fanned the flame of civil war.

Individualism and Intellectualism

Individualism and Intellectualism were the two important aspects of this phase. It had far-reaching repercussions in the sphere of education. Renaissance humanism had already glorified these aspects. However, Reformation phase targeted mass at large and popularized humanist methods in varied schools and universities. The famous gymnasiums or secondary schools developed in various parts of Europe and admitted students en masse. Through the spread of liberal arts and humanist teachings, the concepts of Individualisms and Intellectualism were molded in new ways. The debacle of old church resulted in the beginning of a chapter of secularism in Western Europe. It developed the ethic of individualism. Some historians opined that Religious Individualism was just the opposite of Intellectual Individualism, which led to the birth of capitalism.

Economic Development

The Reformation is seen as a watershed in the history of Western Europe. It ushered in the development of nation-states and the subsequent demolition of feudal-based monarchy. The nexus between Calvinism and economic development is highly mooted in the academic circles. In the midst of the 19th century, Karl Marx claimed that Protestantism won due to the capitalist values of thrift, self-discipline, diligence, self-discipline and rationality.

Mercantilism

Mercantilism represents a system of economic doctrine and legislative policy based on the principle that money alone is wealth. Adam Smith, a prominent classical political economist in his famed treatise, 'Wealth of Nations', coined the term 'mercantilism' or 'mercantile system'. Maurice Dobb claims that mercantilism is a system of state- regulated exploitation through trade and considered it an economic policy of an age of primitive accumulation. In the 16th century, mercantilism transformed these earlier concepts of the smaller economic units of towns or guilds to the level of the entire state.

In Retrospect

- ♦ *Reformation* : Reformation is a general name that is given to a set of religious movements, encouraged by the Renaissance that broke out in the later Middle Ages. The movement was led by a Christian priest named Martin Luther.
- ♦ *Causes of the Reformation* : Spirit of Enquiry, Corruption in the Church, Economic burden on the people, resentment of the Rulers, pre-reformation movements against the Church, immediate causes.
- ♦ *Martin Luther and Protestant Reformation* : Luther nailed on Ninety-Five Theses on the door of the Wittenburg Church in AD 1517. His ideas, writings and speeches gradually started the German Protestant Movement.

- **Other leaders of Protestant Movement :**
  - *Ulrich Zwingli (AD 1484–1531) :* Ulrich Zwingli spread Lutheranism in Switzerland.
  - *Henry VIII (AD 1491–1547) :* Henry VIII of England set up an independent Church known as the Anglican Church.
  - *John Calvin (AD 1509–1564) :* Calvin was against all kinds of luxury, feasting, dancing, sports and games and wanted utter simplicity in the religion severe type of Protestantism was known as Calvinism.

EXERCISES

Part-I (Short Questions)

1. What do you mean by the term 'Reformation' ?
2. Who initiated the Reformation movement ?
3. Discuss the corrupt practices rampant in the Church.
4. What do you mean by the 'Sale of Indulgences'? For what purpose was it used by the clergymen ?
5. What was *tithe* ?
6. Who was called as the *'Morning star of the Reformation'* ?
7. Who were the Lollards ?
8. What was the immediate cause of Reformation ?
9. Who translated the Holy Bible into German ?
10. Which practice of the Church did Luther condemned ?
11. What was the Ninety-Five thesis ?
12. What is Diet of Worms ? What did it decide about Luther ?
13. What was Anabaptism ?
14. Name the reformer who was responsible for the spread of Lutheranism in Zurich.
15. In what manner did Henry VIII come into confrontation with the pope ?
16. What was the Act of Supremacy ?
17. Who was John Calvin? What are the names by which the Calvinists are known in different countries?
18. Name the famous literary work of John Calvin.
19. Who wrote *In Praise of Folly* ?
20. What do you understand by the term 'Counter Reformation' ?
21. Who founded the Society of Jesus ?
22. What were the consequences of the Counter Reformation ?

Part-II (Structured Questions)

1. How did the following causes contributed to the formation of 16th century Reformation movement in Europe ?
   (a) Spirit of Enquiry
   (b) Corruption in the Church
   (c) Economic burden on the common people
2. With reference to the Protestant Movement, explain :
   (a) Why Martin Luther rose in revolt against the Church ?
   (b) His literary work Ninety-Five Theses. What was its contribution ?
   (c) His success in mobilising the support of the People and Princes.

3. What was the contribution of the following people in the Protestant Movement ?
   (a) Ulrich Zwingli
   (b) King Henry VIII
   (c) John Calvin
4. With reference to the measures taken to restore the reputation of the Catholic Church, explain :
   (a) What is Counter Reformation ?
   (b) Who took the first organised attempt at Counter Reformation ?
   (c) What measures were taken to introduce reforms in the Catholic Church ?
5. With reference to the impact of the Reformation, explain Religious persecution
6. What do you mean by a Nation State ? Describe how the feudal societies contributed to the emergence of the Nation States in Europe ?

CHAPTER 13

INDISTRIAL REVOLUTION

◆ Industrial Revolution : Definition, Comparative study of Socialism and Capitalism.

Industrial Revolution

Introduction

Causes of the Industrial Revolution

- *Enclosure Movement*
- *Geographical Location and availability of Natural Resources*
- *Increase in the Demands for Goods*
- *Practical bent of Mind of the English Researchers*
- *Invention of Machinery and use of Steam Engine*
- *Improvement in Transport System*
- *Commercial Revolution*
- *British Progressive Policy*

Impact of the Industrial Revolution

- *Growth of Population*
- *Urbanisation*
- *Mistreatment of Workers*
- *Rise of New Social Classes*
- *Socialism*
  - *Factors Behind the Rise of Socialism*
- *Marxist Socialism*
- *Capitalism*

INTRODUCTION

The Industrial Revolution, which spanned from the 18th to 19th centuries, was a crucial event in Europe, Great Britain and World history. It signifies a series of revolutionary changes that took place in the fields of industry and production.

Prior to the Industrial Revolution, manufacturing was often done in **Guild's home,** using hand tools or basic machines for a limited group of consumers. The Industrial Revolution marked a shift to large-scale production of goods through powered, special-purpose machinery and technology for larger groups of clients. This not only brought about an increased volume and variety of manufactured goods and an improved standard of living for some, but also resulted in often grim employment and living conditions for the poor and working classes. It brought about vast economic and social changes by which a medieval agricultural society was transformed into a modern industrial society. In this epoch, demographic growth was intensely massive. Mercantilism had augmented competition among the European states. Governments greatly encouraged agriculture, commerce and industries. During this time, the process of industrialization acquired rapidity and impetus. By the second half of the 18th century, England became a stabilized industrial force in the whole world. She had set a paradigm in the sphere of industrialization. The changes produced were so fundamental and startling that they may be described as 'revolutionary'.

The Renaissance and the reformation movements greatly influenced the development of the scientific spirit. In England scientists undertook laboratory experimentation, careful observation and searching inquiry which led to the invention of several machines. Thus, the period of Industrial Revolution is also known as the **Age of Machines** as the invention of machines brought about a total change in manufacturing and production and revolutionised the Industrial system in England. Thus, industrial revolution can be defined as a displacement of hard labour by machine power in many of the processes of manufacture and mining.

CAUSES OF THE INDUSTRIAL REVOLUTION

The Industrial Revolution began in England and spread to several other countries during the period AD 1750 to AD 1850. Some of the important causes for the origin of the Industrial Revolution are :

Enclosure Movement (availability of cheap labour)

The Enclosure Movement was a push in the 18th and 19th centuries throughout England and Europe, to take land that had formerly been owned in common by all members of a village for grazing animals and growing food and convert it to privately owned land, usually with walls, fences or hedges around it. They claimed that large fields could be farmed more efficiently than individual plots allotted from common land. Several private acts of parliament as well as the General Enclosure Act (1801) standardised the enclosure process. The first Act of parliament that deliberated on the 'Enclosure Procedure' of a village was registered in 1710. Initially, the process was very slow and was accompanied by the development of a series of other acts in the mid-18th century. As a consequence of this movement big Landlords emerged and small farmers now became landless labourers. This forced several people to migrate to the cities in search of jobs. Thus, the surplus supply of labour as a result of the Enclosure Movement greatly helped Industrial Revolution.

Geographical Location and Availability of Natural Resources

The geographical location of England greatly helped in industrial revolution. Its geographical position was suitable for world trade and all parts of the world were accessible to its ships. The rivers were beneficial for internal transport and its coastline offered excellent harbours. Besides geographical location, it is well known that the country had large deposits of coal and iron ores which greatly helped the growth of numerous industries. Also, the location of the coal and iron mines close to each other encouraged the English to evolve new techniques for the manufacture of iron and utilization of the coals. Owing to the several colonies in Africa and Asia, England had huge supply of raw material which was responsible for the rapid spread of Industrial Revolution.

Increase in the Demand for Goods

England started a vigorous accumulation of colonies like India and Canada in the 18th century. These colonies were not merely used as sources of raw materials but as a huge market for the industrially produced goods. The other factors that provided the incentive to produce more goods were the huge profits of expanding trade and the Napoleonic wars. The industry and trade of the continental countries were damaged by these wars. These countries were dependent on England for the manufactured goods thereby stimulating demand and providing a fillip to Industrial Revolution.

Practical bent of mind of the English Researchers

Another factor which contributed to Industrial revolution was that the English scientists and engineers had a very practical bent of mind. They made inventions keeping in view the needs of the time. They concentrated mainly on those inventions of science which had practical utility. This was in complete contrast to the continental scientists who concentrated on research in electricity, chemicals etc. which were not of immediate applied relevance

Invention of Machinery and Use of Steam Engine

The starting point of the Industrial Revolution was the invention of machinery and its application to the process. Kay's *flying shuttle* (1738) not only helped the weavers to weave wider cloth but also to double their outputs. The method of spinning yarn was improved by James Hargreaves in 1765, by means of assembling the Spinning Jenny. Similarly, inventions in iron and coal industries, textile production and in the field of communication and transport brought radical changes in industry and commerce and gave a tremendous boost to the Industrial Revolution.

Though water and wind were earlier used for running machines, neither of them was a dependable source of energy. Besides, these sources of energy could not be used for running large factories. The use of these energy sources to run big factories became possible with the invention of the steam engine by James Watt. This discovery of steam as a power source ushered in the Industrial Revolution. While steam to run locomotives was introduced in AD 1813,

Spinning Jenny

railway trains started running with the help of steam in AD 1830 greatly helping in Industrial Revolution.

Steam Engine

Improvement in Transport System

The transport system was improved in the second half of the 18th century. Transport and communication formed an important factor for the industrial growth and integration of markets. Until mid-18th century, the condition of road transport was miserable and expensive. Christopher Hill opines, 'one horse could draw eighty time as much in a canal barge as by cart on a soft road'. John MacAdam discovered a new process of road building using coal tar. The use of coal tar facilitated hard roads and adequate use of waterways through steamships and steamboats extensively contributed to the development of the Industrial revolution in many European countries. Later, the *Macadamized* roads became popular in Great Britain and also in the USA, Canada and France. Since roads were not sufficient to meet the needs of transportation, railroads became necessary. The invention of railways by George Stephenson in AD 1814 facilitated the transport of material from one place to another easing communication and accelerating Industrial Revolution. The ship had become an important aspect of English transport and it spurred the growth of industrialization and subsequent development of imperialism.

Commercial Revolution

The Commercial Revolution also proved to be very useful to England. England was on the threshold of a golden age of prosperity and power. She established her imperial and commercial superiority by defeating the French in the Seven Years War. In comparison to other European powers, the Government and military establishments of England were free from corruption and more economical and collected revenues efficiently. Moreover, the extra earning of ship-owners and merchants were actively invested in ventures which could be a source of additional profit. Thus, the **Commercial Revolution** brought economic pros-perity with it and was one of the major causes of the Industrial Revolution.

British Progressive Policy

A policy of commerce, trade and empire-building was followed by the British Government. Navigation Acts were passed by the Government to protect the British shipping companies from competition with those of Holland and France. Instead of undertaking trade and commercial activities, the Government left them to private entrepreneurs. Extraordinary zeal and spirit of enterprise was shown by the traders, private manufacturers, colonists and sailors. Besides earning huge profits for themselves, they brought immense wealth to their country. The East India Company not only engaged itself in the profitable oriental trade but also began the task of empire-building in India. Thus the British Progressive policy proved crucial in the success of the Industrial Revolution.

IMPACT OF THE INDUSTRIAL REVOLUTION

The Industrial Revolution brought about considerable changes in the economic, social and political spheres of human life.

Growth of Population

One of the most important after-effects of the Industrial Revolution was the huge increase in Urban Population as well as population all over. This exponential increase in population growth was aided to greater supply of good, made available by the Agricultural revolution. In addition, orphanages, hospitals and improved medical advancements marked decline in death rate, which resulted in a steady growth of population after AD 1740. Perhaps, the most considerable effect was the survival of more children of the lower middle class and middle class parents.

Urbanisation

Urbanisation was one of the direct outcomes of the Industrial Revolution. With the invention of machinery and the advent of technology, factories could be built anywhere in towns and cities. Thus, people from the rural areas migrated to the urban areas looking for work, education, and other social benefits. The cities became the centres of civilization and culture, attracting many people from the nearby rural areas for better living standards. However, this growth had major consequences; death rates in the cities grew significantly and overcrowding combined with poor sanitation led to the spread of diseases and epidemics.

Mistreatment of Workers

The capitalists exploited their workers thoroughly. The lives of the working classes grew miserable and burdensome. Inspite of not getting adequate wages, the workers had to work for fourteen to sixteen hours a day in poor working conditions. They did not even have safety guards on machines which led to frequent accidents and there were no provisions for the care of the injured and the sick. The children and women employed in factories were also underpaid. Profit making became the main objective of the owners of industries. They preferred to employ unskilled workers, since they were cheaper. As a result, the workers hated their employers and thought that they were badly humiliated, unjustly treated and cruelly exploited.

Rise of new Social Classes

The Industrial Revolution polarized the society into two main groups– the haves and the have-nots. Some individuals became capitalists, meaning the owners of the main means of production. The capitalists had power, wealth and prestige. The other section of people created by the Revolution was the class of poor workers or proletariat. This class included those people who migrated to cities in search of employment and lived in inhuman living conditions or slums. Thus, the gap between the employees and the employers became very wide and remained unabridged.

Socialism

A great impact of the Industrial Revolution was the division of society into the working class and capitalists. Social evils sprang up, owing to the factory system and communism. This led to the rise of Socialism which aimed at eliminating the capitalist class and substituting some form of working class ownership and control of the means of production. With the awakening of the factory workers, there was a demand that the employers should be the only owners of the means of production so that the wealth produced can be shared more fairly. Several socialists stood up to remove these evils such as Saint Simon, Charles Fourier, Louis Blanc and Robert. They were called the **Utopians**. In this manner, Industrial Revolution gave rise to many doctrines of Socialism including Marxism. The workers of the world were called upon by Engels and Karl Marx to unite and fight against exploitation of the capitalists. The socialists wanted to set up such a society that would be free of class divisions and exploitation. A number of factors led to the development of Socialism.

Firstly, it developed as a reaction to the vices of Capitalism. The society came to be divided into two different classes, namely, the *Proletariat* and the *Capitalists*. The socialists not only demanded better living conditions for the workers but also tried to save them from exploitation by the capitalists. They realized that the employers benefited from the mass production but the workers were living in poverty.

Secondly, the British Government was forced by the strong Trade Union Movements to recognise the workers' rights. It was demanded that the workers should be provided better working conditions, security and should also be relieved of poverty.

Lastly, the Chartist Movement that took place in the first half of the 19th century demanded a worker's right to vote. In the mid-19th century, the movement declined but offered a good model for further socio-political reforms.

FACTORS BEHIND THE RISE OF SOCIALISM

Marxist Socialism

Karl Marx (AD 1818-1883) is the most outstanding figure in the whole socialist movement. He was a German economist and political philosopher. In 1844, he met Frederick Engels (1820-1895), his longtime associate, in France.

In AD 1848, Karl Marx and Engels issued the

Karl Marx

Communist Manifesto which introduced scientific socialism or Communism. In this book he explained that the, exploitation of the lower class is the motivating factor leading to the communist movement. Marx's vision of communism was a classless, stateless system based on common ownership and free-access, superabundance and maximum freedom for individuals to develop their own capacities and talents. He believed that a socialist economy would not base production on the creation of private profits but would instead base production and economic activity on the criteria of satisfying human needs, i.e., production would be carried out directly for use. As a political movement, Marxism advocates the creation of such a society and concludes : *"Let the ruling classes tremble at a Communistic revolution. The proletarians have nothing to lose but their chains. They have a world to win. Working men of all countries, unite!"*

Later, in AD 1867, Marx and Engels published the first of three volumes, entitled *Das Kapital*, in which they explained the sum and substance of Marxian Socialism or Communism. The ideas of Marx influenced world thought. Thereafter Soviet Russia adopted Communism, while other European countries like Britain and France began to follow socialism.

Capitalism

The Industrial Revolution triggered certain changes, due to which the arrival of Industrial

Capitalism was witnessed by Britain. The theory of free trade or Laissez-Faire came to the forefront, as a result of the Revolution. Encouraged by this theory, the traders and capitalists wanted the least intervention of the state in economic affairs. Owing to the Industrial Revolution, a new class of people was formed, known as the Capitalists. The input used for making more wealth is known as *capital* and the *capitalists* are the owners of this capital. Capitalism is the economic system in which individuals or groups of individuals own and controls the means of production like raw materials, labour, machines and tools. The motto of the capitalism is Profit-Maximisation. It could only be achieved through exploitation of the industrial Proletariat. Under capitalism, one man's loss was another man's gain. The loser was the hapless worker bound to work more than 12 hours a day under inhuman conditions and the gainer was the capitalist. Capitalism increases individual productivity through 'the division of labour' which divides productive labour into its smallest components. The result of the division of labour is to lower the value, in terms of skill and wages of the individual worker. Infact capitalism had serious economic, social and political consequences. It in turn led to Imperialism.

TABLE SHOWING THE INVENTIONS IN VARIOUS INDUSTRIES

Industry	Name	Invention	Year
Textile Machinery	John Kay Hardgreaves Richard Arkwright Samuel Crompton Edmund Cartwright Ely Whitney Elias Howe	Flying Shuttle Spinning jenny Water Frame Spinning Mule Power Loom Cotton Gin Sewing Machine	AD 1763 AD 1764 AD 1769 AD 1779 AD 1785 AD 1792 AD 1846
Coal and Iron Industries	John Smeaton Henry Bessemer Sir Humphrey Dave	Blast furnace Steel Safety Lamp	AD 1760 AD 1850 AD 1816
Field of Power	James Watt George Stephenson	Steam Engine Locomotive	AD 1736-1819 AD 1781-1848
Field of Transport	John Mc Adam	He used a mud birder to build a type of hard surface road	AD 1756-1836
Communication	Alexander Graham Bell	Telephone	AD 1876

In Retrospect

- **Introduction :** Industrial Revolution, which took place from the 18th to 19th centuries was crucial event in Europe, Great Britain and World history. It signifies a series of revolutionary changes that took place in the field of industry and production. Manual production was replaced by mechanized production.

- **Causes of Indstrial Revolution :** Enclosure Movement, Availability of raw material and natural resources, Invention of machinery, Increase in the demand for Goods, Use of steam, Improvement in transport System, Commercial revolution and British progressive policy.

- **Impact of the Industrial Revoltuion :** Growth of Population, Urbanization, Mistreatment of workers, Rise of a new social class, Socialism and Capitalism.

EXERCISES

Part-I (Short Questions)

1. What do you mean by the term 'Industrial Revolution'?
2. Do you agree with the fact that the starting point of Industrial Revolution was the invention of machinery and its application to the manufacturing process?
3. Mention how the increase in the demand of the English goods led to the invention of new machines?
4. State the inventions of which machines led to the development of Industrial Revolution.
5. In what manner did the availability of raw material and abundant natural resources contribute to the Industrial Revolution?
6. Explain how the colonial policy of Britain contributed to the spread of the Industrial Revolution?
7. State the contribution of immigrants to the Industrial Revolution.
8. State how urbanisation took place as a result of Industrial revolution.
9. State any two economic impacts of Industrial Revolution.
10. With which invention is James Hargreaves associated?
11. Name the two classes of society that were created by the Industrial Revolution.
12. What do you mean by Capitalism?
13. How did the Industrial Revolution give birth to Socialism?
14. Give any two causes of Socialism.
15. Name the author of the book *Das Kapital*.
16. What is socialism according to Karl Marx?

Part-II (Structured Questions)

1. With reference to the Industrial Revolution that marked a change to machine work from hand work and to factory system of production from domestic system of production, discuss the following factors that ushered in the Industrial Revolution:
   (a) Availability of Raw Material
   (b) Invention of Machines
   (c) Improved Transportation
   (d) Demand for English goods
2. With reference to the impacts of the Industrial Revolution, mention:
   (a) Urbanization
   (b) Mistreatment of workers
   (c) The formation of new social class
3. With reference to the rise of Socialism, discuss
   (a) The causes for the rise of Socialism
   (b) Who was Karl Marx and what was his contribution to Socialism?
4. Discuss how Industrial Revolution led to the growth of Capitalism.